BOWHUNTING PRESERVATION ALLIANCE

THE BOWHUNTER'S
>FIELD MANUAL <

Tactics and Gear for Big and Small Game
Across the Country

JUDD COONEY

Foreword by M. R. James
Preface by James Dougherty

SKYHORSE PUBLISHING

DEDICATION

To my daughter Lisa and son-in-law, Mike Kraetsch, for unconditionally allowing me to share a lifetime of knowledge and outdoor experiences with the next generation of bowhunters, my grandchildren, Zane, Cole and Magan, and to revel in their unbridled energy, limitless curiosity and boundless enthusiasm during our ventures in the great outdoors.

■ ■ ■   ■ ■ ■

As a bowhunter who has spent countless irreplaceable days enjoying the great outdoors with bow and arrow in hand, I'm honored to be a part of this worthwhile endeavor where a portion of the money you spend for this book is returned directly to the Bowhunting Preservation Alliance. This non-profit organization works to enhance our present bowhunting situation, develop new bowhunting opportunities across the nation and recruit new bowhunters into this challenging and rewarding sport. These ongoing efforts, in turn, will help preserve our bowhunting heritage for us and future generations to follow.

–Judd Cooney

■ ■ ■   ■ ■ ■

Bowhunting is like religion—once you've seen the "light", you want others to find that special sense of accomplishment and challenge that only bowhunting offers. The Bowhunting Preservation Alliance works to put archery into every community, invite every beginning archer to try bowhunting, and wants every bowhunter to find opportunities to hunt where they live. Your purchase of this book will help provide the means for us to spread the "good news" about archery and bowhunting and ensure that, long after you've left the woods, others will experience the adrenaline rush and genuine satisfaction shared by all who've hunted with stick and string. Thanks.

–Jay McAninch,
CEO/President, Archery Trade Association.

TABLE OF CONTENTS

FOREWORD

Judd Cooney is a living, breathing anachronism. Those of us who know him best universally agree that he would have been just as much at home toting a .58 caliber Hawken back in the 1800s as he is heading afield today carrying a modern compound bow, scope-sighted rifle, or auto-loading shotgun. Likewise we know that Judd would have been just as comfortable clad in beaded moccasins, fringed buckskin shirt, and brain-tanned trousers as he is in Windstopper camo and Vibram-soled hunting boots. And there's absolutely no doubt in anyone's mind that he would have chatted as friendly-like across some high-country campfire with famed frontiersman Jim Bridges as he did across the dinner table with legendary bowhunter Fred Bear.

So, just who is this contemporary mountain man who likely was born a century or two too late? Honestly, it's impossible to pin a single label on Judd Cooney. Outdoor writer? Yes, and a darned good one. Wildlife photographer? Arguably, one of the country's best. Hunting guide? Yep, a top-drawer professional. Conservationist? Definitely, but in the purest sense of the word (don't ever confuse Judd Cooney the conservationist with one of those misinformed Yuppie "preservationists" who learned all about nature by watching Walt Disney movies and who believe animals talk to each other while coexisting peacefully in an outdoor world as lush and innocent as the biblical Garden of Eden).

And don't forget other appropriate labels, either: serious varmint hunter, deadeye shot (with most any weapon you can name), extraordinary game caller, and, oh yes, passionate and knowledgeable hunter with both gun and bow.

Finally, mix in such terms as loyal friend, devoted husband, proud father, and doting grandpa, and you can sketch a pretty good mental image of this rugged, square-jawed individualist who possesses a devilish sense of humor and always calls 'em exactly as he sees 'em—often with the subtlety of a kick in the groin.

Judd Cooney intimately knows and bluntly speaks the truth about nature. He has learned about wild birds and animals firsthand, observing them throughout a long and active outdoor life that spans more than six decades. From his early boyhood days hunting, fishing, and trapping in his native Minnesota... through his formative college years in South Dakota (where he kept a pet fox in his dorm room and sometimes cut morning classes to jump-shoot ducks or bowhunt bottomland deer) . . . to his postgraduate conservation work in Alaska, his later years spent afield as a Colorado game warden and a successful free-lance photojournalist—Judd Cooney has been there, done that. Again and again. Over and over.

It is Judd's familiarity with wildlife and successful hunting techniques—erudition gained from myriad personal experiences during long decades spent in North America's fields and forests—that set him apart from his peers. Combine a God-given writing talent with a hunter's instinct and artist's eye, and you have perhaps the only man who could create this comprehensive bowhunting field manual so honestly, so well.

I first met Judd Cooney some three decades ago. Over the ensuing years, we shared numerous antelope, deer, bear, and turkey camps. In Colorado. California. Alabama. Illinois. Iowa. South Dakota. And Canada, too. Hardly a year passes that we don't team up on yet another bowhunting adventure. Somewhere. Anywhere. And after all this time, I am still amazed by Judd's knowledge and his innate ability to impart useful information to others.

For anyone dreaming of hunting trips to faraway places—or simply wanting to improve backyard-hunting skills—this new book offers on-target assistance and serves as an invaluable reference source. It's intended to be read. And reread. The writing, you will quickly discover, is vintage Cooney. Crisp. Honest. Understandable. Sprinkled with appropriate anecdotes and no-nonsense advice. Every page, in fact, shines with the author's knowledge, talent, and complete understanding of the subject.

I consider *The Bowhunter's Field Manual* to be the ideal package—good reading and generous information offered by an outdoorsman who has lived the words he chooses to share. Now read on—and learn. You'll be a better bowhunter for the experience. That's a promise.

—M. R. James
Founder, Bowhunter Magazine

PREFACE

Many years ago, as a young beginning bowhunter with a dream list of bowhunts I wanted to make and big-game animals I hoped to encounter, there was nothing like this *Bowhunter's Field Manual* to serve as a guide in answering my How-to-Go-About-It questions. Sure, there were recounts of hunts to be read in *Archery Magazine* by such archery icons as Fred Bear that helped, but they were mostly just narratives on what had been done, with not nearly enough emphasis on the *how!*

In my opinion, this book is the ultimate, practical, how-to guide to bowhunting our North American big game. In support of that opinion, it's important that you understand where it comes from. A book of this scope requires much more than organization and good writing skills. It requires—demands actually—the knowledge and perspective of someone with the sort of expertise that only comes with a lifetime of practical, successful, bowhunting experience. Few, if any, meet those requirements better than Judd Cooney.

I've been fortunate to spend many days afield with Cooney. From Mexico to Canada and a dozen states in between, witnessing (and often envying) his considerable skills. And you will too. In the pages of this book, presented in Cooney's straightforward style, you will be entertained and perhaps vicariously excited, but most valuable, you will learn.

—James Dougherty

PRONGHORN ANTELOPE

Wait or shoot, I contemplated as the skittish, ebony-horned buck started drinking 20 yards below my blind. The sharp scent of sage permeated the air as my camo shirt and blackened face absorbed the sun's torrid rays, causing rivulets of sweat to slide down my torso and drip from my chin.

It wasn't the 75-inch pronghorn, within easy bow range, that caused my consternation; it was the high-horned buck loping toward the tank. I'd glassed the buck minutes earlier as he topped a distant ridge, and I was instantly intrigued by his unusually tall horns. As he closed to 50 yards I lost interest in the buck watering nearby and concentrated on the newcomer.

When the buck topped the dam, at 35 yards, and paused to watch the milling group below, the moment of truth had arrived. I would have preferred letting him move down and drink, providing a 20-yard shot. However, there was also the possibility he'd follow the herd leaving the waterhole and ruin my chance.

I didn't waste time thinking as I jerked to full draw and sent the Thunderhead-tipped xx75 on its way. The fluorescent-crested arrow blurred across space and disappeared behind the buck's shoulders.

A few minutes later, I was staring awestruck at the largest pronghorn I'd ever taken. Had I realized his enormous size when I shot, I'd probably have missed him by three feet. The buck's horn length was 17 2/8 inches, with a basal circumference of 6 4/8 inches. His official score was a whopping 85 0/8, which tied the world record. Always said, "I'd rather be lucky than good."

Antilocapra americana or pronghorn antelope are the "aristocrats" of North American big-game animals. Their ancestry dates back five million years and they're the only surviving family member roaming the earth in modern

One of the most sought after trophy big game animals is the pronghorn antelope. Bowhunting these fleet-footed animals takes plenty of patience and perseverance.

times. Before the arrival of the first settlers, there were about 40 million pronghorns and an equal number of bison across the grassy prairies of the continent.

Pronghorns are genetically closer to the goat family than to true antelopes because they lack dewclaws. However, the fact that pronghorns annually shed their horns, not antlers, sets them apart as the sole member in a unique category. They only shed the outer horn sheath, consisting of agglutinated *(glued together)* hair, while retaining the solid, bony core. The outer sheath continues to grow until being sloughed in November. The horns on a buck killed in a late November season will have greater length and mass than the same buck taken in August or September.

Colorado's first statewide "archery-only" antelope season ran in November of 1971, when they were in wintering herds of 200 or more animals. Annually, a group of us rendezvoused near the Little Snake River in the northwestern corner of the state to bowhunt antelope. We soon learned the most successful tactic for bowhunting bunched pronghorns was to subtly push or drive them past hidden hunters. Half would sneak into position in gullies or sagebrush thickets out of sight, while the remainder would spread out across the prairie behind a group of pronghorns. We gradually moved in on them and, when possible, used the newly erected BLM woven wire fences to funnel the animals to waiting hunters.

On one drive, a member of our group arrowed a running buck not realizing it only had one horn, but what a horn! The unshed horn measured 17 inches long and seven inches around the base, with an eight-inch prong. We spent most of a day trying, unsuccessfully, to find that shed sheath. If the measurement of the shed side had approximated the unshed horn, this buck would have exceeded Archie Malm's world-record pronghorn by more than *five inches*.

The pronghorn antelope is the most beautiful, flashy, and colorful of North America's big-game species. Its buff-colored back and snowy white belly and rump patch, combined with distinctive facial marking and glossy black horns, are truly unique. Its bright coloration seemingly contrasts with the muted prairie colors, but in reality, antelope standing in belly-deep grass, sagebrush, or greasewood, or bedded on open, rocky hillsides, blend perfectly with the dusty, barren countryside.

Antelope are the fastest of big-game animals, with a top speed estimated between 60–70 miles per hour. This speed is exceeded only by Africa's cheetah. Pronghorns have a cruising speed of 35–40 miles per hour that can be maintained for several miles. They easily accomplish this feat by utilizing an enlarged windpipe and oversized lungs and heart to push up to three times the normal amount of oxygen through their system. Don't let the pronghorn's spindly legs and lightweight build (bucks go 100–130 pounds and does 75–100 pounds) fool you. Their leg bones have the highest tensile strength of any big-game animal, exceeding that of an elephant. Their running gear is further protected by thick layers of shock-absorbing gristle in the hooves.

An antelope's eyesight is matched to its speed and is similar to that of a person using 8x binoculars. The large dark, eyes protrude, giving antelope a full 180 degrees of vision with each eye. They can pick up an approaching coyote over a mile away.

It's frustrating to make a perfect stalk on a trophy buck through washouts and cactus-filled creek bottoms, only to ease your camouflaged head up and find your quarry staring at you. When a spooked pronghorn flares its white rump hair, the warning signal can be spotted by other antelope several miles away.

Due to wise and aggressive game management, antelope numbers have rebounded, from 14,000 animals in the 1920s to over 1,000,000 today. Bowhunting opportunities have never been better, and all pronghorn-producing states have archery seasons.

Wyoming is the top pronghorn-producing state with a thriving population and the highest number of antelope licenses available. If you're looking for

Wyoming, Colorado, and Montana are top states for pronghorn bowhunting. The rougher the country, the better your chances of finding some of the biggest bucks.

an exceptional buck, concentrate on remote rugged areas rather than open, flat country where "goats" are easily accessible. It's tough to draw an archery license in many of these trophy-producing areas, but getting a chance at a really big buck makes the wait worthwhile. Some of the great trophy areas are west of the continental divide in southern Wyoming. The rugged, rocky valleys, canyons, and ravines, as well as cedar- and sagebrush-covered slopes and ridges, make it tough for gun-toting, vehicle-riding hunters to corner wary bucks. This country gives mature bucks a chance to age and grow trophy horns.

Colorado is the second largest producer of record bucks. It's hard to beat the northwest corner for superb pronghorn bowhunting, but drawing a license is a long-term proposition. With the preference-point system, however, a determined bowhunter is guaranteed a license if he sticks with the drawing long enough.

Montana has excellent pronghorn opportunities in the northern part of the state. A bowhunter willing to expend some time and effort may find an area totally untouched by bowhunters. Stick to rough country for the biggest bucks.

This same philosophy holds true for New Mexico, Arizona, Nevada, and North and South Dakota. These states have produced many top qualifiers for the Pope and Young record book over the past several biennial competitions. They don't have the total number of antelope that roam Wyoming, Colorado, and Montana, but they've had a restrictive license lottery system for years and the reduced hunting pressure has produced some monstrous bucks.

In New Mexico, some of the great trophy areas are found on private

Pronghorns live in flat and rolling areas where they can see well in all directions. Treat every hill you top and every bend in a draw you round as if the pronghorn you are after will be right there—because he very well might be!

lands where licenses are available, *for a price*! Wyoming and Montana also have large private land holdings where savvy landowners are producing quality bucks with good game management and harvest techniques. Don't overlook private land when searching for a trophy hunting experience.

ANTELOPE HUNTING TACTICS

Bowhunting pronghorn antelope is an exercise in patience and perseverance, from start to finish. Once you start poring over literature and maps to find the best bowhunting area, scout your chosen area to find a trophy buck, and determine an ambush site, to the instant you release an arrow at a record-book buck, your greatest asset must be *patience*.

Most antelope reside in semi-arid prairie or desert with minimal ground vegetation and mile after mile of open country. With acute vision and awesome speed, they can be extremely difficult to approach within bow range and even tougher to hit once you get close.

If a pronghorn sees you, chances of hitting him with an arrow are slim to none. A pronghorn's reaction time and speed make a deer look like they're moving in slow motion. The only difference between a pronghorn standing still and one running 30 miles per hour is a single step!

The wide-open spaces, dry country, and homogenous vegetation, providing adequate browse in every direction, makes patterning antelope feeding forays an unpredictable venture. Fortunately for bowhunters, antelope usually have a limited supply of *water*! Roughly 50 percent of pronghorn bucks entered in the Pope and Young record book are taken from blinds overlooking a water source.

A waterhole during a hot, dry summer and early fall is the center of the pronghorn's universe. Unlike other game, pronghorns don't move or feed much at night. They are up at first light, browsing the rapidly drying vegetation as they work toward the nearest waterhole. The most active time at a waterhole during warm weather is from 7 a.m. to noon and from 4 to 7 p.m. In scorching heat, antelope will often loaf around waterholes for several hours and water several times before wandering back to their home range.

In the rut, which peaks mid-September, bucks indicate their breeding grounds by marking boundaries with scrapes similar to a whitetail buck. Pronghorn bucks are extremely territorial and will challenge any buck trespassing these borders. When two pronghorn bucks tangle, it's a vicious, high-speed, knock-down, drag-out" attack that must be witnessed to be believed.

Waterholes are "neutral ground," however, where rival bucks tolerate one another, drink side-by-side and mingle with each other's harems unchallenged.

Antelope prefer a flat, muddy waterhole in the open, where they can observe approaching danger at long distances, to a clear spring in the bottom of a wash or gully, where visibility is limited. Most waterholes have one or two specific areas where pronghorns prefer watering, so it's important to thoroughly check tracks and signs before choosing a blind location.

Spend a day glassing a waterhole from a distance with binoculars or spotting scope and let them show you where they prefer to water. Keep the breeze in mind when locating a blind on a waterhole. I use a powder bottle, filled with talcum powder, to check a blind location for updrafts or downdrafts that might screw up an ambush.

PIT BLINDS

A spade, shovel, and pickaxe are indispensable for pit-blind building. The more time and effort you expend on a proper blind, the luckier you'll get. Choose a spot on the waterhole where you can cover the most heavily used section of the shoreline. Antelope depend mainly on their keen eyesight and speed to keep them out of trouble, but their sense of

Some of my best pronghorn were taken from a pit blind—where all the time and effort building one paid off!

smell is on par with other game animals. Keep the prevailing breeze in mind when bowhunting waterholes.

A properly placed and constructed pit blind is effective immediately. On many occasions, I've had antelope drink within 20 yards while I was digging a pit.

Don't hesitate to dig a blind in areas devoid of ground cover. Antelope are less spooky in low cover with unlimited visibility and a low-profile pit blind is readily accepted as part of the environment.

The oblong pit of my blind measures six feet long by four feet wide by three feet deep. The size can be enlarged to accommodate another bowhunter, cameraman, or non-hunting companion. Comfort is important for extending hunting time and effectiveness. Dig an 18-inch by 18-inch bench seat along the rear of the pit to provide a backrest and seat, allowing you to slide around and cover different shooting lanes.

When I dig the pit into a slope or face of a tank dam, I pile most of the dirt around the front edge to hold brush or grass camouflage. If a pit is dug in level ground, pile dirt evenly around the pit and leave at least 12–18 inches between the pit edge and piled earth to keep dirt from falling into the hole and to provide a shelf for extra gear.

On level ground, hunters may add another foot or two of depth to keep the profile as low as possible and still offer room to draw a compound, recurve, or longbow without the bow tip rising above the top of the blind.

Once a pit is dug and cleaned out, drive four foot by 3/8-inch rebar rods at intervals along the back, sides, and front of the pit. Six or eight rods should be plenty for the largest blind. String a single strand of wire between the rods and tie your brush covering to the wire and rods to keep it from blowing away.

Fill the gaps between the brush with clumps of prairie grass. This durable grass will often take root and grow, providing cover for following seasons. I generally put two shooting lanes in front of the blind to cover as much area as possible.

A dark brushy background is more important than the front covering, and I occasionally leave the front uncovered when an overhanging, dense, shady background is available. The rebar rods can be bent toward the center and covered with tumbleweeds or camo netting to darken the inside of the blind.

Camo paint or headnet covering a pale face and blending with the shadows eliminates any chance of nearby "goats" spotting a motion when you move into shooting position and draw. In a properly constructed and positioned pit blind, a hunter could wear a tuxedo with a white shirt and red bow tie, with little chance of being spotted by a pronghorn. The top covering makes for a cool, comfortable wait even under the hot mid-day prairie sun.

After the hunt, remove the stakes and wire. *Do not* toss the brush into the pit and cover it with dirt. You'll cuss your stupidity if you decide to use the blind again and have to dig out the buried refuse piece by piece. Stash the brush nearby to be used as a foundation next time you build the blind.

BLINDS

I've used portable, pop-up blinds on waterholes with excellent results for several years. Antelope adapt readily to a new structure if they can observe it for a few days and adjust to its presence.

A pop-up blind must be opaque to prevent a hunter's outline or movement from becoming visible in strongly backlit situations. The blind must be constructed to remain taut, even under strong prairie breezes. Canvas or nylon flapping and popping will definitely scare antelope.

Blinds also can be made of plywood, hay, and straw bales and erected near the waterhole as a semi-permanent hide. Outfitters often use this type of blind on private leases they hunt yearly.

Portable and semi-permanent blinds are vulnerable to damage by range cattle and mustangs sharing the waterholes with pronghorns. To eliminate this problem during your bowhunt, drive four steel posts six to eight feet out from the blind and string two strands of barbed wire around them. Rig the wire so you can easily take the front portion down while bowhunting.

Windmills are another alternative for ambushing antelope at waterholes, as pronghorns have no concept of danger from above. A word of caution: Make sure you *lock* and firmly secure the operating mechanism before climbing to the upper platform. A sudden gust of wind could cause the blades and fin to swing and knock you off the platform. Always wear a safety harness when bowhunting from a windmill. They weren't built with bowhunters in mind.

Antelope approaching a waterhole can drive a bowhunter bonkers. When I'm sitting in a blind and

Even if there is little ground cover near a waterhole, antelope will more readily accept a low-profile pit blind that does not block their view of the surrounding area.

An ideal size for a pit blind for one hunter is six feet long by four feet wide by three feet deep. If time allows, include an 18- by 18-inch bench seat along the rear of the blind for a seat.

spot antelope, I get on them immediately with binoculars and start judging the size of the bucks as they approach. If none meet my criteria, I sit back and enjoy the activity. This is an excellent opportunity for great wildlife photos or video. It's also an ideal opportunity to practice moving and drawing on the antelope as they water. Practice doesn't get any better than this.

If I decide an incoming buck is a shooter, I focus my total concentration on getting ready for a shot. When the antelope finally get to the water, be patient.

Antelope hate waterholes as they instinctively realize their vulnerability. A skittish buck will stick its nose in the water for a second then jerk its head up trying to catch movement or sign of danger. They may do this several times before settling for a prolonged drink. I once timed a buck that drank four minutes without raising his head. However, it took this buck two hours to cover the final 200 yards. When your target settles down, pick a spot and don't rush the shot.

A major problem arises when several groups of leery antelope join together near a waterhole. Sooner or later they'll converge on the water en masse, and hunters may be faced with 10 to 100 critters milling around and watering within bow range. The largest buck almost always is in the middle of the mob. To make such situations even more tense and nerve wracking, the whole shebang may spook for no apparent reason and charge out of the waterhole in a flurry of mud, water, and dust. The second or third time this happens, a bowhunter may discover the meaning of *buck fever.*

Settle down, be patient, and concentrate. *Don't* take a chance on skewering more than one animal or hitting one you didn't want. Wait for the right shot and make it count. Pronghorns don't hang around once they finish drinking and usually leave a waterhole on the run. Remember, patience and persistence pay.

The "huntability" of a waterhole can be altered considerably by weather conditions during the season. Bowhunter adaptability is an asset that can turn crisis to conquest. Pronghorns gather around major waterholes in ever-increasing numbers as seeps, pools, and puddles disappear during dry weather.

Thunderstorms are common during early fall, and a local storm can inundate the area around a waterhole, filling washes, ditches, and depressions with water. The animals disperse from the proximity of a primary waterhole and return to their home territories where they get their daily drink from various sources created by the rain. This is considered a disaster by most bowhunters, but 'tain't necessarily so.

Over the years, we've taken many superb bucks from small puddles and pools miles from major waterholes. Pronghorns often show less caution using these small water sources in the open country, where their visual acuity is maximized.

They generally use an isolated puddle until it dries up, then move to another or return to the main waterhole.

When we glass a trophy buck using such a source, we'll arrive at night and dig a pit blind 20–25 yards downwind of it. We'll take a buck off the

Even when a pit blind is placed at a water hole that attracts plenty of pronghorn, you must place it downwind . . . or a sight like this is one you won't see.

waterhole in the next day or so, fill in the pit blind, and move on.

On several occasions, we've found a small intermittent waterhole that attracts an inordinate number of pronghorns including several large bucks. Heavy use and hot, dry weather can quickly turn these *"honey holes"* from a prime ambush site to just another dust bowl on the vast prairie, unless your ingenuity and determination can keep the waterhole functioning. We've occasionally hauled 55-gallon drums of water to these primo spots every few days to keep water available until we kill a buck or two. On one occasion, I flagged down a tanker hauling water to oil rigs and paid $25 to have him dump 2500 gallons of water in a rapidly disappearing waterhole near camp. The load of water filled the small hollow to overflowing and inundated the pit blind in the gully below. A week later, my daughter shot a gorgeous 70-inch buck from that blind.

If your bowhunting area has streams or creeks that make waterhole hunting improbable, try to find crossings or travel ways where an ambush site can be set up. Although pronghorns are not as predictable as whitetails in their daily habits, they will feed in specific areas or fields, cross creeks or water at preferred sections, and loaf in particular locations. The observant and enduring bowhunter can often locate such favored areas and set up an effective ambush. Ravine crossings, openings in sagebrush- or greasewood-filled draws, gates in woven wire fences, and saddles on ridges are other locales where it's possible to ambush the buck of your dreams.

The successful stalking and killing of a pronghorn with a bow is the epitome of the bowhunting challenge, and it can be accomplished by persistence in habitat where there is sufficient cover for a stalk. The key to this method is locating the animal of your choice before it sees you.

This requires quality binoculars and spotting scope for judging a trophy buck and planning your stalking route with finite precision. Patience and persistence are of extreme importance in executing a successful stalk. You may spend hours or days glassing and waiting for the right buck to get into proper position with adequate cover and proper wind direction for a successful stalk. Become impatient and try to push the envelope and all you'll get is a look at the flashing white rump on the south end of an antelope headed north.

Keep the wind in your face, the sun at your back, and luck at your side and you might get a shot. 'Course, then all you have to worry about is hitting the critter before he sees the arrow coming.

Decoying pronghorns becomes more popular each season and can provide unsurpassed action during the peak of the mid-September rut. Antelope bucks in the rut are extremely aggressive and territorial and will attack any buck that approaches their harem of does. To be effective, a hunter should be within 200 yards of a herd buck before popping up the decoy. Good glassing technique, meticulous planning, cautious approach, and the patience to wait for the opportune moment are the keys to successful decoying.

Utilizing the "buddy" system for decoy hunting is often more effective than going it alone. Decoying action can be fast and furious when you show the decoy within sight of a belligerent herd buck.

An agitated buck charging an imagined interloper can cover 200 yards in less than ten seconds. This doesn't give a lone bowhunter much time to firmly set the decoy and get ready for the shot. Making a good shot on a buck charging at 50 miles per hour isn't the easiest thing to accomplish under the best of conditions. One hunter manning the decoy while the other takes the shot is much more effective.

It's essential to stay out of sight until you're within decoying distance. Plan your approach so there are no steep gullies, high brush, or fences between you and the buck, or he may hang up and wait for the challenger to come to him. Hiding directly behind the decoy is best, as the slight motion of drawing and rising for a shot won't spook an approaching buck. He's expecting move-

Antelope bucks will respond well to decoys especially during the peak of the rut during mid-September. An agitated buck can cover 200 yards in less than 10 seconds when responding to a perceived threat by a decoy buck.

ment from his rival. When the buck catches the movement, he'll stop and present a broadside shot, often at point-blank range.

A pronghorn's coloration pattern was designed for bowhunters. Placing an arrow behind the shoulder on the line where white belly hair meets brown upper body hair, results in a down-and-out pronghorn in short order. After a hit, it's important to keep the animal in sight. If you've made a good hit, the antelope will go down quickly. If the hit is questionable, keep the animal in sight and make use of your binoculars or spotting scope to determine the location and severity of the hit.

A paunch- or "gut"-hit pronghorn will bed quickly. *Leave it alone.* If it's still mobile at dark, do not disturb. It will be in the same vicinity the following morning. It may take a paunch-shot animal 18–24 hours to expire, so be patient. Leaving a gut-shot antelope is tough, but the alternative, losing the animal entirely, is worse.

With all other hits, keep the animal in sight and moving. A superficially wounded, high-strung pronghorn can often be pushed long enough, on foot, to cause dehydration and shock from blood loss or nervous exhaustion. At this point, a hunter can sneak close for a finishing shot.

Over a decade of guiding antelope bowhunters in northwestern Colorado, I've had many dogged bowhunters recover record-book bucks with minor wounds. In one such case, a lady bowhunter hit a buck in the lower leg about mid-morning. She followed my advice and immediately pursued the buck on foot. At 4 p.m. and five miles from the blind, she sneaked up on the exhausted buck and finished him.

Another client and I followed a buck, with a cheek wound, for three hours and several miles through sagebrush, rocky draws, and cedar-covered slopes before he eased close enough for a killing shot at the spent buck. Fortunately, my client was a dedicated sportsman that wouldn't let dehydration from the hot prairie sun or near exhaustion deter him from his quest. His endurance and tenacity paid off with a superb, well-earned Pope and Young buck.

A bowhunter should *never* lose a wounded pronghorn unless the hit is a minor nick or scratch. When you quit an antelope or any arrow-hit animal, be assured, in your mind, that you've done everything possible to find the animal and its chances for a full recovery are excellent.

JUDGING TROPHY PRONGHORNS

Antelope horns must score 67 to qualify for the Pope and Young record book. Measurements consist of horn length, circumference around the base and equidistant along the length of the horn, and prong, or "cutter," length. The spread may equal but not exceed the length of the longer horn. *Big* bucks and *little* bucks are easy to judge. It's borderline buggers that give discriminating bowhunters problems.

Length and mass are the most important considerations. A pronghorn's ear length is roughly seven inches from base to tip. Use this measurement to estimate total horn length when field judging a buck.

Horn mass is crucial for a high score because there are four circumference measurements. A one-inch difference in circumference equates to a four-inch gain: Twice the measurement obtained from a horn 16 inches long, as opposed to one that is 14 inches, is a very noticeable difference on a live buck. Short, massive horns will generally outscore tall spindly horns. A prominent prong will also help the score. Horns 13 inches long with five-and-a-half- to six-inch bases and four- to five-inch prongs will meet Pope and Young minimum.

Every pronghorn roaming the prairie is an admirable trophy. Taken from a blind, by stalking or using a decoy, buck, doe, or fawn, the challenge, excitement, and exhilaration of bowhunting the pronghorn antelope is an experience long remembered. ■

BEARS

Bear bowhunting seldom lacks in challenge or excitement, whether you're following a pack of trained bear hounds, spotting and stalking a bruin across a salt grass flat in Alaska, stand-hunting over a bait in Saskatchewan, or calling a ravenous bear with a predator call in Arizona.

Bears are unique animals that have many habits and characteristics totally different from other big game. They are the only species of big game that spends the cold winter months in hibernation. They are soft-footed, silent, solitary animals that prefer the most rugged terrain and inhospitable, impenetrable jungles of brush and vegetation, negotiating and surviving in this habitat with ease.

Black bears come in many different color phases, ranging from light blonde to reddish or cinnamon, chocolate brown, and coal black. Black bears on Kermode Island, off the coast of British Columbia, have evolved into a predominantly creamy white color, and the rare "glacier" or "blue bear" phase near Yakutat, Alaska, is a beautiful and unusual bluish-gray color.

There are areas of Canada, Alaska, and the eastern United States where the bears are predominantly black, and getting a color-phase bear is a rarity, while in central and western Canada and the western United States, color-phase bears make up about 40 percent of the population. One spring I had a sow bear bring three beautiful blonde-colored yearlings into a bait site with her when she appeared in the early spring. She abandoned the cubs in mid-June, when she was ready for breeding, and by September, two of the cubs had shed their blonde fur and were dark brown, while the third remained a light-blonde color with dark lower legs, a phenomenon I had never witnessed before.

Grizzlies and brown bears (actually the same species) vary in color as much as black bears but display the grizzled or variegated-colored hair that gives them their name. I've observed black bears that had a grizzled-color appearance and grizzlies that were solid brown or black, so color is not a reli-

Like a lot of other big game, black bears prefer southern exposures for feeding grounds when they first leave their dens.

able species identifier.

The most dependable identification characteristics are the roman nose of a black bear, compared to the dished-in face on the grizzly, and the rounded shoulders of the black bear as opposed to the grizzly's predominate hump. A black bear's claws are short, and if they show at all in the tracks they will be very close to the toe pads, while a grizzly's claws are long and usually leave a mark at least an inch or more in front of the toe pad.

When a bear first rouses from its long winter's nap, it's pretty lethargic. Its feet are very tender (I've heard that bears completely shed their footpads during hibernation but haven't observed this personally), and their digestive system needs reconditioning. For the first few days, they stay close to the den, resting and nibbling. As time progresses, they venture farther and spend more time satiating their growing appetite. A spring bear may spend four hours a day roaming and feeding, while a fall bear preparing for hibernation will spend four hours a day resting or sleeping and 20 hours voraciously feeding on anything that doesn't bite it first.

Bears are completely omnivorous and have an amazingly varied diet, from bugs to berries and grass to the grossest carrion around. They are also very efficient predators and are very capable of killing other big-game critters. There are several studies that show black bear predation on elk calves to have a major impact on elk populations in areas of the west.

One spring, I had a bowhunting client who almost called me a liar when I told him that black bears were very capable game killers and especially effective on elk calves. As we were approaching a bear bait for his late afternoon hunt, I spotted a pile of fresh bear sign in the trail, and right on top of the pile was the small, undigested hoof of a calf elk. The proof is in the poop, you might say.

The black bear's secretive, reclusive nature and preference for impenetrable habitat would make it an exceptionally difficult adversary for a bowhunter, if it weren't for the bear's escalating appetite after it comes out of hibernation in the spring. Spring has long been a favorite time of year for hunting bear. It's generally the only hunting season available at this time of year, and the bear's pelt is thick and glossy after being protected from the elements and light during the winter's hibernation.

BEAR BAITING 101

According to the last Pope and Young biennial records, over 60 percent of the bow-killed black bear are taken with the use of bait. Baiting spring bears is not rocket science and it's a technique that can be mastered by most bowhunters. There is, however, a tad of injustice to such mastery.

An accomplished golfer, tennis player, or even fisherman is often referred to as a master of his sport. Just think how you'd be referred to as an accomplished baiter.

I never claimed to be a good bear outfitter or guide, but I was a good garbage hauler and scrounger, and that equated to success when it came to killing bears con-

Baiting for black bears still requires a bowhunter to be very careful with movement. Even though a bear is coming in for the food, he is very wary and will spook easily.

sistently for clients and myself. I've often heard comments that bears like nothing better than a maggoty, rotten carcass to feed on, and I can guarantee you that nothing is further from the truth. Bears are very persnickety eaters when they have a choice.

One spring I worked as a conservation officer for the Colorado Division of Wildlife and was inquisitive about every aspect of bear behavior. I placed the fresh carcasses of road-killed mule deer and elk alongside those of a horse, steer, and sheep at one of my well-used bait sites, where there were several bears actively feeding. The bears completely ate the deer and elk carcasses before touching the horse. I replaced the remaining steer and sheep carcasses with more recently deceased ones, and even with the fresher carcasses, the bears completely cleaned up the rapidly ripening horse before starting on the steer.

They completely cleaned up the bones and bits of meat from the other carcasses before touching the sheep (which shows good taste on their part, as I feel the same way about mutton). I've also watched bears pick through a large box of edible scraps from a café, much as you and I would pick out our favorites on a buffet line. They scrounged out the chicken and meat scraps first and then moved to the fish, fruit, eggs, toast, rolls, pie, cake, etc. Potatoes were generally the last edibles munched.

In my experience with over 30 years of baiting, citrus fruits and lettuce are a total bust for bears. Fish is another item that some swear by, and I suppose if you have an inexhaustible supply it will do the job, but I've found that fish rots quickly and gets ruined in short order by flies and maggots. It's just not worth the effort.

I used to haul several trailer loads of killer ponies from Texas each spring to use as bear bait (probably a felony in this day and age) because I always wanted fresh meat or bait on the site when a client was hunting. A bear that leaves a bait still hungry, with the bait completely gone, is a lot less likely to return regularly, and I wanted them to know there was always something to eat when they came back . . . regardless of the time of day.

My favorite bear baits were edible scraps from the local cafés. I would pay the kitchen help a couple of bucks per five-gallon pail and then freeze the scraps for later use. Bears would walk right past a fresh horse or colt carcass to get to the edible scraps; they were easy to haul and use and didn't rot down or attract flies too badly.

For several years, I got loads of "end-of-run" candy from a company and was afraid I might be creating a population of diabetic bears. One of the best baits I ever used were 50-pound blocks of hard candy from the Jolly Rancher company in Denver. At the end of a production run, they would empty the machines into a plastic bag inside a box, creating a solid block of candy.

I put these sweet chunks in the bottom of the barrel, where a bear could scrape off a smidgen of the candy—just enough to pique his taste buds and keep him working the bait, even when all the other goodies were gone. The bears couldn't get the solid blocks through the holes in the barrel, and a block of candy would last all season, making sure there was always a bit of delectable and appealing bait left in the barrel. Unfortunately after a couple years, the company went to computerized candy making and did away with this long-lasting, fly-free, easily handled, un-spoilable, inde-structible, and irresistible form of bear bait.

For a number of years, in addition to edible garbage, I hauled pickup loads of outdated pastries and bread for bear bait. To add to the drawing power of these delicacies, I poured old honey, diluted 50 percent with water, over the whole mix. Honey is a great additive to all types of bear bait, and a good supply can be obtained from any beekeeper at a reasonable cost. The old honey keeps well, and if it turns sugary or solid, just adding hot water will make it pourable again.

I have burned honey on many a bear bait and had bears walk right up to the dense black cloud of cloyingly sweet smoke and actually burn their noses on the hot honey can. The past few years, I've added smoking scent sticks to my bear-baiting set-ups, as the dense, sweet, berry-flavored or anise-flavored smoke carries for considerable distances downwind.

The pungent smoking scent sticks can also be placed on both sides of the tree stand to help mask your scent or confuse the bear's sensitive olfactory organs at close range.

Grease is another additive that can enhance your bear bait. I've poured used grill and cooking grease from cafes and barbeque restaurants very effectively to enhance bread products for bear baiting. Grease garbage and bread products are great for advertising your bear baits far and wide. A bear stirring around a greasy bait site gets his paws and leg hair coated with the odiferous, oily stuff. When the satiated bruin saunters around his domain he leaves a strong, moisture-resistant scent trail clinging to everything it brushes up against. Any bear crossing or passing downwind of this trail has little trouble backtracking it right to the source—your bait site.

I know of several bear hunters and outfitters that simply dump grease on rotten logs or pour it on the ground and consider this a bear bait. Sure, bear will hit the grease site and dig around, licking up bits of greasy dirt and vegetation, but they aren't going to hit such a site regularly enough for my money, or that of my clients.

When I first started bear baiting, I simply dumped or placed my bait on the ground and then built a V-shaped corral of logs behind the bait to force the bear into position. If I was using a carcass of some kind, I wired or chained it to a tree to keep the bear from dragging it off. Birds and other critters devastated my baits, so I eventually switched to 55-gallon barrels with 7-inch diameter holes cut in both sides and a chain run through the holes and around a tree in a way as to keep the barrel locked in the upright position. The snap rim lids made filling these barrels a piece of cake and yet kept the bears out. During our first year of bear baiting in Saskatchewan, we figured we lost 70 percent of the fresh meat scraps on some of our baits to the hordes of rapacious ravens and crows. It didn't take long to switch to bird proof barrels for all of our baits.

The bear could easily dig and pull small quantities of bait through the holes but the ravens, crows and magpies were limited to scraps left on the ground. Barrels also made for a cleaner bait site and were a good gauge of a bear's size and trophy potential, as will be discussed later in the chapter. It didn't take the province of Saskatchewan long to realize the benefit of bait barrels and they are now required for baiting bears in the province.

Also, bear-bait placement is critical to the success of your venture. You can put the best bait in the world where a bear doesn't travel or is unlikely to locate the bait and your chance of success will be between zero and none.

Because bears prefer heavy cover, that's where your bait should be. However, there are several other factors that can increase your chances of success in placing a bear bait. Bears, like other big game species, require food, water, and protective habitat, so confine your baiting to areas near the other two essentials.

Bears, like other big-game species, require food, water, and protective habitat, so confine your baiting (food) to areas near the other two essentials.

I like to have a bait at the edge of, or near, a small clearing or opening for one simple reason. The ravens, crows, and magpies that can raise havoc with loose bait can also be your best advertising agents. When I first start bait, I place loose scraps where the birds can see it from the air. Their raucous racket will often attract bears that cannot see or smell your bait.

I don't want my bait site in the open or where a bear has to cross large open areas to get to it. A bait in such a location might get hit, but only late at night when the bear feels protected by the cover of darkness. Keep your baits close to escape cover and near a source of water, where the prevailing wind can carry the scent into the cover and the birds can advertise the bait's presence to every bear within hearing, and you'll earn your master's badge in baiting in short order.

Stand placement over bait is also critical to the success of a bear bowhunt. Remember, a bear has a very discerning nose and hearing as keen as any big-game animal. Many people would have you believe a bear has poor eyesight, but I don't subscribe to that theory at all. I have had bears pick up my camouflaged form at several hundred yards on numerous occasions. I think their vision is much better than they are given credit for, and I will continue to operate under that assumption until I can be convinced otherwise. I feel that a very high percentage of the bears taken over bait are fully aware of the hunter in the stand, but simply don't give a darn, as long as the hunter doesn't make any quick, noisy, threatening movements.

Wind is without a doubt the most critical factor in placing a bowhunting stand. The distance from hunter to bear is generally 20 yards or less, and a slight whiff of pungent human scent at that distance can put even a dominant old boar on red alert. I generally put my bear tree stands 16 feet above the ground and in a position where the least likely avenue of approach is behind the stand. In Saskatchewan, we were hunting along the lakeshore, so it was easy to place stands where we had both the prevailing breeze and the open shoreline working for us.

If you have to make a choice, choose the stand location with the wind in your favor at the time you will be bowhunting from the stand. Quite often, the prevailing breeze is from one direction during the day, and then it will switch directions toward evening. Make use of this anomaly to get your stand where the wind works for you. You can use scent blocker or eliminator and wear the best scent-suppressing clothing—all this helps—but the real key to success is hunting with the breeze in your face.

I constantly make use of a small, plastic squeeze bottle filled with scented talcum powder to check the wind currents and breezes from the stand location at a time of day when I will be hunting from the stand. A very simple procedure, but an extremely important one that can make the difference between a huge bear rug on the den wall or a blow-up photo of your mother-in-law.

Another crucial factor in choosing a bear stand location is the light direction. The best time to bowhunt bears over bait is in the late afternoon, so place your stand where it's fully shaded during the prime time. You certainly don't want to be lit up like a store window mannequin in the late afternoon light, where your slightest movement will be illuminated and intensified.

Once your stand is in position, inspect it thoroughly for the slightest squeak or scrape and get your bow and gear hangers situated where you can place and retrieve your equipment with a minimum of movement. The less disturbance you make when getting in and out of the stand, the better your chances of success.

'Course, there are exceptions to every rule. As a bear hunting guide and outfitter, I'm able to spend much more time working the baits on a regular basis than an individual hunter. Sometimes this can be used to a client's advantage.

In Colorado and Canada alike, both my guides and myself make little attempt to approach a bait site quietly and often drive a truck, boat, or four-wheeler as close to the bait as possible. We rattle the bait cans and barrels noisily while baiting and leave as much scent around as possible before leaving with a maximum of racket. This habituates the feeding bears to both noise and human scent around the bait. It also tunes them into the fact that when they hear the noise, they'll find fresh food at the bait. I make it a point to *never* go to the bait without leaving fresh enticement.

Sometimes bears can get a little too keyed to your arrival and departure, and numerous times in Canada when we were hunting wilderness areas where bears had little if any human contact, we'd pull up to the bait in a boat or on a four-wheeler and literally have to chase the bears while we were baiting the bait. Several years ago, Larry, one of our guides, got chased back to the boat by a big boar that met him at the bait. That evening, Larry accompanied a hunter back to the bait armed with a shotgun and pepper spray, and the client killed the 19-foot bear half an hour after Larry dropped him off.

When we take a client to the bait by boat or four-wheeler, we drive as close to the stand as possible and leave the engine running while we bang and clatter around, adding a bit of fresh bait to the can while the bowhunting client slips into the stand. When he is situated, we leave the site, making no effort to be quiet. Numerous times, before our truck or boat is out of sight, a hungry bear will be approaching the bait. Proper advertising pays off.

Anti-hunters have been quick to jump on bear baiting, hound hunting, and spring bear hunting in general as unethical, unsporting, and detrimental to the burgeoning bear populations. Which is total hogwash. Unfortunately, they were able to get this issue on ballots in several western states and convince the uneducated and unwashed masses, through lies and misinformation, that bear numbers were declining and spring hunting killed an abnormally high number of females with cubs. Consequently, spring bear hunting of any kind has been eliminated in many of the prime bear-producing states of the western United States, such as Colorado, Utah, and New Mexico.

FALL BEAR BOWHUNTING

The fall of the spring season has meant a spring in the fall season, with more bears roaming the western states than ever before. Bowhunting fall bears is a totally different proposition from hunting spring bears.

When a bear comes out of hibernation, it will spend four hours feeding and moving and up to 20 hours sleeping or resting. In the fall, the process is reversed, with the bear active and feeding up to 20 hours a day, taking minimal down time for rest or sleep. This gives a bowhunter who is willing to put in the time and effort ample opportunity to take a prime fall bear.

Food is the chief motivator for fall bears, so the obvious tactic is to bowhunt near food sources such as berry or acorn patches and grain fields. Water is also a critical element in many areas during the fall season, and man-made tanks, springs, and seeps are also superb places to ambush a thirsty fall bruin. When you can locate a water source adjacent to a food source, your chances of finding and arrowing a fall bear increase dramatically.

The best time to ambush a fall bear in a feeding area or waterhole is

Shot placement is critical on a bear, as it has a thick layer of fat and a long coat of hair.

during the late afternoon. Even though bears actively feed most of the day and are out and about at daylight, the mature bears likely will confine their feeding and movement to heavy cover during the daylight hours.

The warmer the weather, the less likely a fall bear will be found in the open during the day. The morning dew and dampness of the vegetation will generally fulfill a bear's water needs until later, after his siesta. In hot, dry weather, a bear may slip into a waterhole to slake his thirst mid-day, but the behavior is unpredictable, which makes waiting for one an iffy proposition at best.

The erratic, swirling mid-day thermals are another reason to stay away from a honey hole until the odds are loaded in your favor. When you find a prime fall bear ambush location, be patient and hunt it only when the conditions are the best possible. A woods-wise trophy bear can be as leery and spooky as a whitetail buck. Let him know you're in the area hunting him and lurking around his favorite feeding or watering spot, and he'll pull stakes and vacate the area in short order.

CALLING BEARS

Calling bears with a predator call is a way of hedging your bets during the autumn season and adding a whole new challenging dimension to your fall bear bowhunting. I carry several predator calls with me at all times during the fall and have called in a number of bears for clients and myself.

Fall bears are dominated by their appetite, and the alluring sounds of an animal in dire trouble might just bring them within bow range. For fall bear calling I prefer a call with a deep, raspy tone that imitates a deer fawn, calf elk, or big-game animal in distress. My favorite bear calls are the Circe/Lohman triple voice call, the Burnham Brothers Black Magic, and the Critt'r Call magnum.

Bears may respond to calling on the dead run or saunter in to the call with aggravating slowness. Bear calling takes a lot more effort than other types of game calling, as the best results come from almost continuous calling. Bears have a short attention span, and when the calls sound stops for extended periods of time, they lose interest and stop coming. When I set up to call bears, I stay for an hour to give a distant bear time to get within sight. Once a bear is spotted responding to the calling, I adapt it to his actions. When he stops or slows down, I call louder and more frantically. As long as he's headed my way, I make my calls just loud enough for him to hear, which keeps his attention focused.

Bear calling can keep the hackles on the back of your neck standing straight up, especially when an approaching bear suddenly disappears in the brush and you know he's close, but can't see him.

My first bear-calling adventure was the most potentially dangerous situation, with a darn good lesson. I was working on Afognak Island, Alaska, as a stream guard for the Alaska Department of Fish and Game at the time. I'd seen lots of cross and silver fox on the beaches and along the streams scrounging and decided to call some in for movies.

I picked a bright sunny morning, and as soon as it was light enough for filming, about 4:00 a.m. there, I eased my skiff into a small inlet and hiked a couple hundred yards to the edge of a clearing that was several hundred yards long and about one-hundred yards wide. I scrunched back under a spruce, got my camera ready for action, and ruined the peace and quiet of the morning with an agonizing series of distressed rabbit squealing and squalling calls.

The ear-ringing sounds had barely been absorbed by the impenetrable underbrush and moss-laden trees of the forest when a huge brown bear bounded out of the trees across the clearing from me and stood with his head swinging back and forth, trying to locate the source of the enticing sounds. One look at the size of that huge, hungry predator was all it took for the ignoramus source of those sounds to slither soundlessly and speedily away from the clearing, my tongue stuck to the roof of my mouth, and the predator call buried deep in a jacket pocket. As soon as I got a short distance from the meadow, I ran like heck to my boat, expecting at any minute to be overrun by the 700-pound fox I'd called up. If that bear had come in behind me while I was calling, there's a good chance I wouldn't be writing this book.

Any bear attracted to a predator call, expecting to find something warm, fuzzy, and edible to munch, has to be treated as a potentially dangerous adversary, whether it's a black bear or grizzly. Prudent precautions should be taken to make sure you end up the victor and not the victim. In northern Saskatchewan where I operated a black bear hunting camp, the backcountry bears rarely encountered humans and were "king of the bush," with little innate fear of man or beast. We had a number of close encounters and our clients either carried magnum canisters of potent pepper spray or a 12-gauge stoked with 3-inch magnum No. 4 copper-plated buckshot loads as back up. The same advice would be well taken when you're setting up to call bears with a predator call.

Calling with a partner is an excellent method of fall bear hunting and two sets of eyes are always better than one for spotting an incoming bruin. Several years ago, I had a bear-crazy client and his wife bowhunting elk with me in southwestern Colorado. When one of my guides stated he'd seen several different bears along a road while bringing his elk hunters in for a midday break and breakfast, I decided we'd better take a look. I figured there must be a steer carcass or a patch of ripe service berries near where the bears were spotted. It was noon when we got to the area and a gorgeous brown phase bear ran across the road in front of my truck to vanish into the dense oakbrush above the road. The sight of the bear had my client couple hot-wired to the limit, and as I drove another half mile down the road, they were jabbering non-stop about trying for the bear that evening. "Got a better idea," I stated as a pulled into the shade of a ponderosa along the road. "We'll sneak back and set up, and I'll call the bear in for Jerry to shoot." I quipped confidently.

Half an hour later, we'd eased to within 200 yards of where the bear had crossed and set up on an oakbrush-covered bench. I put the client 20 yards in front of me and had his nervous wife sitting by my side in the shade at the base of a huge ponderosa pine. I'd advised Jerry that if the bear came on the run, I'd stop calling when the bruin was in position for a shot, which should stop the bear. My plan worked almost too well. The first series of agonized squalls brought the bear into an opening 100 yards away, and when I cut loose again he came bolting right at Sharon, the hunter's wife, and me on the dead run. When he was 30 yards out, I cut back on the volume and intensity of my calling, which slowed him to a fast trot. When the bear hit the 15-yard mark, I stopped calling, and by the time the bear stopped, he was facing a very nervous Sharon and me at 10 yards. He was also broadside to Jerry at 10 yards. The instant he came to a full stop Jerry's arrow zipped through him non-stop and successfully ended the confrontation—much to his wife's relief.

BEAR HUNTING WITH HOUNDS

Not many bowhunters are in position or have the time to raise and train a pack of bear dogs. Consequently, they miss out on the challenge, frustrations, camaraderie, and rewards in seeing such endeavors come together in forming an efficient bear-hunting team.

Clients hiring an outfitter that hunts with hounds also do not get to see the hunts average out the way the dog man does. I've had clients whose hunt was over the first morning after an easy, quick chase and cooperative bear. Several of these unenlightened bowhunters complained they would never hunt with hounds again because the bear didn't have a chance against the well-trained dogs. Little do they know.

The next hunter may spend five days of trudging over mountains and through canyons listening to the distant dogs trailing a hound-wise bear on

Hunting bears with hounds is an exciting adventure and requires a hunter to be in top physical condition. Also, remember to practice shooting that will simulate shooting a treed bear.

hot, dry hillsides without ever seeing a hair of the bear. Some of these clients have left camp with their tail between their legs vowing never again to try and hunt the abominable, "un-bayable" black bear unless it's from a tree stand over a bait.

Only the outfitter in any hunting situation gets to see enough action and different situations to have any comprehension of what the "average" hunt is like.

The best advice I can give on preparing for a bear hunt with hounds is to get yourself in good physical condition, because the longer you can last on the hunt, the better your chances of bringing home a trophy bear.

Feet are the first to go on a bear chase. Most bowhunters have probably spent the winter months in front of the TV without tromping around much, keeping their legs and feet in condition. Spend some time climbing the bleachers at the football stadium or up and down the gravel piles at a local gravel pit with a hefty pack on your back. A little conditioning at home will make a big difference when it comes to negotiating rough country on a bear chase. Don't plan on breaking in a new pair of lug-soled boots (a prerequisite on a hound bear hunt) on your hound bear hunt; do it at home where the consequences won't be as disastrous.

I've had pro football players and marathon runners who thought they were going to die on a bear chase because their legs, feet, and muscles weren't conditioned to climbing over logs and rocks while hiking up and down the mountainous terrain that a black bear calls home.

A black bear can outrun a horse on flat ground and has the stamina to stay ahead of a pack of bawling bear dogs all day long, especially if he's survived previous hound hunter encounters. When a mature bruin is being pursued by a pack of hounds, he'll head for the most inhospitable habitat he can find and negotiate the rugged terrain with ease. Most bear chases are determined by Murphy's Law, so you can bet the better shape you're in, the closer to the truck the bear will tree. If you're looking for a tough, day-after-day, ass-dragging bear hunt with hounds, just show up for the hunt out of shape and hoping for a quick, easy time of it.

Practice your shooting on the ground, but also do some shooting that will simulate shooting a treed bear. I've had good bowshots shoot up all their arrows at treed bears without drawing blood because of the excitement, bear fever, and the impossible angles involved.

When you go on a bear chase, take a *full* quiver of arrows, and if you've got any apprehensions, have your outfitter or guide carry an extra handful. My guides and I have walked many miles retrieving extra arrows from the truck or camp because a shook-up bowhunter couldn't seem to get an arrow and a bayed bear in the same place at the same time.

SPOT-AND-STALK BEAR HUNTING

Spot-and-stalk is the ultimate challenge in bowhunting any species. When you're dealing with hairy critters that have the equipment, ability, and often the temperament to do serious damage to your tender young body, spot-and-stalk hunting for bears takes on a whole new dimension. It is the leading method for taking grizzly, brown, and polar bears and is equally effective on these species in spring and fall alike.

The first prerequisite for successful spot-and-stalk bear hunting is to see your adversary *before* it sees you. Bears may not have the best eyesight in the realm of big-game animals, but I've seen them pick out a camouflaged hunter at 100 yards and disappear in a heartbeat on more than one occasion.

I've had several grizzly licenses in Alaska when bowhunting other species and blown several stalks on them. The times I've been in a situation to arrow one of these tremendous trophy animals, they had me pinpointed. Shooting a black bear at point-blank range

When still-hunting black bear in the fall, their color variations blend in well with the tans and browns of fall vegetation. Unlike when you are hunting a deer, you won't see the white flicker of a tail or a white rump patch that gives a deer away.

when he knows you're there may not be real smart, but doing the same with a grizzly or brown bear is more like suicide.

Good binoculars and a spotting scope are essential to spot-and-stalk bear hunting and the propensity for letting your eyes do the walking until you spot a stalkable bear. Once you spot a shootable bear, be patient, take your time to watch his movements and plan your stalk to the last detail. Keep the wind and sun direction in mind and use your spotting scope to study terrain features you can use to get within bow range of your quarry. I would venture that over 90 percent of the blown stalks on big-game animals are due to impatience and "pushing the envelope" to get the shot. Patience is next to godliness when it comes to spot-and-stalk hunting, especially when your adversary is armed with formidable teeth, claws, and attitude.

JUDGING TROPHY BEARS

Bears are without doubt the toughest big-game animals to judge for the record book. It's extremely hard to accurately determine the size of a bear's skull under a thick covering of hide and long hair, especially if you haven't

When bears first emerge in the spring, they are intent on eating and will be in places where spring growth is abundant, along stream banks, ponds, lakes, and swampy areas.

encountered many bears in the wild under hunting conditions. When I first started guiding and outfitting for bear hunters, I bought a spring scale to get an accurate weight of all the bears killed. I got rid of the scale after the first season because all the bears weighed less than half what the hunter estimated, and I figured it was better for business if they claimed to have killed a 400-pound behemoth bear rather than one that actually weighed 160 pounds on the scale.

"Ground shrinkage" is probably more acute with bear hunters than any other type of big-game hunting. We used 55-gallon drums for bear-bait containers and advised our hunters that, if the top of a standing bear's back reached the second ring on the barrel, it was an average-sized bear. If the top of its back was between the second ring and the top of the barrel, it would be close to record-book class. And if the top of its back was *above* the barrel top . . . shoot quickly.

A large boar bear is easy to judge because of its massive bulk, low-slung build, and broad, heavy head. A lean, gangly, leggy young bear is equally easy to judge. It's the large, bulky females with their hefty build and smaller skulls, and the equally bulky mid-sized males with skulls that might just make the record book, that are the stinkers to judge down to the last inch.

To add to the confusion, there are long, lean, lanky bears that aren't very impressive looking, with long skulls that will measure better than they appear, and then there are short, stocky

Bears spend time looking for insects in downed trees and under rocks. Still-hunting with the wind in your face in potential feeding areas will get you a bow shot like this.

bears that look massive, with short, wide skulls that measure less than appearances indicate.

There isn't any magic formula for accurately judging the difference between a bear with a skull measuring 17 3/4 inches and one with a skull measuring 18 1/4 inches that qualifies for the Pope and Young record book.

Any bear, regardless of skull measurement, is a trophy. The condition and color of the pelt may be more of a determining trophy factor than skull size to many bowhunters, myself included. I've often had clients take a smaller bear with a prime, unblemished pelt or different color phase over a larger animal with a scruffy, badly rubbed hide. Beauty is definitely in the eye of the beholder when it comes to bear pelts. The only person you have to please on your bear hunt is *you*.

Bears are tough critters with tremendous vitality and endurance. Couple these factors with the sometimes impenetrable habitat in which they thrive, and it's not hard to see that a bad hit or inferior equipment is going to lead to a less-than-desirable experience and a lost animal.

I've had bowhunters take bears with longbows, recurves, crossbows, and compounds, so any bow you can shoot well will do the job on a black bear when a good broadhead is properly placed. Several of my lady clients have made clean kills on large bears with 42-pound bows, shooting two-bladed, razor-sharp, cut-on-contact broadheads.

Bows and arrow shaft type are not critical as long as you can put the arrow where you want it. But broadheads are extremely critical, and so am I. I prefer a cutting type broadhead to penetrate a bear's thick fur, heavy muscle, and fat layers, and my clients and I have made many clean kills with these heads. I do not like mechanical broadheads for anything other than turkeys and did not allow them in my bear-hunting camp, nor do I allow them in my whitetail camp in Iowa. There are simply too many things that can go wrong for me or one of my clients to take a chance on wounding and losing a bear because a mechanical broadhead malfunctioned.

Almost all the wounded and lost bears I have encountered over the past 40 years of bear hunting and guiding have been hit too far forward. I admonish my clients constantly to keep away from the massively muscled and heavy-boned front shoulders. The likelihood of recovering a bear hit too far back is much greater than a front-end hit bruin. Bears are built similarly to humans, and their lungs extend much further back than most hunters think. A sharp forward-angle shot behind the shoulder can be deflected by the outside of the rib cage, or can slice along it, exiting the front of the chest. Unless the shooter is lucky enough to cut open the brachial artery down the inside of the front leg, the bear is going to get away.

Proper shot placement and a razor-sharp broadhead are critical to penetrating a bear's thick layer of fat and into its vitals for a clean kill shot.

Several years ago, I had a client make just such a shot on a gorgeous blonde-colored bear while bowhunting with us in Canada. He had a video camera mounted in the tree behind him and got a perfect shot of the hit and the bear running off. After watching the video numerous times and seeing the arrow strike in a seemingly perfect hit behind the shoulder, the hunter was convinced we would find his bear. I wasn't. I'd trailed the bear for a quarter mile, then lost the blood trail entirely and figured the hit was non-fatal. However, I don't give up on a wounded animal easily, and the following morning, six of us did a grid search for four hours where I'd lost the blood trail. I became even more convinced that, despite what it looked like on video, the hit did little damage to the bear.

Late that afternoon, the bowhunter killed the very same bear on the same bait. The previous hit had gone in behind the front shoulder, grazed off the ribs and exited through the front of the chest . . . just what the blood trail indicated. Both entrance and exit holes were sealed over and were starting to heal. If we hadn't seen the bear on video and identified it by its unique markings and color, we might have missed the 24-hour-old wounds entirely. Bears are unique and tough animals. Treat them with the respect they deserve and you'll never have an unsuccessful bear bowhunt. ■

ELK

Majestic or magnificent would have to be the words that aptly characterize a bull elk, with his head thrown back, colossal, rapier-tined, ivory-tipped, mahogany-brown antlers caging his heaving chest and flanks. His high-pitched bugling whistles and deep, growling grunts echo and reverberate across the valleys and float up the steep mountain slopes. Add a landscape of frost-sparkled meadows corralled by shimmering gold-leaved aspens, intense green spruce, and pine against a backdrop of snow-capped mountain peaks, and an azure sky flawed only by puffs of clouds, and it's understandable why thoughts of bowhunting the wily wapiti run rampant in almost every bowhunter's aspirations.

If I really and seriously had to choose a single critter *(heaven forbid)* that is the ultimate bowhunting challenge year after year, and one that I never tire of bowhunting, it would be the bull elk. Elk are large, tough, intelligent beasties with survival instincts unrivaled by any other hoofed big-game animal. A mature bull can sport a set of antlers liable to give even an experienced bowhunter the adrenaline rush of a lifetime and the shakes and shimmies of a Greek belly dancer. Best of all, elk meat is about as delectable a table fare as there is, and there's lots of it.

Elk were originally foothill animals that roamed most of northern and western North America, but due to their size, herd instincts, availability, and edibility, the vast herds were quickly decimated by market hunting and the survivors were forced into the most remote reaches of mountains to escape annihilation. Today, through wise and often lucky game management, the wily wapiti have expanded their range and numbers and have been reintroduced to many former haunts where they were previously eradicated.

Elk are broken down into three distinct subspecies groups, the largest and most extensive being the Yellowstone elk, which was reclassified in the mid-2000s as the American elk as far as the Pope and Young and Boone and Crockett record books are concerned. The Roosevelt or Olympic elk resides in the rain forests of Washington, Oregon, and southern British Columbia,

Canada. The Tule elk, whose range is limited to the confines of California, is found in such limited numbers, with equally restricted hunting access, that it is not listed as a separate category in the Pope and Young record books, although Boone and Crockett does have a separate Tule elk category.

The American elk range extends from British Columbia, Idaho, and Nevada eastward through the Rocky Mountains and into the prairie states of North and South Dakota and Nebraska. American elk have been transplanted back into their native haunts as far east as Pennsylvania and southward to Oklahoma. Poaching and lack of the huge tracts of land needed have been the major drawbacks to some of these transplanted herds expanding fully and re-establishing themselves. For the most part, these transplants are holding their own, and in some cases the increasing numbers allow for limited hunting seasons.

American elk are by far the most numerous and widespread members of the wily wapiti family and the most sought after by the bowhunting fraternity.

Elk country is immense. Your toughest challenge will be conquering the steep and heavily forested land where these majestic animals live.

One would think that with hunters, from the earliest native Americans to the current compound-wielding bowhunters, pursuing them, the trophy quality and size of these majestic mountain dwellers would have declined somewhat. Nothing could be farther from the truth. Under modern game management and the wily wapiti's propensity for self preservation and reproduction, American elk are more numerous than ever, and the trophy quality of bulls in many areas has never been better.

I've often heard hunters claiming to have killed a 1000-pound bull elk, but a bull that size is a rarity. One fall on a private ranch in the south San Juan mountains of Colorado, I guided Billy Ellis to a huge 6x6 bull that about did us in packing it out. When we got the four skinned quarters to the processor, minus the legs, head, hide, and antlers, the quarters weighed a whopping 449 pounds.

It's usually figured that the four quarters without hide, head, and legs will weight approximately 50 percent of the live weight. That would put this bull's weight at 898 pounds, which stood as the heaviest four quarters weighed at that processing plant for many years and may still be the record.

Most mature bulls weigh 600 to 800 pounds live, with large mature cows in the 500–700 pound class. You don't really appreciate an elk's size until you get one down three miles from the truck on a hot September morning and wonder how the heck you're going to haul it out before it spoils or gets fly blown. Unfortunately, many elk hunters are not prepared for this chore and end up losing some of the best eating on hooves.

I've had a lot of clients who figured that bowhunting and killing a critter the size of an elk would be easy. Wrong! An elk's sense of smell will rival or exceed that of any big-game animal, including a mature whitetail buck. I've had a herd of elk wind me from half a mile away and not even hesitate in getting the heck out of Dodge. Their eyesight is superb, as is their hearing. Elk have the brain capacity and honed survival instincts to instantly add all the input from their superlative senses into an escape and evasion plan that often leaves bowhunters wondering "wha' happen?" Throw in the elk's tremendous strength, stamina, and penchant for covering miles of rugged terrain with ease, and you have a game animal worthy of the best of your bowhunting efforts.

When I was guiding and outfitting for elk bowhunters, one of the most common questions asked by potential clients was: "What do you guarantee on your guided elk hunts?" My usual comment was: "Nothing. In fact, I don't even guarantee you'll have a good time on your elk hunt." When you're a flatlander covering miles and miles in mountainous, foot-blistering terrain at airplane altitudes, even when you see elk and maybe even kill one, I certainly couldn't call the pursuit of this indomitable member of the deer family fun. Bowhunting elk is hard work—and the harder you work, the luckier you'll be.

Elk are herd animals, especially during the fall breeding period or rut. Like other antlered big game, the bulls of summer remain alone or in small bachelor herds while their velvet-covered antlers grow to fighting size. An elk's antler growth is one of nature's most phenomenal occurrences. The bulls don't shed their antlers until February or March, and their awesome headgear is fully grown by August. The only other cells that divide and grow as fast as elk antler cells are cancer cells, and much cancer research has evolved from the study of fast-growing elk antler cells. Asian people have long praised the soft velvet-covered elk antler as a cure-all for many things and as a powerful aphrodisiac.

In August, as the bulls' testosterone levels rise and their antlers harden, they move into pre-rut mode by rubbing the velvet from their antlers, fighting trees and brush, and sparring with each other to build up neck and shoulder muscles. The larger bulls move in and start hanging out with small groups of cows and calves and asserting their dominance over any bull that approaches their harem. Their cow-attracting and competitor-intimidating bugling and grunting activity increases and peaks somewhere between September 15 and October 1 in most elk areas of the West.

It's a no-brainer that calling in a belligerent, bellowing bull elk and arrowing it at point-blank range is the epitome of the elk-bowhunting experience. However, elk are out and about 24 hours a day, 365 days a year, and the peak of the rut isn't the only time to bowhunt them. In fact, it may be the toughest time to kill an elk.

EARLY-SEASON ELK-AMBUSHING TACTICS

Archery season in most of the elk states generally opens before the bulls are fully into rut mode, filling the countryside with their high-pitched challenges and announcing their whereabouts to anything with ears. Hunting silent elk is a whole different ball game from bowhunting bugling bulls. The weather during the early part of the archery elk season is generally on the warm-to-hot side, and this can be the key to getting your arrow and a bull in the same place at the same time.

Over the years, my clients and I have had a much higher success rate per elk encounter when hunting from ambush than using any other method. During the early season, elk wallows, waterholes or springs, natural mineral licks, and travel routes are deadly places to set an ambush. Elk are not quite as habitual in their daily movements as some of the other species of big game, but they do have favorite haunts that they use regularly enough to make patiently hunting them a worthwhile endeavor.

Pit blinds have long been one of my favorite methods of ambushing elk. Whether they're in an oak brush thicket where there aren't any trees big enough for a tree stand or in an open meadow at the edge of a wide-open pond, pit blinds are the most deadly elk tactic in the book.

Several years ago, I was bowhunting with outfitter Dick Ray in New Mexico in the early season, when it was hot and dry. I'd passed up several small bulls and called in a nice 5x5 for one of Dick's hunters but still hadn't found the one I wanted. I had several days left to bowhunt when Dick told me that some ranch hands building fence on a high bench covered with dense

Elk will retreat to the deep timber shortly after day break. You may find them in small clearings in basins where the hunting pressure is light or non-existent.

oak brush motts had seen a 6x6 bull watering two afternoons in a row at a tank dam in the middle of a wide-open pasture. According to them, the bull came from one direction one late afternoon and the opposite direction the following afternoon.

The next afternoon, one of Dick's guides and I drove to the area and found the waterhole pounded by elk tracks. There wasn't a speck of cover within 100 yards of the small pond. We finished the three-hour chore of digging a spacious pit blind into the face of the dam and camouflaging it with oak brush and were settled in its shaded interior by 5:00 p.m. At 5:30, I arrowed a huge 6x6 that walked out of the oak brush 200 yards across the meadow and came straight to the waterhole without giving our blind a second glance. I'll trade three hours of digging for a bull like that any day.

Pit blinds can be used almost anywhere you can get a hole in the ground. Elk are accustomed to danger approaching or appearing above ground level, and they tend to overlook things below eye level. A few years ago, my secretary, Dawn Walker, bowhunted a pit blind we'd dug 25 yards from a spring in an open valley within a mile of my house. She wasn't going to be fussy and intended to take the first legal elk within bow range. The first afternoon she sat in the blind, a half dozen elk charged off the oak brush slopes to water just before dark. There were several cows and a nice 4x4 bull drinking 20 yards from her, and she couldn't shoot because there was a spike bull (protected in Colorado) standing *five feet* away, right in the shooting lane, and another just a bit farther out. They shuffled around in front of her, almost kicking dirt into the pit, completely unaware of her presence. The others finished watering and wandered into the meadow to feed and then moved in to water. The next afternoon, she arrowed a hefty yearling and had to call on reinforcements to help her get it out.

A pit blind is about as simple and easy an ambush site as you can get. When possible, I dig them to the same dimensions as covered in the antelope chapter and usually cover them over entirely with sagebrush, tumble weeds, oak brush, or pine boughs, so the bowhunter is sitting in the dark. An elk's sense of smell is acute, so choosing a pit blind location downwind is very important. However, I've found that scent control is much easier hunting out of a pit blind. Unless there is a stiff breeze, human scent tends to hang in the cooler confines of the pit. The surrounding covering, sprayed liberally with scent eliminator or scent killer or doused with a potent elk scent, helps dilute or cover the dreaded human odor. On several occasions, my clients and I have had elk munch on the leaves and branches covering a pit blind. Talk about a heart-thumping encounter.

The other end of the elk-ambushing spectrum is the use of tree stands. I've had clients take a number of elk from tree stands over wallows, springs, mineral licks, and well-traveled trails over the years, and they can be one of the most efficient and effective methods of bowhunting elk. Elk won't hesitate to look up, so movement, or the lack thereof, is a crucial factor.

A lightweight, portable tree stand is an essential item if you're planning an elk bowhunt. Leave the climbers at home, because most western tree types have too many limbs to make them usable, and even though they can be used on quaking aspen, care should be taken to keep your safety belt in constant use because the spongy, soft bark of an aspen can peel out from under the stand and give you a rough ride to the ground.

Background is extremely important when putting up a tree stand for elk. Elk are well-tuned to the dangers associated with the human shape, and getting skylined is a sure way to end your elk bowhunt on a sour note. I've had elk taken from tree stands in cedars and junipers that were only eight feet off the ground because the almost solid background and dense shadows made the bowhunter invisible to the elk. Height isn't nearly as important as good background cover and concealment.

There have been a lot of pros and cons written about how effective it is to bowhunt elk wallows, and there is no pat answer that covers all conditions. I've taken elk bowhunting well-used wallows and spent many fruitless hours sitting over a seemingly "hot" wallow without seeing hide nor hair of a wily wapiti.

Elk are liable to use a wallow at any time of day or night, and there doesn't seem to be a peak time to hunt at one. I've found that during hot and dry weather, bowhunting wallows late morning and early afternoon seems to pay off about as much as any other time. Locating and hunting over a well-used fresh wallow during mid-day is a good way to spend time between your early morning spot-and-stalk or bugling hunt and your late afternoon hunt.

SPOT-AND-STALK ELK BOWHUNTING

Spot-and-stalk bowhunting is the second most productive method of putting an elk on the ground with a bow and arrow and can be a real test of your bowhunting skill and perseverance.

Elk are big animals and live in big country, and this combination is what gives spot-and-stalk hunters nightmares. I've heard it said that 90 percent of the elk live in 10 percent of the country, and while that may not be true under all circumstances, it's a pretty fair summation of the situation. Most first-time elk hunters can't comprehend the vastness of elk country and the ease with which these long-legged ungulates roam their home habitat.

A number of years ago, immediately after quitting the Colorado Division of Wildlife, I took over management of a piece of elk "heaven" called Catspaw. The ranch was 60,000 acres of prime elk habitat. A wide mountain valley bordered on the west side by the 9,000-foot Chalk Mountain range and the Continental Divide on the east. The elk on the ranch were relatively undisturbed and fed in the lush meadows bordering the Navajo River as it meandered down the valley bottom. Even these un-hunted elk would move a mile or more up the valley slopes to bed in the heavy timber during the day. If an undisturbed elk normally moves a mile or two from feeding to bedding areas, imagine what elk that are harassed will do.

Many whitetail bowhunters try the same tactics on elk and come up short because they don't cover enough ground. My spot-and-stalk philosophy is to get into the area I intend hunting in the pre-dawn darkness and try to cover

If you hunt public land, let other hunters move the elk around during the mid-day hours. Keep posted during your lunch break where you can glass an area where elk may show.

as much ground as I can until I locate elk, either by sound, fresh tracks and droppings, or smell.

Since I am very careful to take advantage of the slightest mountain breeze and hunt with the wind in my favor as much as humanly possible, I can often smell the sweet, licorice-like smell of elk before I see them. I've had clients follow me around for days without realizing that I'm constantly checking the wind with my trusty powder bottle filled with talcum powder. Sometimes all it takes is a small shift in direction to keep the wind in your favor, and it's senseless to try stalking or still-hunting elk if they have the slightest chance of smelling you.

Many times I've glassed elk that spooked at a hunter's scent while the hunter was a half-mile or more away. Doesn't take much human scent to pollute the pure mountain air to the point of spooking a hunter-shy elk. The problem is seriously compounded if you're bowhunting when the elk are herded up and the number of eyes, ears, and noses is multiplied. Keep this fact in mind on your elk hunts: *When the sun goes up, so does the wind, and when the sun sinks, the late afternoon breeze flows downhill.*

I'm always amazed when a client shows up for an elk hunt and doesn't have a good pair of binoculars. Many bowhunters feel binoculars are for use in wide-open country and from a stand, but I make constant use of them when spot-and-stalk or still-hunting through the woods. I glass every nook and cranny that might harbor a hidden elk, looking for anything that could possibly be the ear, nose, rump patch, or antler tip of a hidden elk.

Even binoculars are not infallible when it comes to dealing with elk. One fall, I was poking along through a dense patch of thick downfall timber when I spotted a light patch of color against the dark background. I froze in mid-stride and glassed the patch for a full 30 minutes, trying to tell whether it was an elk or a patch of sunlight against the rotted end of a stump. A dozen times I decided it had to be the side of a bull elk and two dozen times I decided it was the end of a stump. After half an hour, my eyes burned like someone had poured salt in them as I tried vainly to find ears, antlers, or anything that resembled part of an elk. Finally my patience gave out and I convinced myself that no self-respecting elk would lay there that long without some hint of movement. Even then I wasn't convinced and decided to backtrack and approach from a different angle. Hah! The wily elk was more patient than I was, because the instant I took a step backward, a 5x5 bull crashed out of its bed and vanished.

Don't waste your money on a small cheapie set of pocket binoculars, because they'll just cause you grief and maybe cost you a trophy elk. Binoculars are a once-in-a-lifetime purchase, so get a second job, save your money, and buy the best set of binoculars you can afford. For elk hunting, I prefer a set of quality medium-sized 7x42 or 8x32s. These glasses are powerful enough for long-distance glassing but gather plenty of light for early-morning and late- afternoon glassing, and they are especially useful in dark-timber situations. Don't just buy them and carry them in your fanny pack or daypack. Get used to using them regularly. They can make a big difference in the success or failure of your spot-and-stalk elk hunt.

High-country, above timberline, spot-and-stalk bowhunting is the epitome of the elk-hunting challenge. There's no way an elk hunt in such country can be anything but successful, even if you never kill an elk.

Fortunately or unfortunately, there are no figures on just how many spot-and-stalk elk hunts are blown by impatience. Judging from my own experiences, I'd say the figure is above the 90 percent level. It seems no matter how long you wait, it's not long enough. If you err, do so on the side of patience.

Spotting elk in the high country can be easy or difficult, depending on how smart you work your spotting. Trying to pick out elk in the early morning or late afternoon grayness of a shadowed mountainside is exceedingly difficult when you're trying to glass *into* the sun. Glassing elk when the early-morning or late afternoon sun is at your back, with its gilding rays of warm light lighting up the scenery and the elk's light-tan hide, is a piece of cake. There are places where I only glass when the morning sun lights up the countryside and any elk around glow like neon signs, and there are places where I only glass in the early evening for the same reason.

There are places where I have to change locations a few hundred yards as the sun moves up or down to see into pockets, valleys, clearings, and hidey holes with the light working for me. Make the shadows and light work for you, rather than inhibiting your ability to pick out the shape or form of an elk long before it has a chance to pick you out. The key to success in spot-and-stalk bowhunting any critter is to pinpoint your quarry *before* it spots you.

Another key to long-distance, high-country spot-and-stalk elk bowhunting is having and making use of a good spotting scope. I have two favorites. The first is my Nikon 15x-45x, 72 mm ED Field Scope with an accessory 60x eyepiece for ultra-long-distance spotting, when conditions are optimum and I need the additional power to judge a trophy or pick a foolproof stalking route. This scope is on the heavy side but is superbly sharp and clear at the higher magnification, and I generally use it with a sturdy tripod or window mount on my truck window.

The second is a lightweight, waterproof, rubber-armored Nikon 16x-48x XL Spotter II. This little scope is also very sharp and clear and easily transported in a fanny pack or daypack into the roughest, back country elk terrain. A small, sturdy tripod increases the scope's effectiveness, but I generally use it supported by my hat or pack over a log or rock with equally good results.

ELK CALLING 101

"How the heck can anyone miss an animal the size of a bull elk at 30 yards or less?" my client questioned as we sat down to one of my wife's sumptuous suppers the night before his elk bowhunt started.

"Kind of hard to explain," I replied to the point, "until you've been there."

The second day of his bowhunt, we were slipping our way through the dense oak brush on a side slope in the dark when we heard a bull bugle on the slope above and in front of us.

There was a series of small clearings or meadows interspersed with large and small oak brush motts on the slope, and the bull sounded like he was within a couple hundred yards. I put my client in front of a small clump of oak brush where his green camo would blend with the background and slid down at the base of a Ponderosa a few yards behind him. The breeze was drifting down the slope, so we'd have the wind on the bull unless he circled below us, a definite possibility.

The bull bugled every ten minutes or so, and as soon as there was good shooting light, I waited for a bugle, then immediately answered with some seductive (I thought) cow calls. The bull fired back instantly and I could see by my client's body language that he was fully alert and ready for action.

The bull's next bugle left little doubt he was headed our way. Five minutes later, his tan form came drifting silently through the brush 50 yards in front of us. The cautious bull drifted down hill and stopped just out of bow range, where he locked up and bugled several times, trying to get a rise out of the cow he'd heard, and gave us a good look at his tall, massive 6x6 rack.

Much to the consternation of my compadre, I never made a sound. I'd been frequently checking the breeze with my powder bottle as the bull approached and figured, if I called, he'd likely sidehill below us, just out of range, and pick up our scent. After ten tense minutes, the bull finally lost interest and moseyed back the way he'd come. The minute he was out of sight, I slithered to my client and motioned for him to hustle forward 50 yards to another clump of oak brush, where we quickly set up in the same relative positions.

Once again I cow called excitedly, getting an immediate response from the bull less than 100 yards up the slope. I quickly cut loose with a challenging high-pitched spike-bull squeal followed by several more beseeching cow mews. The bull came crashing through the bushes, stopped behind a clump of brush 40 yards in front of my client and proceeded to thrash the brush grunting and bugling his sex-crazed fury.

I was keeping one eye on my client kneeling ten feet from me

One of the best elk calls is a cow call. Keep the calling light and be ready for action if a bull is within calling range.

and could see his arrow bouncing on the rest as the bull circled around the brush and headed our way. When he stepped into a small opening 30 yards below us, I chirped sharply and brought him to a halt where my thoroughly shook-up bowhunter put an arrow right over his shoulders. The bull vanished as quickly as he came, and we could hear him crashing brush and rattling rocks for 200 yards up the hill.

"That's exactly how people miss elk at point-blank range," I chortled to my chagrined, red-faced client. "Now you've been there."

Every elk bowhunter dreams of bugling a bull within bow range, and I'll be the first to admit this is as good as bowhunting gets. However, calling elk isn't the same as it was when I killed my first elk in the early '60s. Today's elk hunter is far more knowledgeable, with a better understanding of elk habits and idiosyncrasies, and calling techniques and tactics, than ever before. With the proliferation of magazine articles, videos, television programs, and live seminars, the plethora of elk bowhunting and calling information available is phenomenal.

Unfortunately, the elk have learned about as rapidly as their nemeses, and those that didn't learn have been removed from the gene pool.

I bugled in my first bull with a coiled piece of gas pipe that sounded horrible compared to modern calls, but the elk were so uninitiated, they responded readily. Today I call less than ever and rarely bugle, but my percent of response is as good or better than ever.

When I enter the woods, elk hunting during the rut, I try to remain totally undetected by the elk until I am in the best-possible position to seduce or infuriate a bull within bow range. I've observed many bowhunters tooting and chirping their way through the woods like the pied piper of the Rockies, and even if they get a bull to respond to their calling, they don't know it.

During the early part of the bow season in most elk states, the elk are just tuning up for the rut and only bugling perfunctorily. They'll respond to good calling at this time, but guardedly and silently. When I feel I'm close to elk in the early season, I set up and use cow and calf mews and chirps for at least an hour or more without moving.

Later in the season, when the herd bulls have gathered their harems, the rules of engagement change. There are lots of eyes, ears, and noses to defeat getting within range of herd bull, and calling him away from his harem is a tough proposition. I've found the best way to do this is to get as close to the herd without spooking them before making a sound. Start calling too soon and the bull will round up his girls and move them away. By the time the dominant bulls have their harems together, they're ready to forgo the fighting for some *loving,* and if given half a chance will drive their cows away from aggressive bugling.

When I'm hunting a herd bull covered up by cows, I try to sneak as close as possible, making sure the wind is in my favor. When I get close (depending on my whims and the conditions), I'll usually cow call softly in hopes of suckering the bull away from his herd. Squealing like a competing spike at this time might just spook him into flight with his harem or bring him on the run.

Several years ago, I slipped to within 75 yards of a herd with a good bull and managed to get between the bull and most of his harem as they crossed an overgrown logging road. I was kneeling behind some serviceberry bushes with the bull just over the ridge above me. When I cut loose with a spike-bull squeal, that dang bull charged down the hill and sideswiped the bush I was behind with his awesome antlers. Try staying in place when that happens. By the time I got my heart off the roof of my mouth and my arrow back on the string, the whole herd had vanished.

Later that same fall, I followed a 5x5 with his herd of cows up the slopes on Catspaw, and when I got within 100 yards, I started cow calling. The herd bull came off the slope and crossed a small clearing and stopped 30 yards from me behind some quaking aspen trees. How an 800-pound animal can hide behind a six-inch tree is beyond comprehension, but a bull elk is a master at it. I froze in position and as the bull turned to head back to his harem I jerked my bow to full draw, released, and sideswiped a stump that suddenly appeared between us. My aluminum arrow ricocheted off the stump and slammed into an aspen. The startled bull got to the far side of the clearing before I could get my hyper cow call in action, but at the first sounds, the bull whirled and headed back for another look-see. This time I was at full draw when he paused in an opening at 30 yards, and my Phantom tipped XX75 caught him in the center of his chest and put him down within 50 yards.

As I mentioned, my first elk call was a coiled gas pipe. I went from there to a modified Herters metal-reed deer call that I had to blow so hard to get the breaking bugle, the insides of my cheeks often ended up bleeding at the end of a day of elk calling. A diaphragm turkey call and 36-inch piece of 1 1/4-inch PVC pipe as a grunt tube put the variety into elk calling. With this combo,

Using a two-man approach to calling in a bull elk will allow a hunter to concentrate on the bull and his own movement, while the other partner does the calling. Close encounters like this are not uncommon!

I could bugle, squeal, chirp, and mew to vary my calling to suit the situation. Today I use the Primos palate plate and Quaker Boy diaphragm calls along with Woods Wise and Quaker Boy Hyper cow calls, with a Primos grunt tube for most of my calling. There are hundreds of superb elk calls of every type to choose from, and all will work some of the time; none that I know will work all of the time.

Each and every rutting-elk encounter requires its own strategy and tactics, and while you can learn *how* to call and bugle elk from the profusion of available information, learning *when* to call elk is the key to putting that bull at point-blank range, where you can't possibly miss. And that comes from experience.

DECOYING ELK

Elk bulls today are much more cautious and circumspect when they respond to calling, and over the past 10 years, I've had few that came on the run looking for trouble. Most will come in slow and easy looking for the cow or bull that is making the racket. When they don't see the sound source, they tend to get spooky and, at best, circle downwind to scent-check the area. At worst, they just get the heck out of Dodge.

I've hunted with decoys of various sorts all my life, and for years I felt an elk decoy would work wonders in allaying an approaching elk's suspicions and bring him the final yardage needed for a good bow shot. However, I didn't relish the thought of carrying a full-body taxidermy mount or archery target through the woods at 9,000 feet to accomplish this purpose.

When I met and discussed this with Dave Berkeley, owner of Feather Flex decoys, it didn't take long to come up with prototype lightweight foam elk decoys that could be rolled and transported easily. The silhouette decoy we came up with was full-sized, without a head for ease of design and portability. The decoy fastened between two trees with lightweight bungee cords, and the elk looked as if its head was hidden by the tree trunk or brush.

This new decoy worked extremely well and brought a number of elk within bow range for me and my clients, but it still lacked the prime ingredient: extreme portability. I've had several manufacturers approach me for advice on elk decoys, and the one thing I stress is that the decoy has to fit in a daypack or fanny pack. This is a tough requirement, but if you can't take it with you when you leave the truck in the morning and pack it all day every day, chances are you aren't going to have it with you when you really need it.

Jerry McPherson, owner and designer of Montana Decoys, solved that problem with photo-realistic cow elk decoys that collapse in a hoop and are small and light enough to be carried all day, every day, of your elk bowhunt. And they really do work.

On one of my first attempts to decoy a bull, I left my prototype decoy hanging between two immature spruce bushes along the edge of a meadow while my hunting partner and I went pursuing a bull that had come in behind us. When we returned several hours later, another bull had come along and evidently made a pass at my silhouette decoy, tangling his antlers in the cords and the flip-floppy decoy. According to the profusion of skid marks in the meadow, the bull threw a fit for 50 yards trying to get the clinging decoy out of his antlers.

Adding a decoy to your calling set-up and appealing to both the bull's hearing and sight might just tip the balance in your favor when you're dealing with a curious but cautious or wary bull. As an added attraction, I use elk scent around the decoy to appeal to or confuse the elk's sense of smell.

Using a decoy will help tip the odds in your favor. Place the decoy where it can be spotted from a distance as the bull comes in to your calls.

I make sure my decoy is set where an approaching elk can spot it from some distance, as I've found that a decoy suddenly popping into view will spook an elk or arouse its suspicions. When they can see the decoy for some distance and at the same time they hear elk sounds, it arouses their curiosity and they are much more liable to come closer. When decoying and calling elk, I try to position myself where it is difficult or impossible for an approaching elk to sneak around behind me, and the path of least resistance puts him in good shooting position.

I try to place me or my client off to one side and between the incoming elk and the decoy, but not in direct line of sight between the elk and decoy. I've had elk so engrossed with the decoy, I was able to draw and let down several times within 20 yards without them paying any heed to my slight movement. Decoys can be a deadly and effective addition to your elk bowhunting arsenal, but only if you carry it with you each and every time you go elk hunting.

SHOT PLACEMENT AND EQUIPMENT

Elk are *tough*! I've bowhunted many species of big-game animals, and in my experience, none are tougher nor more survival-driven than elk. Where a hard-hit whitetail buck will travel 200 yards, a bull elk with the same hit can go half a mile. The heart-lung kill zone on bull elk is roughly twice the size of that on whitetail deer, 20 inches to 24 inches. This means that a 40-yard shot on a bull elk is equivalent to a 20-yard shot on a whitetail, *if* you spend the time practicing at the longer distances.

I've had many eastern and Midwestern clients who stated they wouldn't take a shot over 20 yards. I can appreciate their discretion, but they are

The kill zone on a bull elk is about twice the size as that of a whitetail. Practice shooting at 30 to 40 yards with a kill zone target area of about 20 to 24 inches.

cheating themselves and decreasing their chances of success. In the wide-open spaces the wary wapiti call home, shot distances may be extended considerably, and you need to practice, practice, practice at the longer distances to increase your chances of scoring on a bull.

You might surprise yourself at how well you can shoot at 60 yards with a lot of practice, and conscientious practice at these distances will make a 35-yard shot seem close. Also, practice from a variety of shooting positions. Shoot from your knees, sitting, twisted sideways, and to the off side. Elk have a way of coming from the most unpredictable angles, and practicing these shots will prepare you for such an eventuality.

I've had clients take elk with longbows, recurves, and compounds, and the type of bow makes little difference. One bowhunter made a clean one-shot kill on a 5x5 bull with a 42-pound bow. The bow that you shoot the best is the one you want to use for elk hunting. While there's a lot of latitude in bow type and weight for bowhunting elk, the one equipment factor where there is absolutely no leeway is broadhead dependability and sharpness.

I prefer and have taken many elk with *"cut-on-contact"* broadheads, such as the Zwickey, Bear Razorhead, Phantom, and Steel Force. My clients and I have also made clean kills on a number of elk with Andy Simo's trocar-pointed Thunderhead. I *do not* like or recommend mechanical broadheads of any kind. Why base the success or failure of your elk bowhunt on a head that may or may not work, when there are many solid and proven heads that leave no doubt?

Bowhunting elk is the supreme western big-game challenge, so make sure you're prepared for the encounter. ■

MULE DEER AND BLACKTAIL

T aking a trophy mule deer with a bow and arrow just may be today's toughest bowhunting challenge. Throughout much of the west, the mule-deer population is in a drastic decline, and finding a trophy buck that will make the Pope and Young record book is getting tougher with each passing year.

If the game and fish departments don't start taking a closer look at the present predator situation in the major mule deer–producing states and provinces, and come up with some workable solutions to the predator problem, poaching, changes in habitat and people infestations in historical deer range, competition from elk, and CWD (Chronic Wasting Disease), hunting for mule deer will become a dream of the past. I personally don't hold out much hope for the return of the fantastic mule deer hunting of the sixties, because most of the wildlife agencies have gotten themselves between a rock and a hard spot by trying to remain politically correct and make everyone happy. Consequently these agencies have lost much of their capability to properly manage the mule deer populations within their boundaries.

What this boils down to for the bowhunter looking for the best opportunity to arrow a decent mule deer buck is more critical research and care in choosing areas that have a recent history for producing record-class mule deer bucks. It used to be that a bowhunter could head west and hunt almost anywhere in the mountains of Colorado, Utah, Wyoming, or Montana and have a decent chance at seeing lots of mule deer and getting a chance or two at a good buck. Those days are long gone.

A look at the statistical summary of the last Pope and Young biennial recording period and last record book can provide a wealth of information, not only about where the best bucks were taken, but also the most successful method of hunting them. As a point of comparison, there are roughly eight times the number of whitetails entered into the record book as mule deer. This means putting a mule deer in the book is eight times more difficult than taking a Pope and Young whitetail. These figures should give you an idea of the task you've chosen if you decide you want a mule deer buck for your trophy room wall.

Colorado is still the top trophy-producing state for mule deer (both typical and non-typical), followed by Utah. Wyoming, Oregon, and Idaho also produce many typical and non-typical mule deer, and Alberta is number three in the production of non-typical mule deer.

I can swear by this statistic. Several years ago, I was bowhunting whitetails with my good friends Drew, Mary, and Bob McCartney in north-central Kansas, and I rattled in a 180-plus, non-typical muley buck. The curious buck came right up to my whitetail decoy and stood broadside at 20 yards, while I cussed Kansas law, that prohibits non-residents from taking mule deer on a non-resident archery deer license.

Today you might have a better chance of arrowing a monster muley off the back porch of an urbanite, living on the edge of one of the small towns in the foothills along the front range of the Rockies, than in one of the remote, hidden, high valleys on the western slope. The mule deer have moved close to human habitation and actually invaded many of the small mountain communities to escape from constant pressure by the escalating mountain lion, coyote, and bear populations.

I used to make an annual trip to Estes Park, Colorado, in late November and early December to photograph the huge bucks that migrated to the lower reaches of Rocky Mountain National Park and then into the city limits, as winter and coyotes pushed them down from their high-country homeland. It wasn't uncommon to find 20 to 30 bucks, from a hefty 170 points to monsters well over 200 points, in the area, along with plenty of does and fawns.

During the fall of 2003, I swung through Estes on my way back from Iowa (for Thanksgiving at home) in hopes of photographing some bucks. Ha! In two days of driving around, I found a dozen mule deer (total) and only two small bucks. According to the local conservation officer, Chronic Wasting Disease (CWD) had wiped out most of the deer in the area, and the few that were left by this insidious disease were further hammered by the coyotes and big cats.

Many of the historically famous mule-deer areas are no longer good bets for bowhunters, and some areas that haven't been noted for producing big mule deer are gaining ground. Many of the prairie states and provinces are producing big bucks, simply because they are out of cougar country and the bucks get a chance to grow to trophy proportions, especially on private ranches and areas where there is still predator control of some sort.

Don't overlook eastern Colorado, New Mexico, Wyoming, Montana, and the Dakotas in your search for a prime mule deer bowhunting location. Alberta is also high on the list of trophy mule deer producers, and there are some areas of the province that offer excellent, non-resident bowhunting opportunities. Start planning well ahead of time, so you can thoroughly research your mule deer bowhunt. It will be time well spent.

Mule deer are open-country, migratory critters that live in and roam much larger expanses of habitat than whitetails, with a far less defined home range. The muleys' yen to roam makes them more unpredictable than whitetails and more difficult to pattern and ambush. However, the broken, more open country they call home makes them an ideal subject for spot-and-stalk bowhunting. Roughly 60 percent of the mule deer bucks entered into the Pope and Young record book were taken by the spot-and-stalk method.

SPOT-AND-STALK MULEY HUNTING

The key to successful spot-and-stalk bowhunting is just what the words imply. First you have to spot the buck and then you stalk him. Sounds simple, but considering some of the large-scale and inhospitable country the big muley bucks call home, bowhunting them by this method can involve lots of time and plenty of patience, not to mention a good share of luck. For my money, spot-and-stalk mule deer bowhunting in the high country, above timberline, is the quintessential bowhunting experience.

If you bowhunt properly using this method, you're going to be spending most of your time spotting, judging, planning, and plotting rather than stalking. The most important part of your bowhunting equipment will be your optics. Good binoculars and a quality spotting scope will make the job of spotting a trophy mule deer much easier and more comfortable. I've often stayed in one location, glassing for a big buck in good mule deer country, for eight to ten hours at a time. A cheap pair of binoculars with poor-quality lenses will have your eyes feeling like they've been sandpapered and salted after a concentrated couple of hours of glassing slopes

Wherever you hunt muleys, you''ll need excellent binoculars. Your bare eyes won't pick out mule deer (or parts of mule deer) in the draws, gullies, canyons, and other hidey holes they favor.

and ridges, trying to pick out the well-camouflaged form of a stalkable mule deer buck. Buying a pair of quality binoculars is a lifetime investment, and if you choose carefully, it may just be the most useful and valuable single item of equipment in your bowhunting arsenal.

Any quality binoculars in 7x, 8x, or 10x will work for glassing mule deer. For the longer distances usually involved, I prefer 10x binoculars like my Nikon Superior E glasses. These sharp, center-focus binoculars are tough, lightweight, and medium-sized, and they gather light unbelievably well, all prerequisites for mule deer spotting.

A lightweight, good-quality, variable-power spotting scope is essential for critical long-range spotting, pinpointing deer locations, judging trophy quality, and choosing a stalking route to your quarry. I found that 15-45x is the best all-round power. The lower setting isn't too powerful for general scanning and spotting; yet the higher setting is strong enough for critical long-distance trophy judging and picking out details in terrain features. I have a 60x eyepiece for my 60mm spotting scope, but this is only usable under perfect conditions with a rock solid rest or tripod.

The next most important element of your spot-and-stalk mule-deer hunt is *patience*! It's difficult for any bowhunter in spectacularly open muley habitat to master sitting in one location and have his eyes do the walking and work. Most bowhunters want to move out and comb the countryside in an attempt to locate any bucks in the area. Not good. The essential element

Big buck mule deer live in rough, rocky, isolated, and lonely places. Don't forget to glass shady spots where they like to feed, bed, and hide.

to the success of your mule-deer bowhunt is whether you can spot a trophy buck before it spots you. Guess that's why they call it spot-and-stalk bow-hunting.

You'll be a lot less likely to give yourself away to a sharp-eyed muley by sitting quietly and comfortably in the shade of a tree, under a rock ledge, or even in the cab of your pickup, and let your eyes cover the countryside. This is much more efficient than traipsing over hill and dale, rattling rocks, filling the air with your pungent scent, and, in general, letting everything with fur and feathers know there's an intruder in the area.

Locating mule deer is best accomplished during the early morning hours, when the deer are most active and time is on your side. Nothing is more frustrating than spotting a good buck in the late afternoon and not having enough time to get within stalking distance before dark. Of course, this will give you an excellent starting point the following morning and certainly narrow down your search area, so early evening spotting is definitely worthwhile.

Mule deer spend much of their time in the open. They will often bed on an open hillside, at the base of a small tree, under a ledge, or in the shade of a bush, where they have a panoramic view of their surroundings. There are many times when a crafty old buck's bedding or loafing location makes for an impossible stalking situation. *Be patient.* A very high percentage of blown stalks are due to one fundamental faux pas: *impatience.*

When glassing for mule deer, it's important to make use of every little trick you can muster. Always try to glass with the sun at your back, lighting up the area you're glassing. The mule deer's gray coloration was designed to blend with his habitat, and it's unbelievable how well this camouflage works against the broken pattern of shadow, rocks, and brush. The golden rays of early-morning and late afternoon sunlight will reduce the effectiveness of this camouflage and make a muley's hide stand out like a diamond against a lump of coal. Plan your glassing to take advantage of this fact.

Don't sit there in blissful ignorance and figure you're always going to spot a full-bodied, magnificent, heavy-antlered buck perfectly outlined against a grassy background in plain sight! It happens, but you're better off looking for a shape that seems out of place, like an antler sticking up over a bush, a partial rear end patch on the backside of a thicket, or the flick of an ear or tail against a shadowy background. Spot the little things that don't quite fit their surroundings, and then take the time to put together the rest of the pieces and parts with the aid of you binoculars or spotting scope, and you'll locate a lot more mule deer.

The tough part, when patience becomes even more important, is *after* you spot a good buck that has your mouth watering and puts a tremor in your bow hand. This is the time that most spot-and-stalk hunts are blown. The uncontrollable urge to proceed with the stalk often overrides the common sense of taking the time to properly plan it from the first to last step. *Big* mule deer bucks didn't grow to trophy size by being stupid and making mistakes.

A mature buck has super eyesight, a keen sense of smell, and phenomenal hearing, combined with the survival instincts to get him out of danger in the most expeditious manner possible. Don't overlook the slightest detail when planning your stalk.

This is the aspect of your mule-deer bowhunt when a good spotting scope can pay for itself in short order. You can use your spotting scope to choose every inch of your stalking route. Study the smallest detail of the terrain features between you and your adversary without ever leaving your observation post and taking a chance on spooking the deer.

If you spot a buck or bucks feeding in the early morning, unless they are close and in an ideal location for a relatively quick stalk with everything in your favor, it might be better strategy to wait until they bed down for a mid-morning siesta. There are, of course, times in a spot-and-stalk hunting situation where you may have a chance at success by pushing the envelope a bit and getting the stalk on without wasting time. On several occasions, I've located mule deer feeding along a slope or flat, and headed for brush or timber that would make an ideal ambush point . . . *if* I could get there ahead of them. In this situation, go for it, but don't forget the deer's senses of smell, hearing, and eyesight in your stalk and don't rush it.

Once the deer get bedded down and stay put for 15 minutes or so, make sure you know where each and every deer is located. If it's a long stalk over difficult terrain, don't hesitate to draw a rough diagram of the situation and make use of it during your stalk. The countryside and objects look a lot different through binoculars or a spotting scope due to limited depth of field and the compression factor of optics. Make sure you pinpoint the deer's location with a landmark you can identify without question when you get close to where you last saw your quarry. There have been a number of times when failure to fully pinpoint a buck's exact location has let the buck win the encounter. There have been an equal number of times when the untrustworthy deer moved while we were in the process of the perfect stalk, and the buck wasn't where it was expected to be. Stalking mule deer is never cut-and-dried; so don't get overconfident, impatient, or careless at this stage of your hunt. It will cost you dearly!

Spot-and-stalk bowhunting can often be better used by two bowhunters working together. Four eyes are always better than two, and once a deer is located, having one set of eyes glued to the deer while the other bowhunter makes the stalk increases the odds of success considerably. Take the time to work out a set of clear and concise signals to communicate from both ends of the stalk, without miscommunication. Leave the slightest opening in this regard, and you can bet Murphy will pop out of the brush and throw the screws to your best-laid plans . . . big time.

BACKPACK MULE DEER

One of the major reasons for backpack bowhunting mule deer is that it allows you to get into prime mule-deer country that is almost inaccessible by

Plan your spot-and-stalk route well in advance. Keep the wind in your face and wait for the right shot. Always keep an eye out for other deer—deer you originally didn't see that would blow your stalk.

any other method of hunting. One of my favorite mountain bowhunting axioms always has been, "When you get into country where there are no people, you'll find game!" Backpacking for trophy mule deer may just be your best option for that out-west, high-country hunting venture. There's little doubt that a spot-and-stalk bowhunt for a gigantic mountain muley is the epitome of bowhunting challenges, and a backpack high-country hunt has to be the supreme mule-deer bowhunting experience.

Despite what some bowhunters think, a trophy mule deer buck can be as crafty and spooky as a whitetail. Letting such a buck see or smell you in his home area is just inviting him to disappear without a trace. By carefully backpacking into the area, keeping the mountain breezes in your favor, staying on the back side of the ridges in the heavy timber, and setting up a dry camp with a minimum of noise or disturbance, you won't broadcast the fact that you're around to anything bigger than the local pikas and rockchucks.

One of the major drawing cards to a backpack, high-country bowhunt is *cost!* You can't go much cheaper than loading the family car with your hunting equipment—backpack, sleeping bag, 8x10 foot piece of plastic, minimum amount of food, an aluminum pot with sterno stove—and driving to the nearest high-country mule deer habitat. Backpack bowhunting can get you into many areas that are not readily accessible by any other method. You can do it on your own or with a bowhunting buddy, rather than having to hire the services of a professional outfitter or guide, thereby saving money, adding challenge, and having the resulting element of self-satisfaction to your hunt.

The first step in setting up a backpack bowhunt is to pick an area where there is a huntable population of mule deer in country that's suitable for backpacking. Get hunting info from various western states, listing seasons and dates, to begin the process. Most western state Game and Fish Departments also provide harvest data or kill figures on the different game management units within the state. With this info and a general state map, you can begin to narrow down your choices.

Look for units that have low density of hunters and a good success ratio in areas with lots of wild and wooly country. There are many areas in the western mountains where you can park the family station wagon (or minivan) along the highway on a high mountain pass, at a mountaintop microwave tower, campground, USFS trailhead leading to a wilderness area, or on the end of a logging road at the base of a mountain, and go backpacking. No need for a 4x4 pickup, four-wheeler, or horses and trailer to get you close to some of the best big-buck country available.

Another option that's a bit more expensive, but far cheaper than an outfitted mule-deer bowhunt, is a drop-camp high-country bowhunt. This is a great way to get into good mule deer country *if* you do your homework and choose the area you want to be packed into yourself. Leaving the choice of a drop camp up to a horse-packing outfit that doesn't do any scouting, and is more interested in the ease of getting into and out of the back country than its potential for trophy bucks, may not be in your best interest. There are outfitters who have set drop camps in excellent deer country and will pack you in and out for a reasonable price. By far the best plan is to thoroughly research a hunting area and then have a packer cart you and your equipment to *your* chosen location.

STILL-HUNTING MULE DEER

An additional method for bowhunting mule deer bucks is by still-hunting, with approximately 15 percent of the Pope and Young entries taken using this method. This totals up to 75 percent of the bucks being taken by spot-and-stalk and still-hunting methods.

In my experience, it's really tough to differentiate between the two methods. When you're still-hunting through a pocket of timber, keeping your eyes open for a buck, you're basically spotting on the move. When you locate a buck, your still-hunt turns to a stalk even if it's only for a few yards. When you spot a buck from a distance and ease carefully into bow range, are you stalking him or still-hunting him? Who cares . . . as long as you end up with him on the ground?

Still-hunting through a piece of likely mule-deer habitat takes the same patience and locating skills as spot-and-stalk hunting, only this time you don't know for sure exactly where you quarry is located. Remember, you're more likely to see only a portion of a deer rather than the whole animal. Key your thinking to this aspect. Many neophyte muley bowhunters don't even consider binoculars for this type of hunting, but I can tell you from experience that good light-gathering glasses are even *more* important for this type of hunting.

Still-hunting is hunting "up close and personal," in close quarters where a single step can make the difference between success and disaster. Binoculars will tell in short order if a light patch is a deer's rear end or just a sunlit patch of grass, if that slight movement was the tip of an antler showing from behind a tree or bush or the movement of a pine squirrel. Carry binoculars with you all the time and force yourself to use them constantly. Once you find out their value in close quarter still-hunting, you'll never be without them for any of your bowhunting ventures.

Remember the three main detriments to your getting within bow range of a trophy mule deer buck in still-hunting are wind, noise, and movement. *Always* still-hunt through an area with the wind or breeze in your favor. The best way to accomplish this is to use a squeeze bottle filled with talcum powder and let the prevailing breeze dictate exactly how you still-hunt through the area. Try to move as slowly and cautiously as possible, stopping often to survey and glass the terrain you're working into.

Tree-stand hunting for mule deer is not a new phenomenon, but it's one that is rapidly gaining popularity, simply because of its proven effectiveness. Only eight percent of the record-book entries for mule deer were taken from tree stands, while a whopping 78 percent of whitetails are taken using this method. Tree stands for mule deer can be deadly when properly placed.

There have been numerous occasions when I have been still-hunting or spot-and-stalk hunting and have seen a good buck in an ideal location where a tree stand would work, or come upon a mineral lick or heavily used trail from a feeding area that is an obvious location for a tree stand.

A well-placed tree stand with good background cover and good tree-stand hunting techniques is a highly effective mule-deer tactic. Ideal tree-stand locations are overlooking waterholes, travel ways leading to feeding areas or croplands, in saddles and cuts where deer travel from one range or drainage to another, and other locations where a muley's travels are narrowed down to a specific ambush point.

With the mule deer's propensity for open country with sparse tree cover, there are often ideal ambush sites in saddles or along creek beds or meandering streams, on trails leading to a bedding area in the middle of the wide-open spaces, and a million other excellent locations with little cover available and *no* trees. Don't give up!

Get yourself a shovel, pickaxe, and good brush cutter and put in a pit blind or ground blind. This is probably the most overlooked method for bow-hunting a trophy mule deer and yet it can be one of the most adaptable and effective methods employed. I have used pit blinds in situations where it would seem impossible to get within bow range of a cautious, open-country, mule deer buck and had them walk within a few yards of the blind within hours of its construction.

CALLING MULE DEER

Two percent (or less) of the mule deer entered into the record books were taken by some method of calling. Mule deer are not territorial like their whitetail cousins, nor are they as aggressive during the rut. The mule deer buck's mild manner makes it tough to get one fired up with rattling antlers or grunt challenges to suck them close enough for a bow shot. I've rattled in a few bucks, but they responded out of curiosity more than anger. Several eventually worked their way close enough for a good shot, but the percentage of responses certainly didn't make this one of my favorite methods of bowhunt-ing muley bucks.

I've had much better results using a coarse-toned predator call to imitate the distress bleats of a deer. This is a viable method for bringing in a buck or doe early in the season, when the fawns are still with the does. I've had several good bucks respond when I was calling coyotes early in the fall and again during the winter.

Again, during the late season, I feel it's more of a curiosity response rather than one of aggression or anger, although my late-season calling has brought in some real trophy bucks. I always carry a predator call with me when bowhunting and wouldn't hesitate to try to coax up a trophy buck if he was in sight, with no alternative way of getting close enough for a shot. Calling may not work often enough to use it as your main method of bowhunting trophy mule deer, but it does work and might give you a chance at a trophy buck when nothing else seems feasible.

In states with late-season mule deer hunting, driving is another viable method of putting a trophy buck within bow range. This method can be well used where the mule deer tend to congregate in their wintering areas–along river bottoms, shelter belts, or along wooded slopes or valleys. A mule deer's natural tendency is to move uphill or to more open ground, so take this habit into consideration when choosing your ambush points.

It doesn't take a whole crowd of pushers to move muleys out of cover. In fact, one or two bowhunters moving slowly through a patch of prime, late-season mule-deer cover, with the wind at their backs, will be far more effective than a larger group. Wise old bucks have a propensity for sneaking up side draws, small gullies, or other inconspicuous escape routes, so keep your eyes open for such locations when setting up your late-season drives.

COLUMBIAN BLACKTAILS

Columbian blacktail deer are found in California, Oregon, Washington, and lower British Columbia, with Oregon and California producing a major portion of the record-book bucks. California's archery deer season opens in mid-August, when the bucks are still in velvet; consequently, almost all the record-book Columbian blacktails in velvet are taken in California.

The majority of the Columbian blacktails (like their magnum-eared cousins) are taken by spot-and-stalk bowhunting, with the second most effective method being tree-stand hunting.

Most of the foregoing techniques used for mule deer are equally applicable to Columbian blacktails. However, when I bowhunted them again in Oregon, I found that they responded to calling and rattling far more readily than mule deer.

On one occasion, I was bowhunting a densely wooded ridge overlooking a wide valley where the visibility was severely limited by the dense jungle-like vegetation. At mid-morning, I set up along an overgrown logging road and commenced rattling and grunt calling, as if I were whitetail hunting. Within minutes, a heavy, dark-antlered blacktail stuck his head out of a fern thicket 30 yards from me, trying to locate the source of the sound. What I wouldn't have given for a decoy.

That buck appeared and disappeared in the verdant vegetation in front of me for the next 20 minutes while I tried to coax him into the open for a shot. I'd see patches of hide, antlers, or rump, and occasionally a head, but never enough for a good shot. After half an hour of inactivity, I figured the buck was gone and started rattling again. An even larger buck appeared in a small opening at 40 yards, but before I got my wits working and came to full draw, he melted into the background like his compadre. I bleated and grunted softly and got several momentary glimpses of him twice more before he, too, was engulfed by the green labyrinth.

A tree stand would have put me in position to see down into the dense jungle ferns, vines, and moss-shrouded trees and given me a good shot at either record-book buck. I did manage to call in a couple of forky bucks, but after an encounter with the two boomers, I just couldn't bring myself to take the shot.

SITKA BLACKTAILS

Sitka blacktails are found in the northern section of British Columbia and the coastal regions of Alaska. Kodiak Island is definitely the place to go for a record-class Sitka blacktail buck. When I worked for the Alaska Department of Fish and Game in the early '60s, there weren't any blacktails on Afognak Island and darn few on Kodiak Island. Their population exploded shortly thereafter, and not too long ago, the limit was seven deer per hunter. The lush vegetation and abundant food supply make for a high population of fat, healthy deer, but the lack of minerals doesn't do much for antler growth. Consequently, a bowhunter needs to look over a lot of deer to find a Pope and Young qualifier.

Bowhunters weren't the only ones to benefit from the population explosion of the Sitka blacktails. The humongous predatory brown bears were quick to take advantage of the burgeoning red-meat supply and actually learned that gunfire usually meant a fresh gut pile or carcass. This unusual response added a whole new dimension to hunting blacktails for gun hunters, as the voracious bruins started showing up unexpectedly at the site of a fresh deer kill. These close-quarter encounters in the jungle-like thickets of alder and devil's club resulted in a number of fatalities, both human and bear.

Fortunately, a bow doesn't make much noise when it goes off, but I've talked with a number of bowhunters who have lost deer to brown bears. On one occasion, a bowhunter arrowed a deer a bit far back and watched it move slowly into an alder thicket, where it bedded down. The bowhunter backed off and positioned himself on a hillside several hundred yards above the downed deer, waiting. He spotted a brown bear in the valley half a mile above the deer's hidey hole, but didn't think anything about it.

An hour later, he spotted the bear moving purposefully down the valley with his nose in the air and realized he was wind-scenting the wounded deer and headed right for the thicket. A few minutes later, the frustrated bowhunter watched the huge bear carry his record-book blacktail over the hill and out of sight. He was frustrated but darned glad that he hadn't been in the thicket gutting or quartering his deer when the bear showed up to claim the kill.

Almost all Sitka blacktails are taken by spot-and-stalk bowhunting using the same techniques, tactics, and equipment as mule-deer bowhunters. The coastal areas of Alaska are noted for their atrocious weather, so waterproof rain gear is essential for comfort, as is a pair of quality, ankle-fit hip boots that you'll more than likely be wearing day after day.

According to Ed Russell, a bowhunting compadre residing in Anchorage, Sitka blacktails respond readily to bleats and squalls in imitation of a doe or fawn in distress. Ed was one of the first to seriously bowhunt blacktails on Kodiak and has taken a number of bucks by calling them. His favorite call is simply a blade of grass stretched between his thumbs. A variable-tone deer call would work just as well and be easier to master. However, unless you're bowhunting an area with good distant visibility, hunting with a partner who has a brown-bear license and a *big* rifle, or are crazy, calling Sitka blacktails in brown bear country may not be the best bet for putting a trophy blacktail buck on your den wall.

SUMMING IT UP

In my opinion, the future of mule deer in the west is not good, with everything from predators to human encroachment working against them. However, there are still many good mule-deer areas with enough boomer bucks roaming around to fulfill your wildest bowhunting dreams. Don't procrastinate, start planning that mule deer bowhunt *now*. When planning for blacktails, do your homework, research over the Internet, and plan well in advance. ■

WHITETAIL AND COUES DEER

Where do you start on a chapter for the most dominant and important big-game animal in North America? Whitetail deer are the greatest game-management coup in the world, and there are more whitetails roaming more area now than ever before in history.

When I was a kid growing up in Minnesota, there were very few whitetails roaming the river bottoms and sloughs in the farm country of the southern portion of the state and western Iowa. I bowhunted the first archery season in southwestern Minnesota in 1954 and chased what few deer there were around the gravel pits and creek and river bottoms around my hometown. Today, these same areas are on the verge of being overpopulated with whitetails.

For years, Wisconsin, Michigan, and Minnesota were the states to bowhunt if you wanted a record-book buck. These northern states led the country in producing record-book bucks for both bow and gun hunters. Over the past 10 years, the breadbasket states of Iowa, Illinois, Ohio, and Kansas have moved into the equation. Iowa has now replaced Minnesota as the top contender in producing Boone and Crockett bucks for gun hunters in spite of the fact that Wisconsin and Michigan produce three to four times as many deer and have three times the number of hunters.

Long time compadre and outdoor writer Jim Zumbo asked me a few years back why Iowa was able to produce so many big bucks for bow and gun hunters.

Most of the central states have the genetics for producing big bucks with an abundance of nutritious feed, rich in the vitamins and essential minerals needed for good antler production. But the three major factors in putting more trophy bucks in the woods for bowhunters are:

1) Restricting firearms hunters to muzzleloaders and shotguns only (not the case in Kansas). When gun hunters can't reach out and kill a buck at 300-plus yards, the bucks have a chance to become older and wiser and reach maximum antler growth and body size. My thought is that if a buck is missed a few times by a hunter with a shotgun or muzzleloader, then he'll become a nocturnal, virtually unkillable ghost.

2) Firearms seasons are after the peak of the rut, when bucks are less susceptible, have had a chance to recover from their sex-crazed "stupids," and are worn down to where they are only interested in rest and a full belly (very much the case in Iowa). Pressure these bucks and they'll head for the most unsuspecting hidey hole they can find, only venturing forth when hunger drives them to it, and then only during the hours of darkness. With the aid of a night-vision scope, I've watched many of these trophy bucks enter a food plot an hour after full dark, feed for an hour, and then disappear back into their sanctuary. It takes extremely cold weather, finesse, and one heck of a lot of luck to put a buck like this on the trophy-room wall.

3) Sloppy hunting techniques by local hunters more interested in meat for the freezer than trophy bucks. Many of the deer drives I've witnessed are carried out with a minimum of planning, poor execution, lots of noise, and little attention to wind direction. Every encounter a mature buck survives and learns from makes him just that much tougher to corner the next time.

One of the major problems in several of the top whitetail bowhunting states is the difficulty of drawing a nonresident archery license. Iowa, Kansas, and Illinois are all on a draw-only basis at this time, so you may have to plan your bowhunt several years in advance to get a license. The rest of the top whitetail bowhunting states sell archery licenses across the counter, but make sure you double-check the regulations well in advance, so you know exactly what the licensing situation is where you've chosen to bowhunt. The Canadian provinces all require the services of a licensed outfitter to bowhunt whitetails.

MORNING VS. LATE AFTERNOON BOWHUNTING

Information obtained by the Pope and Young club shows that twice as many record-book bucks are killed during late afternoon bowhunts as in the morning. I prefer early evening bowhunting myself, because I hate getting out of a warm bed to go out and sit up in a tree like some demented owl in the pre-dawn darkness.

Even though morning whitetail bowhunting isn't my favorite time, I rarely miss a morning hunt when conditions warrant. When we have clients in camp, we hunt just as hard in the morning as in the late afternoon and simply adjust our bowhunting tactics to take advantage of morning movement and conditions.

It's almost impossible to bowhunt deer successfully in the morning in many places where their feed grounds are adjacent to their bedding areas. The high risk of spooking the deer while you're getting into position or sitting

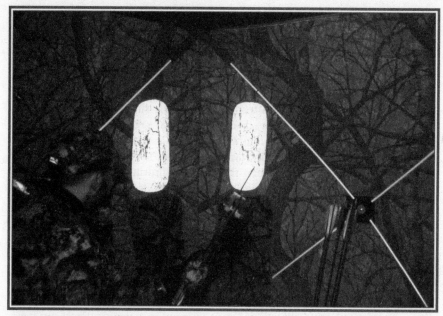

Pop-up blinds are portable, easy to set up, and weatherproof. If using one, set it up at least one week prior to the hunting season so that the deer will get used to it.

in your stand isn't worth the chance. Wait until mid-day, when the deer are safely bedded, and silently get into position in a set up where scouting has indicated the best location for a late afternoon stand or blind. Always take into consideration the wind and weather conditions.

In areas where deer move a considerable distance from their bed grounds to feeding areas, your best tactic for a morning hunt is to place a stand or blind along their travel route, a safe distance from both the feeding and bedding areas, to ambush them as they return to bed for the day.

The best situation, if you're lucky enough to be bowhunting private land you're leasing, or where you have permission to place semipermanent stands, is to get your stands into position as soon as you've thoroughly scouted and located the best place to ambush a trophy buck. Letting a stand or blind "age" for a week or two before hunting it is by far the best tactic. Set several stands in key locations to account for variations in wind, weather, and big-buck quirks. Remember, the best time to hunt a stand is the *first* time, even a stand that has been in place for a while. I've learned that deer pattern hunters just about as quickly as hunters pattern deer, so don't burn your stands byabout as quickly as hunters pattern deer, so don't burn your stands by overhunting them.

BLINDS, STANDS, AND HOLES IN THE GROUND

Roughly 80 percent of all record-book bucks are taken from tree stands, but don't let that fact put you in a mind-set where you have to have both feet off the ground to feel like you're bowhunting. Over the years, I've used about every type stand and blind imaginable for bowhunting whitetails and convinced a lot of fellow guides and outfitters, as well as clients and friends, that trees aren't an absolute necessity for killing record-book whitetails.

In Alberta one fall, I convinced my outfitter he was missing a bet by not digging pit blinds on waterholes in the middle of open fields for bow-hunting whitetails in the low-bush country. He wasn't really sold on the idea, until I took a 150-class buck out of a pit blind in the low brush at the edge of an open field, where there weren't any trees. His wife took a 125-class buck from a pit blind on an unhunted waterhole, and if she'd waited another two minutes, a 170-class buck would have watered at the same spot where she shot the smaller one. Now the outfitter uses as many strategically dug pit blinds as he does tree stands—on waterholes, in fence lines, on travel routes, and at the edge of feeding areas.

In South Dakota, I bowhunted from a blind rigged to imitate a round bale sitting along the edge of an alfalfa field the deer were hammering. When I ran into a situation in Alberta the next fall, the outfitter and I built a round bale blind out of wood, wire, and burlap covered with oat straw to simulate a real bale, where the oats were baled up heads and all. Three days after placing the bale in the open harvested oat field, one of his clients killed a tremendous buck out of the blind at 20 yards. On our Iowa leases we use a combination of portable tree stands, ladder stands, tripod stands, pit blinds on foodplots and waterholes, and pop-up ground blinds.

The past few years, we've been making more and more use of pop-up ground blinds, as they are extremely portable, adaptable to many unique situations, easy to set up, weatherproof, warm and comfortable in extremely cold weather, and very effective when it comes to killing deer.

The Double Bull blinds are by far the best on the market as far as I'm concerned, but I've also had excellent results with the Invisiblind. If you're going to use a ground blind, try to set it in position a week or so before hunting to give the deer time to get used to it. I've had deer walk within a few yards of a newly set up blind, but why take chances with a trophy buck?

Another phenomenal and uniquely portable type of blind is one of the Shaggy Suits or Ghillie suits. These burlap-covered outfits are among the best moveable ground blinds I've ever used, and I make more and more use of one each fall. Wookie suits, as I call them, are great for still-hunting through the woods and especially effective for on-the-go rattling and grunt calling. I've had deer and turkey come so close that I could almost touch them with my bow. Shaggy suits are as effective for concealing the human shape in a tree as they are on the ground. I guarantee, once you try one you'll never be without one again.

THE INVALUABLE WIND-INDICATOR BOTTLE

Make use of all the scent-elimination tactics, clothing, and boots you can; none of it hurts, and it may help greatly under the right conditions.

However, as a back up, make constant use of a simple powder bottle filled with scented talcum powder to keep you abreast of the slightest wind variances while you're bowhunting. I use scented powder for a very good reason: I want to be able to smell it, and a deer smelling the flowery aroma has already gotten a whiff of your pungent odor, so that aspect is null.

There have been many times when being able to smell the powder has helped me change hunting tactics to compensate for subtle changes in wind, drafts, or air currents. Quite often, when bowhunting a tree stand or ground blind, I'll check the wind with my bottle and, a few minutes later, pick up the faint smell of powder drifting back to me, indicating a change in wind direction. This can be good or bad, but at least I know there's a change and can act accordingly. The same holds true when still-hunting through the woods or stalking a critter. You have to know what the wind is doing, and the scented powder is your best bet for keeping informed.

The powder bottle is especially useful for proper placement of stands and blinds, for providing finite information as to the prevailing breeze, updrafts, downdrafts, convection currents, etc., at the stand or blind position at the time of day you intend to bowhunt it. Doesn't make sense to set a stand and check the mid-day wind situation when you'll be bowhunting the location early morning or early evening with a totally different wind pattern.

Obvious weather changes, such as storm fronts and shifting cloud cover, will change the wind patterns at the site of your stand or blind. Not many bowhunters realize that ditch banks, black or bright-green fields, downed logs or sloping hillsides, gullies, or fields of crops can also alter or produce almost undetectable wind and air current changes that can drastically effect your bowhunting success.

SCENT SENSE

Relatively few bowhunters really understand the idiosyncrasies of scent and its use. They simply buy what the manufacturers promote as the ultimate scent that will make them the deer slayers they've always dreamed of being. With glassy-eyed intent, these bowhunters slather this potent potion all around their stands, blinds, and on their boots, and then sit waiting for the buck of a lifetime to come leaping tall fences and bounding over small rivers to their waiting ambush. If they kill a buck, they'll sing the praises of the infallible elixir to anyone who'll listen, and if they get skunked, they feel guilty, because they failed at becoming the bowhunter the scent manufacture promised. Yahoo! If only the use of scents were so easy.

As a long-time trapper, I know that properly used scents work very effectively. However, getting a scent to work when and where you want it to is a different story. Some scent products will work some of the time, and some won't work any time, but none of them will work all the time, even when properly used.

Wind characteristics are more misunderstood in utilizing scents than in general bowhunting. If your chosen scent product doesn't get to a deer's nose, you've wasted your time and money. A deer can walk 10 feet from the most potent and alluring scent on the market, and if he's downwind, he can't smell it.

I had a disgruntled bowhunter tell me about his totally unsatisfactory scent experience with a pricey guaranteed-to-bring-in-the-bucks lure. He'd sneaked to within 200 yards of a couple of bucks fighting over a doe and chosen his ambush spot along a trail they used regularly. He carefully doused the brush and trees with his sure-fire scent and waited for the action. After two hours, the bucks moved his way, and when they were 50 yards out, veered off and disappeared into the woods. He let me know he was furious with the worthless scent and was going to get his money back. Duuhh! If the bucks and does didn't wind him from 200 and then 50 yards, it was obvious they were upwind of him and didn't have a clue there was a new irresistible scent in the air.

I've used about every deer scent on the market and created a few of my own, and they will work if you keep in mind the wind and the intent of the scent product. I've had deer react and pause long enough to give me a good bow shot for such crazy things as sardine oil, Butterfinger candy bars, Ben Gay, strawberry jelly, toothpaste, and a host of others you wouldn't believe. A deer is a curious animal, and if you can get a new and appealing smell to his nose, he is liable to give it the once-over and maybe pause long enough to give the innovative bowhunter a shot.

One of the most effective scents I've used in the past few years has been smoke scent. When I first saw this I thought, "What the heck will they come up with next?" On second thought, it made sense: Smoke is a solid and would be an ideal carrier for different scents. The inept nose of any bowhunter can tell the difference in the smell of burning leaves over that of burning tires or garbage, so why shouldn't a deer be able to discern various odors and flavors through smoke?

Exhaustive testing showed this stuff really worked and would draw deer from a quarter mile downwind. The oily scents used in the Deer Quest scent sticks actually left a residue on anything the smoke touched (including careless bowhunters) that could be backtracked by the deer to the source of the smoke. Another major advantage of the smoking scent sticks was visibility. Pour or spill liquid scent on a limb or scrape, and it becomes invisible from a few feet away. The white smoke spiraling above the smoke canister (used to mix and concentrate the scent and keep it out of the direct wind) acts as a visual attraction. I've had deer, elk, bear, and other critters spot the smoke from 100 yards upwind and come in for a look without ever having smelled the smoke.

Another feature of this scent is its ability to override and confuse human odors. The oily smoke molecules actually coat the sensitive scent receptors in an animal's nose and reduce their capacity for differentiating between scents. I usually place several of the smoking sticks on either side of me for this purpose. The drifting white smoke is also a constant reminder of wind changes and drifts.

I could go on and on about this unique scent, but give it a try and test it yourself. You won't be sorry. I prefer the Wild Berry scent for most of my deer hunting, as its sweetness attracts both bucks and does to the smoking scent sticks. The new Curiosity blend works equally well and has a strong berry scent, with just a bit of deer scent added to pique a buck's interest even more.

I like experimenting with scent and scent products, and every fall I get new insight into deer's responses. I always use scent of some sort when setting out decoys and when I am in a stand or blind. You never know when that perfect scent that works all the time might hit the market.

RATTLING AND GRUNT CALLING

Rattling and calling whitetail deer should be a no-brainer for bowhunters; nothing to lose and everything to gain. But I'm amazed at the number of bowhunters I encounter who have never tried rattling or calling.

Some of these hunters feel that they don't want to take a chance on spooking deer that might be lurking nearby or on the way to their ambush. Others feel that effective rattling is a skill better left to the experts. Hogwash! An "ex" is a has-been, and a "spurt" is just a drip under pressure. There aren't many antler-rattling deer-calling bowhunters who would own up to being experts under that definition, although I have personally met several who fit the criteria perfectly.

Deer calling and rattling is not rocket science. All it takes is a set of antlers, either real or synthetic, a deer call or two and a modicum of action and wind, along with lots of patience and perseverance. Many bowhunters give deer calling and rattling a perfunctory attempt during the season, and when they don't get an instant response from a monster buck, they give up. My rattling antlers and calls stay in my daypack from the first day of bow season in mid-September until the last day of season in mid-January, and they see lots of action the entire time.

Calling and rattling expands your bowhunting reach considerably and can entice neighboring bucks from a mile away. I personally feel the main reason many bowhunters aren't successful at calling and rattling is their reluctance to make lots of racket. Each fall, I have clients who arrive at our hunting camp toting a pair of six- or eight-point rattling antlers. These might pique the interest of a small eastern buck, but sure won't cut the mustard with a big Midwestern whitetail. If you're going to arouse the ire or curiosity of a dominant or trophy-size buck, you've got to make him think the sounds he's hearing are emanating from bucks worthy of his interest and large enough to present a challenge to his dominance.

I personally feel the main reason many bowhunters aren't successful at calling and rattling is their reluctance to make a lot of racket. Each fall, I have clients that arrive at our Iowa hunting camp from back east toting a pair of six or eight point rattling antlers. These might pique the interest of a small eastern buck but sure won't cut the mustard with a big Midwestern whitetail. If you're going to arouse the ire or curiosity of a dominant or trophy-size buck, you've got to make him think the sounds he's hearing are emanating from bucks worthy of his interest and large enough to present a challenge to his dominance.

I prefer a set of real deer antlers for my rattling, although I've successfully rattled in bucks with synthetics and would rather have them than a lightweight set of real ones. My favorite pair are hefty eight-point sheds. I've filed the brow tines down to keep from mashing my fingers when I get over exuberant and left the antler tips on so I can tinkle and chatter them lightly when need be. These antlers fit perfectly into my daypack and reside there throughout the deer season, ready for almost instant action.

When a couple of big bucks get into a knock-down-drag-out fight, the racket they produce is incredible, both in volume and intensity. These fight sounds are not likely to be produced by a mere bowhunter with a grunt call or rattling antlers. One of our clients almost jumped out of his tree stand when two huge bucks met head-on within 100 yards of him. He described the sound as that of a Mack truck hitting a tree trunk at 30 mph.

When I start a rattling sequence, I begin with fast action but only a light clattering of the antler tips to imitate the tentative antler contact of smaller bucks. As time progresses, I start banging and clashing the antlers harder and harder with each sequence. If I'm really trying to reach cross-country, I'll smack the back sides of the antlers together as hard as possible.

When I rattle or call to a deer that's within sight (I contact grunt or call to every deer I see during the fall, and a surprising number respond.) I'll start out at very low volume and watch the deer through my binoculars. I'll keep calling or rattling louder and louder until I can see by a buck's actions that I've got his attention, and then I call or rattle only loud enough to keep him coming. When the deer gets within 100 yards or so, I quit rattling and switch to a mouth call only. My favorite for this situation is a small but loud call that pins to your jacket, with a tube that runs to your mouth and pins to your collar or jacket front. The call operates by inhaling rather than blowing and can be used hands-free, with no interference in drawing and holding your bow as the deer moves closer.

When I set up in a tree stand or on the ground, I try to position a bow hanger or tree step by my left hand, where I can hang my rattling antlers and place them with minimum movement if a buck comes in sooner than anticipated. By consistently placing the antlers in this position, I always know exactly where they are and can reach down and tweak the hanging cord to get a bit of rattle for close-up enticement.

Gary Clancy, a good friend and superb whitetail bowhunter, ties his rattling antlers to the pull-up cord on the tree stand so they just reach the ground below it. When he spots a buck approaching, he drops the antlers onto the ground, which generally has no effect on the approaching buck. If a buck hangs up out of range, he simply jiggles the cord to make the antlers clash and thrash against each other in the leaves at the base of the stand. This action further piques the buck's curiosity and diverts his attention toward the disturbance at the base of the tree, and away from the hunter.

The most effective calling and rattling takes place during the pre-, post-, and peak rut, but I call and rattle all season and have had deer come to my calling the first weekend of the season in September and the last day in mid-January. Early and late in the season, I call and rattle with a lot less violence and intensity, as I'm only trying to establish the fact there are other bucks in the area and make a buck curious enough to come sufficiently close for a shot. Often I had bucks appear in a food plot or across an open field, and by using a contact grunt or two and almost imperceptible tinkling of the antlers, I've coaxed them close enough to shoot. Smart calling and rattling, combined with time and patience, can put a whole lot more deer within bow range for those who do than those who don't. Nothing ventured, nothing gained.

DECOYS AND DECOYING WHITETAILS

A decoy can be an extremely effective tool in bringing bucks within bow range and should be a part of every bowhunter's equipment cache. Several of the largest bucks killed on our Iowa hunting operation, including a monster scoring 198 2/8, were taken as a direct result of utilizing the visual attraction of decoys to seduce them within bow range of our clients.

Adding the visual appeal of a decoy to the distance-covering sound effects of rattling and grunting, and the olfactory attributes of deer scents, can create the edge that often makes the difference between bowhunting success or failure.

Rattling and calling are ideal tactics when bowhunting whitetails. If a buck hears what he thinks are the grunts from a competitive buck, you can bet he'll come in to investigate—pronto!

Full-bodied plastic deer decoys can be a pain to transport and haul around and, for this reason, are often ignored by bowhunters. A bad mistake. Today, the decoys available on the market are a lot more user-friendly than when I started deer decoying many years ago with a one-piece, heavy-foam archery field target.

There are a number of lightweight plastic and foam full-bodied decoys as well as several different types of silhouette decoys. For years, my favorite deer decoy has been the lightweight plastic Carry Lite. This full-bodied decoy breaks down into a reasonably compact (once you figure out the method to pack the legs, head, and antlers neatly into the body cavity), portable unit that fits into a blaze orange mesh bag that can be easily, and safely, hauled through the woods.

Newer and more portable and adaptable are the foldable photo-realistic decoys made by Montana Decoys, Inc. A couple of their different body position decoys can easily be carried in a daypack ready for almost instant use when the situation warrants.

The past couple of years, I've been using the ultimate deer decoy: A full-body mount of a doe deer with adapters in the head so I can use it as a buck when appropriate. This is the same type of animated decoy that state game and fish agencies use to catch poachers shooting deer from the road or at night in violations of the laws. The head and tail of this decoy are moveable and operated by a radio remote-control unit. The head swings back and forth while the tail flicks side to side. The radio remote-controlled decoy mounted by Brian Wolslegal of Custom Wildlife Robotics is as deadly effective as a deer decoy can get, and although the remote control is illegal in many states, the deer decoy can be used effectively without it.

When your goal is to put meat in the freezer, aim for the lungs. This shot will ruin the least amount of meat.

I try to keep my decoys as human-odor free as possible, and when we set them out, my guides and I wear gloves or rubber gloves and spray the decoys with scent eliminator when we get them positioned in the field.

A challenging buck will generally circle a buck decoy and approach head on for an eye-to-eye confrontation. Position the decoy so a circling buck will present several shot opportunities as he moves. A slight angling of the decoy facing the bowhunter's position will put the responding buck in broadside position when confronting the decoy head on.

Smaller bucks often circle the decoy and hang back, observing from the backside. This occurs more in timber or heavy cover than in open country. In timber locations, I generally set the decoy at 10 yards angling away from my stand. Don't set a decoy where a buck facing either the front or rear of the decoy will be looking directly toward your stand or blind.

A right-handed shooter should offset the decoy set-up to the left of the stand or blind to facilitate drawing and shooting with minimum movement from a sitting or standing position. The opposite would hold for left-handed shooters. A little experience in decoy placement and close observation of the deer actions around the decoy will get you tuned in and increase your success at putting a trophy buck right where you want him.

Decoy movement can add a life-like dimension to your set-up, and I've tried about everything imaginable, from toilet tissue taped to the underside of the decoy's tail, chin, and belly, to fringe material Velcroed along the ears and tail. Higdon makes a silhouette-type motion decoy that works well when set up properly, and I keep bugging some of the decoy manufacturers to develop a product with a head that bobs up and down to imitate a feeding deer. There are several head-down feeding decoys on the market, but I've found they spook a deer more times than not. It's unnatural for a deer to remain immovable with its head down for extended periods.

Adding scent to your decoy set-up in the form of urine, buck lure, or smoke scent sticks adds another dimension to your decoys and makes them even more effective. The more of a buck's survival senses you can overwhelm with your decoy set-up, the better your chances of luring a buck within bow range.

As with any other method of bowhunting mature bucks, decoying doesn't carry a guarantee of success. It's often frustrating, time consuming, and seemingly ineffective. However, the first time a trophy buck comes barreling across the open countryside with his ears laid back and his hair turned inside out as he stiff legs it up to your decoy, completely oblivious to everything but your decoy, you'll wonder why you hadn't used this "sure-fire" tactic years earlier.

Buck decoys work best because they can trigger an aggressive reaction. Adding a decoy when you're calling and rattling will visually confirm what the buck is hearing.

LATE-SEASON TACTICS

Without doubt, late-season bowhunting whitetails is the most challenging hunting of the whole year. No longer are you pursuing a bunch of unsuspecting, naive, nonchalant critters that are blasé about human encroachment into their habitat or working a buck that has his survival instincts overridden by his testosterone-charged sex drive.

During the latter part of the season, almost all deer that have survived the onslaught of archery, muzzleloader, shotgun, and rifle season have been harassed, pursued, spooked, shot at, and otherwise disturbed by the two-legged adversaries that have invaded every inch of their domain. During the course of the fall seasons, whitetails, from fawns to mossy-horned old bucks, have honed their escape and evasion tactics to a fine edge, tuned their senses of smell, hearing, and sight to the highest level, and adjusted their survival instincts to peak level 24/7, where they're in one-step-forward, two-steps-backward, ready-to-explode mode at all times. Definitely the most challenging and rewarding time to be bowhunting the trophy buck that's eluded you all season.

Late season is a time when the deer are interested in two things: survival and food. Food is the key to getting the odds in your favor on a late-season bowhunt.

On our Iowa, Nebraska, and Missouri whitetail-hunting leases we have many acres of food plots planted specifically to attract deer during the entire season. The food plots are planned and planted to provide lush, palatable, and nutritious green plants such as tyfon, clover, alfalfa, Brassicas, winter wheat, rye, triticale, and soy beans during the early part of the fall hunting season.

As the season progresses and the weather turns cold, the green plants lose their value and the deer turn to the corn and bean fields for their feed. Establishing food plots is time consuming, frustrating, costly, and, at times, marginally effective because of that intangible called weather.

We've been working on food plots on our leases for nine years and have gone to the Keep It Simple Stupid principle with better and better results each fall. In a very brief nutshell (this subject could be a book of its own), we plant Roundup Ready corn, in all our food plots in the spring and keep it sprayed for weeds. The humongous deer populations we're dealing with always manage to eat and destroy a certain percentage of the plots to varying degrees each growing season.

In mid-August, we go back into the plots, disc up any damaged or destroyed corn and replant with Whitetail Institute's Whitetail Clover, Alfa Rack, and NoPlow and Mossy Oak Biologic's Full Draw, Green Patch Plus, and Maximum. We also plant winter wheat, rye, tyfon, and triticale as we see fit. These quick-sprouting, fast-growing mixtures are up and supremely edible during the bow season. When winter hits the Midwest with snow and frigid temperatures, the green plants die back and the deer concentrate on the cornfields.

Sounds simple huh! Well believe me, when you start to combine the unpredictable weather, weeds, overpopulations of deer, and, oh yeah, did I mention unpredictable weather, you have a nightmare in the making. If you're bowhunting private land where a food plot or two might help your situation, your best bet might be to let the landowner plant his normal crops and then dicker with him to let you buy an acre or two in an advantageous hunting location for the going rate of the crop.

Each area of the country is a totally different ecosystem when it comes to growing crops for food plots, with different crops and planting times and procedures. Gather all the info and data pertinent to your hunt area and try to help your late-season bowhunting with a strategically placed plot or two. You won't be sorry.

Late-season bowhunting is more weather dependent than any other time of the season. If the weather is miserably cold, the deer have to spend more time moving and feeding to keep up their energy level, which provides the most opportunity for a properly outfitted and clothed, mentally prepared, late-season bowhunter to take a buck that's forced into activity.

During unseasonably warm late-season weather, the deer are not forced into activity and generally will wait until the last vestiges of daylight before they venture out to feed. Naturally, the does and fawns come first and the bucks are the last to arrive, just before dark.

This is also the time when everything in the woods is as quiet as a feather hitting a snowdrift. If you've ever bowhunted in below-zero weather on frozen ground or snow with nary a breath of wind, you know what quiet is. This is deer hunting at its most challenging and exciting. Late-season deer are ultra spooky and allow no leeway for error, so hunt smart or don't waste your time.

SCOUTING TO SUCCESS

There is no such thing as post season scouting in my book. The day hunting season is over for the year, all scouting efforts point toward next year's bowhunt, so that makes it pre-season scouting.

As soon as the last hunting season is history, the deer start settling down and concentrate on surviving the rest of the winter. This is a good time to get serious about preseason scouting. Start checking your bowhunting area and potential new ground to determine surviving populations, especially individual trophy buck survival. Driving roads in the early morning and late evening and glassing feeding areas in and around your hunting area should give you a pretty fair census of the deer that survived hunting season. Quality binoculars and spotting scope make it possible to observe a lot of country from the comfort of your vehicle. Get family, youngsters, and non-hunting friends involved in your scouting outings. This is also an excellent time to contact landowners about bowhunting permission for the following fall, long before the competition has given thought to such things.

Combine spring scouting with chasing gobblers, shed-antler hunting, bird watching, or mushroom picking. Spring scouting may be the most productive time for preseason whitetail scouting the whole year. The previous fall rubs and scrapes are still visible and the trails and runs stand out like a sore thumb against the dead winter background. During the spring you can follow trails into bedding areas and buck hidey holes and scout out stand locations in these sensitive areas without fear of spooking a skittish buck into leaving your hunting area, as might be the case close to or during the season.

I often get more intrigued by scouting deer sign, trails, and such when I'm turkey hunting than with the turkey hunting itself. This intense interest in spring deer sign keeps me in the woods longer covering the countryside and investigating those outoftheway places. This extra time has often resulted in a late morning or midday gobbler that I probably wouldn't have gotten had I just concentrated on turkey hunting.

Every spring during the Iowa , Nebraska, and Missouri spring turkey seasons I gain new information about the deer travel patterns, individual trails, rub lines, crossings, bottlenecks, travel corridors, waterholes, and deer movement in general in the areas that I bowhunt in the fall. This is a very unobtrusive time for cruising the edges of croplands, sloughs, fields, and meadows in a pickup or fourwheeler checking trails, scrape lines, travel corridors, etc. for potential stand locations at the same time I'm trying to locate a gullible gobbler.

Keep a notebook and record of your scouting trips and findings with locations, maps, dates, and other pertinent data. It's an easy task to refer to these notes prior to the fall hunting season and go directly to the exact location, even though the crops are still in the fields and the leaves obliterate and hide most of the vital sign you found earlier.

Aerial photos are an effective tool for preseason scouting and can provide a wealth of information at a glance. A set of aerial photos covering your hunting area and the adjacent property will give you a broad overview of the entire area and help determine logical areas for deer movement in regards to the lay of the land. Spend time to familiarize yourself with them and mark off the property boundaries of your hunting area with colored felt-tip markers. Identify and mark key landmarks such as farm buildings, roads, ponds, fields, food plots, creeks, streams, or sloughs, etc. It's a good idea to have aerial photos and maps of adjacent lands also as they may play a big part in determining deer movement patterns through your hunting area. Studying aerial photos is an excellent way to pinpoint bottlenecks, likely travel corridors, saddles over ridges, patches of dense bedding cover, and many other terrain features that need to be checked out on foot during your scouting trips. You can mark scrape and rub lines, bedding areas, feeding areas, and such on the photos during your preseason scouting forays. By combining your ontheground knowledge with the perspective offered by aerial photos and USGS topography maps, you'll get a much better overview of your hunting area and the adjacent country. Both USGS and aerial photos can be downloaded and printed free from your computer by going to www.terraserver.homeadvisor.msn.com. You can locate your hunting area or property and get wide overviews or close-ups by zooming in and out. A complete set of aerial photos or USGS maps of your hunting area(s) is an invaluable asset. Also see Chapter 18 for further information on obtaining customized maps and charts.

I hate summer! It's hot, buggy, and muggy, and there aren't any hunting seasons in progress. If it weren't for the fact that bucks need the summer, with its protein and mineral rich forbs and sedges, to grow big antlers and does and fawns need the warm weather and lush vegetation to grow and mature, I'd vote summer out entirely in favor of three more months of fall.

By late summer when the buck's velvet covered antlers have branched and start to show their true proportions, it's well worthwhile to spend some evenings glassing in hopes of locating a big buck or two for some serious indepth scouting later on. This time of year deer are reasonably predictable and can often be found in the same vicinity on a regular basis.

By late August and early September, the buck's antlers harden, their testosterone levels rise, and they're ready to tune up for the rut. The buck's primary goal during this period is to get as much nourishment and rest as they can to sustain them through the rigors of the fall rut. Often, the bucks that have been so much in evidence simply disappear as they become more nocturnal and move around less. Be patient.

When the early archery season opens, don't just spend an evening or two scouting a good buck or two and then think you can move in on them and start hunting. Unless the bucks are located on public land where you might have competition from other hunters, stay with (but away from them) morning and evening for a week or so until you know their every movement and can predict with accuracy a particular buck's movements to and from his feeding and bedding areas. If the buck of your choice is a big, old, mossyhorned monster that's lived through several previous hunting seasons, it's obvious he didn't survive by being stupid. Don't take such a buck for granted. You'll probably only get a single chance to tag him. Give yourself the best shot possible by scouting him as thoroughly as possible, until you can anticipate his movements to perfection. Keep good notes on your chosen buck's comings and goings, morning and evening, especially in regards to wind directions and weather conditions.

If you've located the buck in familiar stomping grounds, your previous hunting knowledge of the terrain and your preseason scouting forays combined with your target's current schedule should pinpoint one or more locations to set up a successful ambush.

LATE-SEASON DEER DRIVES

For a number of years, I bowhunted with a group of guys from Pierre, South Dakota, that didn't even get excited about whitetail bowhunting until Thanksgiving weekend, long after the early-season bowhunters had given up and the various rifle seasons were history. By this time the brutal Dakota winter weather with its blizzards and frigid arctic winds had drifted into the many hidey-hole sloughs and draws on the prairie and driven the deer to the shelter of river bottoms, groves, and shelterbelts.

These guys had driven the deer in this area for years, and while anyone observing their bowhunts would think it was kind of a helter-skelter operation, I can tell you it was anything but.

The first year I bowhunted with them, we were pushing a winding snaky section of prairie creek bottom where the trees were so few and far between an owl would have trouble finding a roost. There's no way any self respecting whitetail buck would consider this a late season sanctuary. The two drivers were going to still-hunt through two miles of the bottom while we set up on the downwind (30 mph arctic gusts) section of the creek. When we got to our blocking area, Jerry, one of the locals, suggested I go and position myself by a stump sitting forlornly in a grassy fence line 100 yards from the creek bottom across an open pasture. There was an open gate and roadway just off the creek that was obliterated with deer tracks and I convinced my host I might be better off there.

An hour later I'd had a dozen does and fawns and one small buck bust by me within a few yards. Everything would have been fine. If it hadn't been for the #$*&$#@, very large ten-point buck that had cut off a curving portion of the creek and waltzed down the fence line and right past the stump where, but for my know-it-all attitude, I would have been sitting. I caught a lot of well-deserved razzing over that screw-up, but you can bet I didn't dispute my host's suggestions after that.

Deer driving for bow and arrow requires a lot more planning, finesse, and pure luck than for gun hunting, but there are many areas of the country where late-season conditions make for ideal deer driving. A thorough knowledge of the country and lay of the land (a good place to make use of aerial maps), along with likely deer movement when pressured, is essential for success in this venture. Such things as weather conditions, wind direction, time of day, light conditions, and direction can all play an important part in the success or failure of a deer drive.

One of the reasons that bucks live to a ripe old age in many sections of the Midwest is the fact that locals do a lot of careless deer driving. They may harvest young and naive does, fawns, and young bucks, but they only add to the education of the older deer by not paying attention to noise, wind conditions and direction, weather factors, and deer-escape routes. This is better for bowhunters who take their hunting seriously.

Driving deer for bowhunters should be a slow, methodical process, with the blockers making use of every skill they possess to keep from being smelled, heard, or spotted while getting into ambush position. The drivers should actually still-hunt their way through the cover as slowly and methodically as if they were the only ones in the woods.

If a deer can see, hear, or smell a hunter moving through the woods and keep him located, the educated late-season deer has a much better chance of letting him pass by or sneaking back past him where least expected. If the driver moves slowly and cautiously, spotting a deer first or getting on top of one that's bedded, he has a better chance of getting a shot or subtly moving the deer where it's supposed to go. A panicked or nervous trophy buck concentrating on the pursuing bowhunter is far more likely to make a mistake that just might take him past a waiting bowhunter.

COUES DEER

Coues, pronounced cows, are a small subspecies of the whitetail deer found only in the southwestern states of Arizona and New Mexico and in Mexico. Most of the coues deer in the Pope and Young record book come from Arizona or Grant County, New Mexico, where the world-record coues deer, scoring 116-0/8, was taken in 1997.

Bowhunting these small gray ghosts is a game of patience. Lots of sitting and glassing trying to spot one of the elusive little deer in the rocks, cactus, and brush they thrive in, and then stalking to

Food plots provide excellent supplemental nutrition for deer and other wildlife. With a well-placed, downwind, stand at the field's edge, you may find some bowhunting trophies like this one.

within bow range. Most of the coues deer taken by bow and arrow are taken from tree stands overlooking waterholes in the arid country they call home.

On my first coues deer bowhunt with a couple Arizona Game and Fish employees, I glassed my first buck early one morning, and when I'd studied him for a while, trying to pick a stalking route, I asked my companion if the little buck in my spotting scope would score in Pope and Young.

After a few minutes of studying the bucks browsing on the distant slope, he drawled nonchalantly, "Oh, he'd probably beat the world record by a couple of inches or so." Needless to say, my trophy whitetail judgment needed readjusting for these desert-dwelling Midwestern deer.

I made a good stalk on the buck, and just as I started thinking about a place to mount him on my den wall, I spooked javelina bedded in the shade of a cactus, which in turn scared the heck out of my intended world record, and that was the last we saw of either animal for the rest of the week's bowhunt.

Glassing for coues deer is the ultimate game of patience. I've sat for hours at a time glassing a slope where my hunting companion knew there was a good population of coues deer, and seeing nothing, and then suddenly the hillside seemed alive with them. Seeing them from a distance and finding them when you get into the area on foot is one of the toughest challenges a bowhunter can face.

Most of the serious coues deer hunters use 15 to 20 power binoculars mounted on a tripod for their glassing, and any binoculars under 10x are a waste of time for trying to sort out these rock- and brush-colored deer from the deer-colored rocks and brush.

On a spot-and-stalk for coues deer in the inhospitable and definitely not hunter-friendly country they call home, buddy hunting is by far the most practical method. Once a shootable deer is spotted, one hunter keeps the little bugger located while the other stalks close enough for a shot. The spotting hunter usually has to guide the stalker through the jumble of rocks and impenetrable brush until he gets within sight of his quarry and can conclude the stalk on his own.

I've been on several bowhunts where even this method couldn't keep the elusive deer located long enough for one of us to get within bow range. Coues deer country is awesomely huge, and these dainty little deer don't take up much room. Even if coues deer were blaze-orange colored, they'd still be one of the greatest bow-hunting challenges in North America.

Most of the coues deer entered in the record book are taken on a morning bowhunt from tree stands placed over waterholes. So the key to success in bowhunting these ghosts of the desert is to choose a good area, scout out available water, and set up a tree stand or blind near the waterhole.

Rattling and grunt calling are also viable methods of bringing these desert deer within bow range, but temper all your calling efforts to a much more subtle and low-key level if you want to attract rather than repel these skittish survivors of the desert.

Late-season bowhunting techniques require hunters to be slow in their spot-and-stalk approach. This time of year, the deer are extra wary and are skilled at either letting a hunter pass by or sneaking back around him with ease.

Bowhunting coues deer may be a tough challenge, but it's one that every bowhunter should experience. ▪

MOOSE

Moose are the largest member of the deer family and sport the largest antlers of any animal in the world. Not only is bowhunting moose an exciting challenge, but the meat is superb and those antlers make an awesome trophy.

There are four subspecies of moose recognized in North America. The largest is the Alaskan-Yukon moose. An adult bull carrying antlers in the fall, just before rut, can be eight feet tall at the top of the shoulder and 11 feet from nose to tail, with a hefty weight of 1500 pounds. As the name implies, this gigantic deer is found throughout Alaska and the Yukon Territory.

The second-largest subspecies is the Canada moose, a term applied to both the western and eastern animals. The western Canada moose ranges from Ontario to British Columbia, while the eastern Canada moose ranges from Ontario to Newfoundland and down into Maine. These two subspecies overlap in northwestern Ontario, a prime area for moose hunting. An adult Canada bull moose carrying antlers in the fall, prior to the rut, can be seven feet at the shoulder and 10 feet nose to tail and weigh in at 1250 pounds, very much in the heavyweight class.

The fourth subspecies, the Shiras or Wyoming moose, found from Colorado and Utah northward through Wyoming and Montana, is the pigmy of the group, but still big! An adult Shiras bull sporting antlers during the fall can stand six feet at the shoulders, be nine feet in length, and tip the scales at 1000 pounds. All moose are BIG!

Moose have considerable attributes that make them a tough adversary to bowhunt under any conditions. Their long-legged, ungainly appearance, with a huge shnozz, dangling fuzzy bell, and humongous rack, may foster the impression of a dull-witted and lethargic critter. Not so. Moose may not exhibit the sneakily alert look of a whitetail buck or the majestic demeanor of a bull elk, but the moose's survival equipment will rival those of any big-game animal.

A moose's first lines of defense are its extraordinary sense of smell and hearing. That stupendous shnozzola can discern the slightest tinge of human scent in the air at phenomenal distances and smell edible greenery under several feet of water.

A bull's hearing is keen enough to pick up the soft, low frequency moans of a cow a mile or more away and the soft snap of a twig at 100 yards. This I know from personal experience. A moose's ears work independently of each other, so it can be checking both the front and back door at the same time. When moose tune in on a sound they want to investigate, they zero both ears and can pinpoint the slightest sound with uncanny accuracy.

Experienced moose bowhunters can also vouch for the acuity of the moose's eyesight. Their daytime vision is equivalent to a human's, but in the dim, early morning, late afternoon, or dark timber light, their vision is far superior to a human's. Their eyesight is highly tuned to picking up the slightest movement, and like their ears, the eyes work independently of each other. A moose's height gives him an elevated perspective that is often underestimated by bowhunters.

On my first Alaska moose bowhunt, I got within 70 yards of a huge bull that was feeding in alders and willows and quickly realized that, from his lofty viewpoint, he'd be able to see down into the dense cover and probably spot my movements. The only thing I could do was trail along behind him and wait for the right opportunity to close within bow range. It never happened.

Even though the monstrous bull was casually munching his way through the dense creek bottom willow and alder thickets, his long-legged strides atop dinner plate–sized splayed hooves allowed him to move faster than I could unobtrusively follow through the thick, noisy brush and spongy, boot-sucking tundra. The last sight I had of the bull was as he strode purposefully across the tundra a quarter mile ahead, headed for another creek in the next drainage, completely unaware of my pursuit.

According to the Pope and Young record book, calling is the most successful method of getting within bow range of a bull moose, and decoying (where possible) can make calling even more effective. To effectively call and decoy moose, one needs to be aware of the major difference in rutting tendencies between the Alaska-Yukon moose and their Canadian and US cousins.

Because of the vast expanses of tundra and more open alder- and willow-covered country, the Alaskan moose is not nearly as vocal as the Canada moose. Biologists tell us that this may account for the larger antler growth of the Alaska-Yukon moose. Moose living on the tundra make more use of their antlers in communication than do woodland moose.

The Alaska-Yukon bulls stake out the mating areas, tend to be more territorial in defending these areas, and gather harems of cows through calling, perfuming themselves regularly in rut pits and wallows, and making showy antler displays. The bulls hold their cows in brushy creek bottoms, along lakeshores or timbered ridges and side hills, where they can keep an eye on them and run off any interloper bulls that try to horn in on the action. Alaskan-Yukon bulls don't spend as much time or energy roaming their territory looking for cows as do the Canada bulls. They spend their time keeping the competition at bay, their harems intact, and their girls well serviced.

A caller trying to lure an Alaskan bull into bow range should use aggressive tactics and bull sounds to incite a jealous bull. Several Alaskan moose guides I know mix a few cow calls with their bull grunts in hopes of stoking a rutting bull into enough of a jealous rage to leave his harem and come looking for a fight.

One Alaskan outfitter uses a small set of lightweight, fake moose antlers to decoy harem bulls to him by flashing and rattling the antlers in the brush to imitate another bull in the herd bull's territory. According to him, when this method works, the action is fast and furious and certainly not for the faint hearted.

An Alaska bull's huge antlers play an important part in letting other bulls know they are in the country and just how big they are. I've glassed several

bulls at a distance challenging each other by simply swaying their heads back and forth to show their opponent the size and width of their antlers. Quite often, this antler display is enough to determine the outcome of the confrontation without any physical contact. In the low Alaskan and Yukon vegetation, a large bull's antlers flashing in the sun can be seen for several miles by both hunters and other moose. This visual signaling alone probably plays a greater

Carry a small squeeze bottle filled with talcum powder when spotting and stalking moose. Their very sensitive nose will pick up your scent in an instant, so keeping yourself downwind of your quarry is of utmost importance.

role in attracting both bulls and cows than hunters realize.

Several studies have been conducted that strongly indicated decoying with a large set of fake antlers worked with bulls that carried equally large or larger antlers, but would spook bulls with smaller antlers. I would love to bowhunt Alaskan bulls with a lightweight, pop-up cow decoy of some form and a small pair of antlers. There's no doubt such a combination could put a trophy bull right in the hunter's lap.

CANADA AND SHIRAS RUT

The Canada and Shiras moose rut is very different from the Alaskan-Yukon moose rut. The main rut usually starts sometime near mid-September, give or take a week depending on the location. It is the cow that controls when mating will take place. Just before coming into estrus, solitary cows stake out breeding areas approximately one-and-a-half to two square miles, and start to advertise their presence by calling for bulls and frequently urinating to leave their scent for the roaming bulls to find. Cows will defend these areas against other cows and try to drive off any cows encroaching on their mating areas. Cows generally prefer territory around ponds, beaver dams, lakeshores, meadows, or logged areas during the breeding season. Naturally, these are prime locations to set up for calling bulls.

The Canada and Shiras bulls, on the other hand, have home ranges that may cover as much as 16 to 18 square miles, with the ranges of various bulls broadly overlapping each other. During the rut, they travel these ranges in search of cows to breed. Rutting bulls are not constant travelers, they often stop in a particular area for long periods of time listening for cows that might be calling. Once the bull hones in on a vocal cow, they travel together until she comes into estrus. When the cow allows copulation to take place, they may breed several times during a 24- to 48-hour period, then the bull leaves to find a new cow. Cow moose that do not get bred in this main rut period will come into estrus again 25-28 days later and start calling and trying to attract a bull all over again. Some Canada and Shiras cows have been known to breed as late as November.

CALLING AND DECOYING CANADA MOOSE

Alex Gouthro is a Canadian moose outfitter and guide, with 30 years of experience guiding hunters and bowhunting moose himself, and he is probably one of Canada's most knowledgeable and proficient moose callers. Alex believes the use of a moose decoy, combined with good calling, is the deadliest combination possible for a bowhunter.

Pulling a Canada bull within 70 yards by calling is okay for a rifle hunter, but it doesn't cut it for a bowhunter. After several years of trial and error, Alex finally got a decoy designed that works well for his type of calling and hunting. Alex's silhouette cow moose decoy is life-size, cut from four-inch thick Styrofoam, and divided into three parts for portability. The realistic body, long-nosed head, and prominent ears present a profile that looks like a cow moose from a distance, particularly during the early morning and late afternoon hours.

As with any decoy, Alex believes that movement is the key to effectiveness. To accomplish this, his moose decoy mounts on a lightweight pipe stake through the center, with 30-yard pull cords attached to the head and tail of the decoy. Pulling on the cords swings the decoy back and forth on the pivot stake and allows Alex to fully control the position of the decoy from his calling location. He can swing the decoy to keep it broadside and more visible to an incoming moose or simply move it back and forth to give the impression of life-like action.

Another Canadian moose guide uses a painted foam taxidermy head form of a cow moose. He carries the moose head strapped to his chest with a shoulder harness. This decoy is equally effective when properly used, and has produced many close encounters for the outfitter and his clients. Several have put the outfitter into hasty retreat mode with an overly amorous Canada bull.

MOOSE CALLING

In addition to the decoy, moose calling tools consist of a birch bark calling horn and a dried scapula or shoulder blade bone. Moose megaphones can be the traditional birch bark, plastic, fiberglass, or rolled linoleum. They should be 14 to 16 inches long, with a mouthpiece one and a half inches in diameter, and the bell end five to six inches in diameter. The moose horn simply amplifies the caller's voice and imparts a moosey timbre to the noise. There are also several excellent commercial moose calls on the market that use a reed or diaphragm to produce cow and bull sounds rather than the human voice. The horn can even be used to simulate a cow moose urinating by pouring water from it onto the ground or into a lake, stream, or pond.

A moose or domestic cow scapula is used to imitate the sound of a bull raking his antlers in the brush or knocking against a tree. A scapula isn't as traditional as a set of real moose antlers, but it's a heck of a lot lighter, less cumbersome, and still has a "ring of bone" sound, almost as good as the real thing. In lieu of a scapula, a canoe paddle also works well for imitating the antler action of a rutting bull, and some may find it even easier to use.

Moose calling falls into two categories: passive and aggressive. Passive calling consists of making cow calls to let the bull know there's a cow in the area. Wary, older, trophy-size bulls often approach the caller cautiously and generally downwind to let their nose verify the presence of the cow or danger. Bulls may respond from a distance by grunting an answer and continue grunting as they approach the caller's location. These are the easy ones. More cautious, mature bulls are liable to come in as silently as a morning fog and suddenly appear right in the caller's lap. Amazing how such a huge animal, with such an awesome set of headgear, can move like smoke through the dense timber and brush, but bull moose seem to manage it with ease.

A responding bull may announce his presence by smacking his antlers with single knocks against a tree or by loudly thrashing them in the brush. The single knocks generally indicate a cautious bull that wants the cow to come to him. Use passive calling tactics with this bull.

The bull thrashing trees and brush with his antlers is aggressive and claiming the cow's territory for himself. If passive tactics don't work, use the scapula, pretending to be a small bull raking his antlers in the brush or limbs. I've also had several bulls come to my calling, grunting every step of the way, leaving little doubt as to their whereabouts.

The sheer size and intimidating nature of a rutting bull moose can often turn an avid hunter into a gibbering wreck and leave a guide wondering if he shouldn't take up guiding bird watchers.

Several years ago, Alex called up a nice, 50-inch bull that came in for one of his clients. The bull was creating a major ruckus, raking bushes and trees and grunting loudly. He was deadly serious about intimidating any other bulls in the area.

Alex hand signaled his client to move closer to him and coaxed him into squatting behind a clump of three-foot-high bushes. Alex then proceeded to call the bull past the shooter, broadside at 16 to 18 yards. *Five times!* The bull would stalk up to the decoy, stop, and eye the fickle female, waiting for her to make some move. Alex was so close, he didn't dare twitch the control cords. Getting no response, the bull would move off until Alex cow called and moved the decoy to entice it back.

As with other big game, the call of a cow in heat will quickly bring in a love-sick bull moose. One of the oldest and most reliable calls is a birch bark megaphone.

As the bull stalked past, the petrified shooter would peek over the bushes and then hunker back down. The bull eventually got tired of going in circles with no visible encouragement from the cow, and wandered off to look for a more cooperative date. When a very exasperated outfitter inquired as to why the hunter hadn't taken a shot, the flustered client blurted, "The bushes were in the way."

Alex pointed out that the bushes were not all that tall and it would have been easy to shoot over them. "Well you didn't tell me that," the thoroughly distraught, badly whupped bowhunter retorted.

When a reluctant bull hangs up back in the woods or approaches following a cow, switch to more aggressive calling tactics. Use soft bull grunts and the scapula to imitate another amorous bull competing for the favors of the cow. These tactics simulate a smaller, younger bull that won't intimidate the target bull and are especially effective later in the season, after most of the cows have been bred and the bulls are hunting hard for the next encounter. Patience and perseverance are probably more important in moose calling and decoying than any other type of hunting.

THE PERFECT MOOSE-CALLING SEQUENCE

Move quietly into position on a good crossing, travel-way, or along a lakeshore at least an hour before legal shooting time. Carefully set up your decoy, if you are using one, set out scented rags or canisters or light up your smoke scent sticks, and place them downwind of your blind or tree stand.

After everything is set, walk slowly and noisily around in the brush, slightly downwind of your stand, and splash loudly in any nearby water to simulate the sounds of a feeding or active cow, just in case there is a bull within hearing. After the racket making, get into your blind or tree stand and wait for things to settle down, listening for any bull sounds.

Float hunting waterways for moose is an enjoyable hunting strategy that will also allow you to take in some stunning scenery. Just make sure the bull is not in the middle of a bog or stream when you release your arrow.

If nothing develops after 15 minutes or so, make a couple of soft communication grunts, using your cupped hands rather than the megaphone. Continue the cow-in-heat calls every 20 minutes, gradually increasing the length and volume of your calling for one or two hours. If there's no action and you're set up near water, quietly leave your ambush, fill your calling horn with water, and loudly pour several containers full into the water, to simulate a cow urinating. The urination procedure can be repeated every hour or so.

If nothing develops by mid-morning and you feel the need for a break, move quietly out of the area, leaving your scent equipment in place. If using a decoy, lay it on the ground and cover with brush.

When you return for the afternoon bowhunt, do so with caution, as occasionally a bull will move into the area during the mid-day lull, looking for the source of earlier moose sounds, and he may still be there. The late afternoon session is much the same as the morning hunt, and if you don't do any good, don't get discouraged. Whether you plan on bowhunting the location again or not, vacate the area as quietly and unobtrusively as possible. Even a bull moose spooked by accident may become more difficult to hunt because of it.

A bull moose, for all his size and bulk, can move almost soundlessly through the thickest timber and brush. Add the disturbance of even a slight breeze, and a distant grunt or antler cracking against the brush or a tree may be muted or obliterated by rustling vegetation. I try to cut down on the chances of an unheard encounter by using a pair of Walker's game ears to amplify the sounds around me. The ability to hear the slightest out-of-place, stealthy step or subtle antler scrape may make the difference between success and being snookered.

Partner calling, where the second hunter does the bull imitating while the first does the cow calling, can add even more realism to the ambush, because the simulated cow and bull sounds are coming from two different places. This double teaming will often coax even the wariest of bulls to sidle in close enough for one or the other to get a good bow shot.

Bulls accompanied by a cow can present a whole new challenge to calling moose. If a bull is following a cow, chances are good she has *not* been bred, and aggressive calling may get the bull riled up enough to come relatively close for a shot. If the cow *has* been bred, the bull will be in front of her leading the way and ready to find another receptive cow. In this situation, passive calling with seductive cow-in-heat groans, and even the calls of an agitated cow begging for attention, may pull the bull into shooting position.

As with elk calling, when a responding bull is arrowed and starts to leave, a flurry of excited hyper-cow calling may stop the bull and hold him in the area until he drops.

Most of the same tactics used for calling and decoying Canada moose are equally effective for the Shiras moose in the lower 48. The Shiras subspecies cows also establish their own territories and the bulls cover a lot of ground in their quest to locate a breedable cow. Pre-season scouting to locate the cows' home ranges or core areas and travel ways, or corridors within their area, can provide ideal locations for calling during the season. Unfortunately, no manufacturer makes a moose decoy that is realistic looking and easily transported in the mountainous terrain the Shiras moose roam, so decoying these moose is generally not a viable option.

SPOT-AND-STALK MOOSE HUNTING

Spot-and-stalk bowhunting is almost on par with calling for producing record-book moose for bow-and-arrow toting hunters.

Spotting moose is a heck of a lot easier than stalking moose. I've flown over thousands of square miles of prime moose habitat in Alaska and Canada and seen hundreds of humongous trophy bulls from the air. Unfortunately, you couldn't get to a high percentage of them from anywhere, and most of them will live and die without ever having encountered a single hunter.

The first axiom for a successful spot-and-stalk bowhunt, as mentioned before, is to locate your antlered adversary *before* it becomes aware of you. An animal the size of a moose, with its massive headgear, is often easy to spot from a distance in the swamps, tundra, timber, or brush country it calls home. Finding the same critter when you're engulfed in the same impenetrable tangle of moose habitat, at the same level, is a whole different ball game.

Good binoculars are essential for locating moose at a distance and a spotting scope can be invaluable for long-range trophy judging and finite route planning of your stalk. Once a shootable moose is located, don't let the excitement and anticipation override your patience and planning. It's easy to do and disastrous to success. Generally, you'll be hunting with a guide or partner on a moose hunt. Take the time to work out a system, whereby one stays put in a well-marked, visible location, while the other stalks the moose. Work out a fully understood set of signals, so the stalker will be able to ascertain the bull's position relative

Spotting moose is hard work. The country moose live in is huge, but they move through rough, log-strewn bogs and sloughs with amazing speed and ease.

to his own, its activity . . . bedded, feeding, moving, etc., and the unexpected appearance of other moose (bulls or cows).

Impatience blows a major portion of the stalks on big game, so take your time and do it right. If the wind changes direction, the moose relocates, or anything unforeseen happens, don't hesitate to back off, reconnoiter the situation, and start over . . . even if you have to wait another day.

Since visibility is often very limited when stalking moose in heavy cover, wind becomes even more important, and I make constant use of my powder bottle to keep the slightest trickle of breeze working for me. A string or feather on your bow won't register slight updrafts or downdrafts, and these are often erratic enough to carry your scent the wrong direction. Use your powder bottle.

MOOSE BOWHUNTING GEAR

Moose are my kind of target . . . *big!* A bull moose is not exceptionally hard to kill with a well-placed, razor-sharp broadhead. However, as big as they are, it just takes them a bit longer than smaller big game to realize they are dead and supposed to fall over. Any type of bow, 50 pound and above, shooting cut-on-contact, razor-sharp broadheads, will make clean kills on the largest moose when the arrow is put into the huge heart-lung zone of a moose.

The large size of the kill zone on a bull moose (30 inches by 30 inches) gives a bowhunter a bit more leeway on range and a 50- to 60-yard shot on a moose equates to a 20-yard shot on a whitetail buck . . . *if* you conscientiously practice and become proficient at these longer distances.

The moose's enlarged dimensions and overall size make range determination a critical factor in moose hunting, and the best tool to take the guesswork and chance out of this important aspect is an accurate rangefinder. Never leave home without it!

Clothing can go a long way toward making or breaking a moose bowhunt, as the weather where these beasties live during the fall can range from miserably hot to miserably cold and wet. The hot weather can be combated by stripping down to the essentials, but for the wet and cold weather, you'd better have effective rain gear and warm, dry, layered undergarments.

All outer garments should be in a camouflage pattern and color that blends with the background, including gloves and facemask or camo paint. Moose country generally isn't plagued with cockleburs, burdock, and some of the more clingy, poky weeds of whitetail country, so my choice is wool outerwear, with thick or thin (depending on temperature) wicking-type underwear. (I hate wool against my tender skin.) Whatever clothing you choose should be soft and quiet as well as warm and water resistant. Scent Lok has come out with items of clothing that are ideal for moose hunting under a variety of conditions, and they help cut down on the amount of human stinkum floating around the moose habitat.

Moose are water creatures, which means your footgear should be waterproof, insulated, and of sufficient height to keep your feet warm and dry. Unless, of course, you have to cross a lake to get to your moose; then a boat would be nice.

When you walk up to a dead bull moose, your first thoughts are going to be, "What have I done and how far is camp and transportation?" You can have all your portable, packable, and foldable meat saws for smaller critters. I want a razor-sharp, full-sized, steel-handled axe at hand for quartering a moose.

Taking a trophy bull moose with a bow and arrow is an awesome accomplishment, and one that every bowhunter should experience. Sinking your teeth into a sizzling, sputtering, fat-dripping, succulent, two-foot-long, campfire-broiled moose rib ain't a bad experience either. ∎

Keeping himself downwind of this record book black bear was a key factor for bowhunter Kirk Brown.

The opportunity to add some challenging upland bird hunting during your big game bowhunt shouldn't be overlooked.

One of the most effective ways to hunt antelope is to ambush them at watering holes. If time allows, build a pit blind with the wind in your face to bag a trophy like this.

Polarized sun glasses are necessary when bowfishing for carp, especially in the spring when carp are spawning or "shoaling" in large numbers.

When bowhunting big game like moose, be sure to aim for the lung/heart area. Keeping calm and remaining focused when game this big is in bow range is key to taking a record moose like this.

Stalking showshoes with a bow is an ideal way to spend the mid-day hours–in between your morning and afternoon deer posts. It sharpens your shooting skills too!

Bowhunting late-season whitetails can prove productive–especially when it yields a trophy like this one. Having pre-selected shooting lanes also helps.

These two successful Merriam turkey hunters know the asset of full camouflage when hunting this quarry with its keen eyesight.

CARIBOU

"Rise and shine, it's daylight in the swamps," I hollered enthusiastically to my supine and snoring companions as I stuck my head out the tent flap and marveled at the vast expanse of fog-shrouded tundra surrounding our minuscule campsite. Man I was pumped and ready to go bowhunting for caribou. The seemingly endless (butt-numbing) 900-mile drive from Anchorage to caribou camp, below the north slope of the Brooks Range, was quickly forgotten when we started seeing herds of caribou at the foot of Atigun Pass, along the famed Alaska pipeline. The area adjacent to this engineering marvel is the largest "bowhunting-only" zone in the United States. A no-firearms-hunting buffer zone extending two-and-a-half miles on each side of the gigantic tube transporting crude oil from the oil fields around Prudhoe Bay; 850 rough and rugged miles south to the seaport of Valdez in Prince William Sound.

It was well after midnight by the time we'd gotten camp set up at Galbraith Lake, eaten a sandwich washed down with a couple of beers to celebrate our arrival and upcoming adventure, and slipped into our sleeping bags for a short snooze. The grueling drive and camp set-up had done little to stem my enthusiasm, and having been in the outfitting business for years, I'd learned to sleep *fast*, especially when it never really got dark. At 4:00 a.m. it was light enough to shoot and I couldn't control my excitement any longer. Unfortunately, my experienced companions didn't share my enthusiasm, and after some dire threats mumbled my way, I crawled back into my sleeping bag, wondering what kind of bowhunters I'd teamed up with and what big-game critter wasn't up and about at the crack of dawn.

Caribou bowhunting is different. It's kind of a cross between bowhunting pronghorn antelope and whitetail deer, depending on the subspecies and terrain.

Sometimes caribou hunting involves a lot of waiting. But, generally, when you see one, there are many more to follow!

There are four subspecies of caribou scattered across the far north, from the northwestern tip of Alaska to the northeastern tip of Newfoundland.

Barren ground caribou are found only in Alaska and are a larger species, in both body and antler size (by a very small margin), over the equally popular Quebec-Labrador caribou found in northern Quebec. The world-record barren ground caribou stands at 448 6/8 inches, while the Quebec-Labrador record is 434 0/8 inches. Central barren ground bulls are much like their Alaska cousins (only a bit smaller), with the world record at 420 6/8 inches. The mountain caribou is right in there with the world record at 413 6/8 inches, while the woodland caribou tops out at 345 2/8 inches.

All caribou look very much alike and you'd have to see the different species side-by-side to spot the slight differences between them. Caribou are the only big-game species where both bulls and cows sport antlers. Their antlers look like they were put together by a committee, and accurately scoring a caribou in the field can drive you to drink. You'll find a bull with long points and good spread with small shovels and bez points, while another bull has wide double shovels and bez with short tines and narrow main beams, etc. Before you embark on a caribou bowhunting adventure, study every photo of caribou antlers you can find. The most valuable time I spent in preparation for several caribou hunts was ogling the numerous record-class antlers at several Pope and Young competitions and trying to figure out why each set scored as they did.

It didn't take me long on my first day of bowhunting barren ground caribou with pros Curt Lynn, Ed Russell, Dave Neel, and John Colway of Anchorage to realize that bowhunting caribou has its own unique set of rules and timetables that differ drastically from normal big-game bowhunting.

This vast luxuriant tundra country is prime habitat for thousands of barren ground caribou, moose, grizzly, ptarmigan, and a host of other critters. The soggy, saturated arctic tundra is also home to Alaska's state bird, the mosquito, and their equally voracious and aggravating cousins, gnats and flies.

Early fall on the spongy, boggy tundra can be a tough place if you're a caribou with wide-open, sensitive nostrils and eyes. These infernal insects make life miserable for caribou by gathering around their heads and crawling into their noses and eyes. The only peace the caribou get is the few hours of twilight, when the coolness

Caribou antlers come in all shapes and sizes. Take a bull caribou that will bring you memories of your thrilling big-game bowhunt.

Stalking caribou over the water-logged tundra or tightly packed, ankle-twisting fields of rocks and boulders can challenge even the most physically fit of bowhunters.

puts the insects down. Once the sun rises and warms things up, the bugs swarm out of their roost in clouds, and start harassing anything warm blooded that moves, and caribou in particular. The insatiable pests literally drive the caribou crazy, which can work for or against a bowhunter, depending on his luck.

My Alaskan bowhunting buddies were aware of the bug phenomenon and knew the best time to locate caribou was well after the sun was up, when the bugs were really bugging the caribou. It didn't take me long to realize that the eyes, nose, and mouth of a bowhunter are almost as sought after as those of caribou. Venturing about without a liberal application of Deet insect repellent is tantamount to bowhunting grizzlies with rubber blunts. I also learned to breathe through my mouth rather than my nose and use my clenched teeth to strain out most of the bugs.

Barren ground caribou bowhunting is a spot-and-stalk situation that calls for a good set of binoculars, spotting scope, and patience. The Alaska tundra is very deceptive country for the uninitiated. Stalking caribou across the quaking, waterlogged mat of vegetation that overlays ankle-twisting, ball-bearing-like rocks and boulders is a lot tougher than it appears. A quarter-mile caribou stalk is the equivalent of a mile or longer stalk in antelope or mule-deer country, and the erratic nature of bug-crazy caribou adds a whole new dimension to stalking.

The only way the caribou can get relief from the airborne pests is to find some shadow or shade where it's too cool for the aerial assault artists. Their favorite bug-evasion tactic is to find a shady spot under a bush, behind a rock, or, best of all, in a small pool of permafrost-cooled water. The caribou stick their heads or noses into these bug-free havens and may stay head down, eyes closed, in this vulnerable position for an hour without moving, or they may get a bug up their nose and run back to where they just came from. This erratic bug-induced behavior makes for some interesting and frustrating stalking.

The first day we must have glassed and judged 200 caribou as we drove along the Haul road. We were all chomping at the bit to try our hand at stalking caribou, but we figured we needed to locate and pinpoint as many trophy animals as possible for the days ahead. Late in the afternoon, a bug-bedeviled, record-book caribou came striding out of the river bottom, crossed the road in front of us, and ran into a small draw several hundred yards above the road. The annoyed caribou jammed his head into the cool shade of a low-growing willow for relief from the cloud of hovering gnats and mosquitoes.

My companions dropped me off a quarter mile down the road and I quickly circled behind the small ridge to approach the caribou from above and downwind, hoping he'd stay put long enough for me to get into position for a shot. When I eased my head around a bush on top of the ridge, the caribou was still head down at 40 yards, oblivious to the world around him.

I came to full draw from a semi-prone position and then slowly raised to my knees for the shot . . . the bull never moved a muscle. I picked a spot, released and watched my fluorescent-fletched and crested xx75 flit through the arctic air and disappear into the caribou rib cage. Zip, zilch . . . no reaction from the bull.

I quickly snapped another arrow onto the string, wondering if the bull was taking me seriously. He was still head down in the bushes and hadn't showed the slightest indication of being hit, although I could plainly see blood around the first arrow's entrance. I concentrated on the first arrow hit and sent a second arrow his way. The second arrow, slicing through the rib cage in almost the same place, made the bull jerk his head out of the bush and take a couple steps before he staggered and went down.

We spent the next week spotting and stalking caribou to our heart's content, and when we ended the hunt, the five of us had arrowed 13 Pope and Young caribou bulls (limit was three caribou per hunter).

Barren ground caribou are one of the few Alaskan big-game critters that can be bowhunted without the services of an outfitter or guide. Many people have the mistaken notion that Alaska is overrun with game and there are critters behind every bush and tree. Alaska is a monstrous chunk of real estate, with vast areas that contain nothing larger than voles and lemmings for much of the year. I have flown thousands of miles over the Alaskan hinterlands without seeing a live beastie, and then popped over a ridge into a valley crawling with furred and feathered game.

Hunting on your own in Alaska is a great adventure, but make sure you do your homework and plan meticulously, or you could be in for the greatest disaster of your bowhunting career. The most prevalent do-it-yourself way to get into Alaska's caribou country is hiring a flying service to drop you off in the bush for your bowhunt. During the early bow season, barren ground caribou are fairly sedentary and not in migratory mode yet.

The key to success in this type of bowhunt is to make *sure* you get dropped off where there are caribou. Some drop-camp flying services will drop you into a lake or area where it's easy for them to get in and out, regardless of whether there are caribou in the area. Not a good situation. Thoroughly check out several flying services and their references. Make sure they understand you want to survey the area before being put down. If there aren't huntable numbers of caribou in the area they want to drop you, fly the area until you find caribou within bowhunting range of where they can drop you off.

A good flying service will check on you periodically, and if you need to be moved they will do so. Make sure you both have an understanding of what's going down *before* you send a deposit, and get it in writing. Doing your research and homework well in advance of your Alaskan caribou adventure can make the difference between the success or failure of your bowhunt.

CARIBOU BOWHUNTING EQUIPMENT

Stalking open-country caribou is an exercise in patience and persever-ance because the tundra doesn't offer much cover, and your stalks have to be meticulously planned and executed. Good binoculars and a spotting scope are invaluable in locating the animals and choosing the best route of approach. Combining the judicious use of quality optics with smart bowhunting tactics and persistence should make your caribou bowhunt a blast.

The tundra is like a giant sponge, soaking up the frigid melt water from the underlying permafrost. You can depend on being damp or wet much of the time while bowhunting and stalking caribou. When crawling through low-growing willows, the icy water running in around your belt, down through your shorts, and out your pants legs does a lot to keep you alert during your stalk. Tough as it is at times, grit your teeth, and as the old Indian in the movie *The Outlaw Josey Wales* quipped, "Endeavor to persevere." Don't let the frigid discomfort or clouds of bugs hovering around your head push you into making a mistake or rushing your stalk.

The damp, breezy arctic conditions make wool or fleece clothing invalu-able. Undergarments that cut the wind, maintain their warmth when wet, and dry quickly are an essential part of your gear. Camouflage clothing or outer garments that blend with the background are also a necessity for caribou bowhunting success.

Caribou have excellent noses, but the prevalent arctic breeze generally makes stalking with the wind in your favor a simple matter. You have to let your conscience be your guide on shooting distances in most caribou coun-try. The more proficient you become at the longer ranges, the better your chance of scoring when the opportunity presents itself. Since I shoot instinc-tively, a range finder doesn't do me much good, but for a sight shooter, a quality laser rangefinder is essential for your far north bowhunt.

QUEBEC-LABRADOR CARIBOU

I've been snake bit when it comes to bowhunting this species. I've had several hunts booked, and something has come along to spoil the trip every time. On one occasion, the outfitter simply disappeared and hasn't been heard from since. Probably a good thing, since his stranded clients were ready to mount his head on their garage wall.

All of the Canadian caribou species require the services of a licensed outfitter, so do-it-yourself Canada caribou bowhunting is not an option. The Quebec-Labrador caribou are generally bowhunted during the fall migration from summer to winter range. Depending on weather conditions, this north-ern Quebec bowhunt can range from fantastic, with thousands of caribou on the move in your hunting area, to famine, where you'll be lucky to locate a few local cows, calves, and small bulls.

The key element in killing a trophy Quebec-Labrador bull is being able to glass and judge numerous caribou, so you can pick and choose the bull

Caribou migrations can vary from year to year, depending upon the weather. Book with an outfitter that can transport you to a new territory if the caribou have already passed through or are not in the immediate area.

of your dreams. The hunts are run from a main camp near historical caribou migration routes. Each day, hunters are transported to various crossings on rivers or lakes, where they set up to ambush caribou as they move to the crossings.

According to the many bowhunters I've talked with, the action can vary from fast and furious, with caribou streaming past everywhere, to very boring, with only a couple caribou a day. Once again, good optics are essential; you want to glass and judge oncoming caribou as far out as possible so you can concentrate on getting in position for the shot.

This can be a lot easier said than done, as a herd of caribou on the move presents a jumble of antlers that all look like trophies. Singling out a "boomer" bull in a migrating herd is one thing, but getting within bow range without spooking the whole blooming bunch is another. Imagine there are times when track shoes would be more useful than rubber boots. Caribou are like most other herd animals in that where one goes, the rest of the herd is likely to follow, and this characteristic can often be used to good advantage to put a bowhunter within range of a good bull.

Pre-hunt planning is of the utmost importance for Quebec-Labrador caribou bowhunting due to the dependence on the caribou migration. You want to book your hunt when past statistics and records indicate the peak of the migration in the area you choose to bowhunt. Start the process of booking your Quebec-Labrador caribou bowhunt at least two years in advance, so you have plenty of time for contacting outfitters and their references. Regardless of how meticulously you research your caribou bowhunt, the weather is still a critical and uncontrollable factor that neither you nor the best-intentioned outfitter can predict.

CENTRAL BARREN GROUND CARIBOU

The central barren ground caribou is the third most popular caribou species pursued by bowhunters and very similar in size to the barren ground and Quebec-Labrador. It is found in the Northwest Territories and northern Manitoba provinces, with by far the best bowhunting in the NWT in the unique and interesting town of Yellowknife. Bowhunting tactics for the central barren ground caribou are a combination of ambushing them on migration routes and spot-and-stalk hunting.

The migration is more of a slow-moving cross country trek, with scattered herds of caribou meandering in a southerly direction, following established routes around and across the thousands of various-sized lakes scattered in the rocky tundra. This seemingly haphazard travel gives bowhunters ample opportunity to glass moving herds of caribou and stalk them or get into position to ambush them as they circle around lakes or move along the narrow eskers (ridges or fingers of wind-blown sand) between the larger bodies of water.

I've been in many bowhunting camps, but Camp EKWO (which means caribou in the Dogrib Indian language), located on Humpy Lake and operated by Joyce and Moise Rabeska out of Yellowknife, NWT, is one of the best I've encountered. The fabulous food and ultra-comfortable and spacious tent accommodations are enhanced by the superb lake-trout fishing, nightly visits by local grizzlies, and the almost-constant passage of caribou on both sides of the strategically located camp. Camp EKWO has produced the world-record central barren ground caribou for archery, muzzleloader, and rifle. Not a bad accomplishment.

The main method of bowhunting the central barren ground is to cruise the extensive lake shores, glassing for caribou, or hike across the tundra to various lookout points and glass for feeding or moving groups. If the caribou are on the move, the guides usually know just where they are headed or will cross, and hustle the bowhunter into ambush position. Feeding or bedded caribou can often be successfully stalked across tundra that's broken by rock and boulder outcroppings and patches of willow, alder, and spruce.

I killed my first bull as they moved through a narrow bottleneck between two lakes, and missed the next two as they moved along the edge of a lakeshore. The largest bull that qualified for Boone and Crockett at the time I killed it was taken 400 yards from the main camp, as it and several other bulls moved along a narrow sandy esker.

WOODLAND AND MOUNTAIN CARIBOU

According to Dave Widby, who experienced a successful woodland caribou bowhunt in the dense timber and brush country of Newfoundland, bowhunting these caribou is akin to whitetail deer spot-and-stalk hunting. Dave and his outfitter would cruise the logging roads and trapper trails through the dense woods on a four-wheeler, trying to spot a good bull. The woodland caribou use these trails and roads as the path of least resistance in their travels and are often spotted moving along or crossing these travel-ways.

Dave, a resident of Anchorage, Alaska, likened Newfoundland's tundra caribou country to the Alaskan bush. The heavy timber is interspersed with numerous open tundra and bog area, where the caribou feed, and allows bowhunters a decent opportunity to spot and stalk them. Spotting a caribou in one of these areas is just half the battle, as keeping them located amongst the willow- and alder-dotted sloughs while stalking can be a problem. Walking up on and spooking an unseen caribou is a regular occurrence on these bowhunts. Binoculars are a woodland caribou bowhunter's best friend, and their judicious, constant use will often make the difference between success and failure.

Woodland caribou populations seem to fluctuate from year to year in different areas, so when planning your hunt, get the latest population information from your outfitter, provincial wildlife department, and bowhunting references before choosing a hunting area and outfitter.

Mountain caribou, as the name indicates, are found at the higher elevations in British Columbia and the Yukon and are bowhunted by the spot-and-stalk method. Binoculars and spotting scope are as essential to hunting these critters as your bow and arrow set. A good spotting scope can save you lots of boot-sole rubber by letting you judge and select your target from a distance. A spotting scope is invaluable in picking the best possible route for stalking within bow range of your chosen trophy.

Again the most valuable aspect of bowhunting a species such as mountain caribou, where an outfitter is required, is the time and effort spent in picking a primo area and the most capable outfitter you can afford. Start your planning well in advance of your bowhunt . . . you won't be sorry.

A prime bull caribou should be mandatory for any bowhunter's trophy room. The caribou's distinctive headgear, resplendent coloration, and unique habitat make it virtually impossible to have an unsuccessful caribou bowhunting experience. So start planning *now*. ■

SHEEP AND GOATS

O nce in a lifetime," I thought to myself as I stared intensely through my spotting scope at the barely legal three quarter-curl bighorn ram bedded in the shade under an overhanging ledge at the tip end of a long rocky ridge, 200 yards below my hidden eyrie. "Damn . . . why can't things ever be simple when you're bowhunting?" Here I was, in excellent stalking position on the bowhunting trophy of a lifetime, and I had to make some hard, fast decisions that could affect my bowhunting for the rest of my life.

I'd lucked out earlier in the year and drawn one of the coveted Colorado bighorn sheep licenses in a unit I knew like the back of my hand: the district where I was a wildlife conservation officer working for the Colorado Division of Wildlife. Part of my job was keeping tabs on the bighorns in my district. I'd flown sheep counts for several previous years in a fixed-wing plane and helicopter and worn down lots of horseshoes riding the high country. I had a pretty fair idea where most of these ridge runners roamed and where to spend my time looking for them.

However, Colorado had just recently passed a law limiting all bighorn sheep hunters to one bighorn kill in a lifetime. If the ram I was ogling had been one of several heavy-horned, three quarter- to full-curl rams I knew lived in the area, and I'd have spotted a ram in that category, there would have been no conscious decision necessary and I would already be putting a stalk on the unaware ram and his two smaller companions. As it was, I had taken a very respectable three quarter-curl ram on Pikes Peak before the "once-in-a-lifetime" regulation had taken effect. The ram I was glassing was just a shade smaller than my first sheep, and I'd made a pact with myself when I first moved to Colorado to hold out for a bigger critter each succeeding year.

I spent four hours mumbling to myself and playing mental gymnastics,

Rocky Mountain bighorn love timber and spend much of their time in the trees.

while the rams nonchalantly chewed their cud and enjoyed the mild fall day, completely unaware of my camouflaged presence. When they finally got up and meandered down into the timber, I congratulated myself on my perseverance and resoluteness.

As they say, hindsight is 20-20 and foresight is never that good. I spent the next two days glassing several groups of sheep and some smaller rams before I located a monstrous seven eighths-curl ram across a steep-sided valley. It took a full day to circle around to get above where I'd last scoped him in a small park, and then the fog and rain moved in and kept my partner and I cooped up in our tent for three days. We couldn't see 10 yards in any direction, and climbing around the steep, rotten, rock slope wasn't a viable (or smart) option. I ended my sheep bowhunt wishing I'd taken the ram I'd located earlier. To add insult to injury, two years later the Division of Wildlife rescinded the "once-in-a-lifetime" ram regulation. They weren't getting sufficient harvest on mature rams because of hunters with the same attitude I had. Damn!

In my humble opinion, sheep aren't the sharpest big-game animals roaming the mountains, but they certainly do live in country that will test your stamina and determination to the limit. Unfortunately, the biggest detriment to bowhunting the sheep species is license availability and cost.

Several years ago, one of my Iowa whitetail bowhunters had just returned from Nevada, where he'd taken a huge desert ram that was the new state record. He'd purchased the governor's desert bighorn tag for $47,000 at the sheep foundation's banquet. One of the cheaper specially allocated sheep tags in the western United States that year. A little out of reach for the average blue-collar bowhunter . . . including me. A good friend, and one of the few bowhunters to take the grand slam of North American sheep with a bow and arrow, estimated it averaged approximately $30,000 per sheep for the slam, and he didn't buy any of the special governor's permits.

Bighorn sheep were the most sought-after game animal according the Pope and Young's 23rd recording period summary. The world-record bighorn taken in Alberta in 1998 scored 199 5/8. The most record-book bighorns are harvested in Colorado, Alberta, and Montana. At present, Colorado allows 10 percent of its bighorn sheep licenses for non-residents on a lottery basis. Alberta and Montana both require outfitters for sheep hunting.

Hunting Dall sheep requires a hunter to pack way in. They are the easiest of all sheep to spot, but they can blend in fairly well when bedded in shaded recesses and niches.

Dall sheep, found in the mountains of Alaska and the Northwest Territories, are the next most popular sheep, with a total of 201 listed in the record books . . . the largest being a 171 0/8 inch boomer taken in the Chugach mountains of our largest state in 1988.

Stone sheep, a cousin of the Dall that range in color from off-white to dark gray with white edging, are found in British Columbia and the Yukon and also require the services of a licensed outfitter. There have been a total of 81 stone sheep entered in the record book, the largest scoring 174 2/8 inches, taken in British Columbia in 1992.

Desert bighorns are found in the arid and barren canyons and mountains of Arizona, Nevada, Mexico, Colorado, Utah, and California, where they are now fully protected. Mexico is by far the top place to hunt for desert bighorns. The world record, scoring 178 6/8 inches, was taken in 2007 in New Mexico. There have been a total of 111 rams entered in the record book: 40 killed in Mexico, 34 in Arizona, 24 in Nevada, and the rest split between Utah, California, Colorado, and New Mexico.

Patience, perseverance, and one heck of a lot of luck are needed to get a coveted desert bighorn tag. I know of one bowhunter who's applied for an Arizona desert sheep permit for the past 23 years without success. That's

Stone sheep are similar to Dall sheep but are fewer in numbers and are more difficult to spot.

about as tough a bowhunting proposition as you'll find in the country.

Bowhunting sheep is pretty much the same kettle of fish, whether you are bowhunting the North Slope of the Brooks Range for Dall or the Pedregosa Mountains in southern Arizona for desert rams. It has to be the ultimate in spot-and-stalk bowhunting, and the key to success is the spotting part of the hunt.

As I stated earlier, I don't feel that sheep are in the same category with a wise old whitetail buck or crafty bull elk when it comes to out-and-out smarts, but the rough, rugged terrain sheep roam gives them a decided advantage against a stalking bowhunter.

SHEEP AND GOAT BOWHUNTING EQUIPMENT

All sheep have phenomenal eyesight, and the only way to over-come their visual advantage is with the best optics you can afford and a willingness to use them to the fullest. I bowhunted sheep in the Absaroka Wilderness area one fall; we would get into a good comfortable position, with the morning sun at our backs just at sunrise, and often stay in one spot for six hours without moving. (A soft seat cushion might also be considered an essential item for sheep hunting.) We glassed lots of mule deer, elk, and sheep, but couldn't find a worthwhile ram.

Sheep spotting and glass-ing is a long-distance proposi-tion. I prefer a quality set of 10x binoculars for the job, such as my favorite lightweight 10 x 42 Nikon Superior E's, accompa-nied by an equally high-quality, variable-power spotting scope. My 15x-45x Nikon ED spotting scope has a 60mm objective lens and extra-low dispersion coated lenses to provide a sharp, clear image at all powers.

For ultra-long distance or critical trophy judging, I carry a 60x eyepiece that really brings in the detail. I've tried numer-ous lightweight camera tripods for supporting the scope on rocks or logs, but they are all too shaky. The best alternative I've found is a rock-solid tripod with a rotating and lockable ball head made by Pentax. The whole unit is only 10 inches

Bring along the finest set of binoculars you can. You'll do a lot of glassing when hunting Stone sheep.

long and packs almost flat; to set it up, the legs are rotated into locked position. It may not stand very high, but when placed on a boulder, log, backpack, or across a saddle, it'll hold the largest spotting scope steady.

The next most important aspect of your sheep bowhunt is your physical condition. The most effective avenue of attack for a sheep bowhunter is from *above*, and since sheep live and thrive on the sides of mountains, you have to get to the top of the mountain for much of the hunt.

Generally it is the hunter's legs or feet that give out, with an occasional bout of altitude sickness thrown in. The only way to get those legs and feet in shape for hunting in steep, rocky, rugged mountainous terrain is by simulating sheep-hunting conditions as closely as possible in your home habitat.

Good footwear is extremely important for sheep hunting north or south. I highly recommend quality Vibram-soled leather climbing or hunting boots. Rubber boots or pacs are great for whitetail bowhunting, but for serious hiking and climbing on rocks, nothing beats well-prepared leather boots. Most of the leather boots on the market today come with a soft Cambrelle cloth lining and insulation, such as Thinsulate, which is fine if you get them early and wear them enough to get them sufficiently broken in.

When I first started hiking and hunting the mountains, I bought the best pair of Rieker hiking boots I could find. These boots were clunkers, with padded leather interiors that really protected my ankles and feet from twists, cuts, and rock bruises. On the advice of an old German shoemaker in Denver, I filled the new boots with warm water and let them set for an hour, then poured out the water and wore the boots all day. They fit like a glove and I never got a single blister. This technique will work with any boots that have a leather lining (works especially well for breaking in or custom-fitting western boots and dress shoes, also) but won't help the cloth-lined boots that are prevalent on the market today.

Get your feet and legs in shape wearing the boots in which you plan to hunt sheep. Start out easy, climbing stairs, bleachers at the local football stadium, or, better yet, sand or gravel piles at the local sand pit or cement plant. If you live in hilly country, so much the better. You're liable to be climbing scree slopes, boulder fields, and through downed timber, so try to simulate these energy-zapping, muscle-cramping situations in your own baliwick, where you have access to Advil, a hot tub, and your own bed, far in advance of your "once-in-a-lifetime" sheep bowhunt.

Start out hiking and climbing sans backpack, until your feet and boots get toughened up and broken in a bit. When your feet and boots meld into a comfortable combination, start toting a lightly weighted backpack and your bow. Gradually increase the backpack's load, until you're carrying as much or more weight than you plan to have sheep hunting. I don't know of anyone that has ever gotten overly conditioned for their bowhunting trip, so don't be afraid of overdoing it.

Weather has probably ruined as many sheep hunts as any other factor, so prepare for the worst . . . cold, wet, and miserable for northern climates and hot, dry, and miserable for the desert sheep. High country is a fabulous, awe-inspiring part of our bowhunting world, but that beauty can become nasty, vicious, and dangerous in minutes when the capricious weather turns against you.

Layering is the key to comfortable high-country bowhunting. I start out with a layer of lightweight, soft, scent-eliminating long underwear over my tender hide. I follow this with a layer of medium-weight wool, camouflage pants, shirt, and shirt jacket, or fleece pants, shirt, and jacket. These materials shed water, and, if they get wet, maintain warmth and dry quickly. I carry waterproof (not water repellent), quiet rain gear in my pack as a backup for wet and cold weather, along with waterproof gloves and a wool cap.

Luck is 99 percent hard work. The harder you work at getting in shape, choosing the proper gear, and practicing for your hunt, the luckier you'll be on your sheep hunt.

ROCKY MOUNTAIN GOAT

I'd worked hard, gotten in good shape, practiced shooting from every position imaginable, had all the right gear to stay comfortable in the miserable weather we'd encountered, and I still got snurgled by the darn record-book billy when the "moment of truth" came.

I'd spotted the lone goat from a mile away early the second morning of our Alaskan goat hunt, shortly after splitting off from my two bowhunting partners. I spent four impatient hours observing the billy casually browsing along the hillside, under a rocky precipice. At the end of the 200-yard long, vertical, rocky outcropping, the hillside sloped into a bowl, liberally interspersed with clumps of willow and alder . . . ideal stalking terrain. As the billy neared the end of the cliffs, I figured he'd continue into the bowl and give me a chance to stalk within bow range. I hot-footed it along the top of the cliff, staying back away from the edge to eliminate any chance of being spotted by the goat.

As I approached the end of the cliffs, I crept up behind a rock and glassed the bowl looking for the billy. Nothing. I spent the better part of an hour trying to find that disappearing goat with no luck. The only place the goat could be was back along the cliff, so I eased up to the edge and peered over cautiously. Sure enough, the billy was bedded in the shade directly below me.

Unlike whitetails, goats have no qualms about looking up. The sharp-eyed billy must have caught the slight movement of my head against the gray sky background, because an instant later he was on his feet staring up at me. I jerked to full draw, tried to pick a spot, but I was 60 feet straight above the goat; not exactly the best angle. I'd practiced shooting from about every imaginable position . . . except straight down. The goat whirled to run, giving me a narrow, downward-angle, top-of-the-chest shot, for just an instant. My Phantom-tipped xx75 sliced a handful of hair from the goat's side and buried

Mountain goat hunting involves tons of physical exertion and the skill to navigate some of the continent's roughest areas.

in the dirt where he had been bedded. When the goat appeared again at the end of the cliff, he was going full steam and headed for a distant mountain range.

That mountain goat bowhunt was one of the toughest physical bow-hunts I've ever been on, mostly because of plans gone awry and miscalculations. Four of us had booked a flying service out of Anchorage to carry us into a good goat area and leave us for a week. I'd tried this venture a year earlier and bad weather in the goat mountains had kept me grounded in Anchorage for the whole 10 days of my scheduled bowhunt.

This time, Jim Jarvis, one of my companions, had been into the area previously and assured the rest of us there were plenty of goats above the lake where we were being dropped. Right. When we got to the lake, it was fogged in and the plane couldn't set us down where we wanted to be. The pilot blithely told us he'd drop us on the beach and it was only about a mile hike to the lake. Right. That mile hike turned into a nightmare, 15-hour climb through impenetrable devil's club and alder jungle.

Nanny and billy goats both sport horns. Billy goats have heavier bases and their horns curve back more than nannies'.

When we arrived at the lower end of the lake, we discovered the rain-swollen torrent rushing out of the lake was uncrossable, and we were on the wrong side of the water to get to where we'd spotted all the goats when flying over the area. We had to climb straight up to timberline in hopes of finding goats on our side of the lake, which had a lot more open ridges and slopes . . . not ideal goat habitat.

Then the rains and fog settled in. In seven days of hard hunting, we saw two goats on our side of the lake; I missed the billy and Jim arrowed a nanny that plunged 500 feet off a cliff, then down a slide chute and another 200 feet onto a rock pile. The goat was nothing but a hide full of pulverized meat and the horns had been ground down to nubbins. Yes sir, goat hunting can be tough.

Rocky Mountain goats are actually not goats at all but antelopes, because they have dewclaws, a characteristic not found on members of the goat family. The goats thrive on vertical cliff faces that would scare a bird, and bowhunting them in such terrain can be a dangerous challenge . . . especially during inclement weather conditions.

Physical conditioning and top-notch clothing and footgear are even more important to a bowhunter pursuing goats than to a sheep hunter. You can almost plan on miserable weather during a fall goat hunt. I've flown to Alaska three times for bowhunting goats and only gotten into the mountains once, because inclement weather shut down flying. Access to good mountain goat country in the lower 48 is generally a much surer proposition, as most of the in-and-out travel is by horseback or backpacking.

There are 731 Rocky Mountain goats entered in the Pope and

Young record book, with the world record taken in British Columbia in 2006. British Columbia is the top goat bowhunting province, with 190 record-book goats, followed by Colorado with 135 and Alaska running a close third with 118. Washington, Idaho, and Montana are next.

The first time I bowhunted Alaska, an outfitter wasn't required and several of us flew into Anchorage, hired a flying service, and went goat hunting. The Alaska Fish and Game commission changed that law just in time to foul up my second goat bowhunt, scheduled with an Alaskan resident who had access to great goat country.

Your best final approach when hunting goats is to get above them. Billies tend to look for danger from below and are less likely to spot you from above.

All goat licenses in the lower 48 are on a limited license lottery basis, so start planning your goat hunt now, because it might take a few years to get a license.

The key essentials to a good sheep or goat hunting venture are physical conditioning, proper clothing and footgear for the best and worst weather conditions in your chosen hunting area, and the best optics you can afford. Of course, it goes without saying that such things as prior planning, enthusiasm, perseverance, a modicum of hunting ability, and skill with your archery equipment will also help. Last but not least, a large passel of luck won't hurt either. ∎

COUGAR AND OTHER PREDATORS

There's nothing quite as exhilarating as trudging through three inches of fresh, dazzling, eye-searing snow under azure mountain skies on a crisp December morning, listening to the distant bawling of a pack of hounds echoing out of the canyons as they try to unravel the zigs and zags of a cold cougar trail.

The sight of the huge pug marks single-stepping across the virgin white—only partially obliterated by the splay-footed tracks of the pursuing hounds—the clamor of the exuberant pack, and the anticipation of eventually seeing the humongous feline treed above the baying dogs was enough to boost my heart rate and skyrocket my adrenaline level. Unfortunately, some of the exhilaration and excitement of that morning was blunted by the fact that, every 100 yards or so, I had to stop and "heave" all over that nice clean snow.

The cougar hunt got a discombobulated start after noon the previous day, when I was cruising a four-wheel drive road through a narrow canyon looking for a fresh bobcat track on which to turn my two Plott hounds. Earlier in the morning, I'd found a couple of small bobcat tracks but held off turning the dogs out in hopes of eventually finding the track of a large tom.

Halfway up the narrow canyon between two high, rocky mesas, I cut the tracks of a huge cougar crossing the narrow roadway. Great! There was only a week left in the year and I hadn't gotten a cougar license or permit for the current season, even though the quota had not been filled and there were plenty of licenses available. The sheer size of the track left little doubt about my trying for him, so I headed the 30 miles to town and purchased a cougar

Cougar populations are booming throughout North America. Hunting with hounds can offer a hunter a shot like this.

license good until the 31st of December. A quick call home had my daughter, Lisa, on the way to town with two more of my bear and cat hounds.

Colorado's cougar (or mountain lion) is on a limited quota system, so the next step was to get a cougar permit, which was required in addition to the license and only available from the area office in Durango, 60 miles away. A phone call accompanied by some serious cajoling and pleading got my signed permit on the way via mail. When Lisa showed up at the local 7-11 with the hounds in the back of her pink pickup, she was dressed and ready for a cat chase.

Somehow I managed to avoid a speeding ticket in getting back to the lion track, and by 2:00 p.m., Lisa and I had the four dogs out of the truck 100 yards from where the cat had crossed and were leading them to the track, letting them clear their heads and noses and build up their enthusiasm for a chase. The keen-nosed hounds were 10 yards from the track when Skunk, my top dog, started bawling and straining at the leash. The dogs' ardor left little doubt about the track being hot enough for a chase. After getting jerked and dragged for 200 yards along the tracks as the dogs got their snouts full of acrid cat scent, we turned them loose.

As darkness descended, we were several miles from the truck and had lost hearing of the dogs amidst a jumble of dog and cougar tracks. It looked like the dogs had cold trailed the cougar we started and had run into another tom on the ridge, and whatever the two cats did, they left enough tracks to confuse the hounds. There were so darn many dog and cougar tracks going every which way that Lisa and I decided to call it quits, as she had to get back for an unavoidable school function the next day and we weren't equipped for a night chase or cold camp in the woods. I knew if the hounds treed the cat that late afternoon, they'd stay with him all night and hopefully the next day.

Lisa wasn't a happy camper about not being able to hunt, but she was president of her class, and when it was decided that she just couldn't avoid the conflict, I phoned my good friend and cat-hunting guide Tony Hoza, from Norwood, Colorado. Being a crazy cat chaser, he quickly agreed to load up a couple of top-notch lion dogs and meet me at the truck stop in Pagosa before daylight the next morning to continue the chase.

Tony drove through a horrendous, high-mountain blizzard all night and arrived at the truck stop several hours before daylight, red-eyed, hungry for breakfast, and ready for a cat chase. We quickly stocked up on a hearty meal of eggs, sausage, pancakes, and plenty of truck-stop coffee. While we were scarfing down the food, I filled him in on the previous day's events. By the time we got to the lion crossing in the canyon, my stomach was bubbling and boiling in protest of something I'd eaten.

On the hike in, I vomited several times and was miserable to say the least. When Tony and I, accompanied by three fresh and eager hounds, arrived at the location where Lisa and I had turned back the previous afternoon, and could work out the mish mash of dog and cat tracks, we discov-

The cougar is a master stalker and kills all his prey—from rabbits to elk—with this finely tuned technique.

ered my Plotts had split off on the fresher lion track and headed in another direction. The newer track was almost as large as the original, but not quite.

We agreed that Tony would stay on the larger track with the dogs, and if they treed the cat, he would stay at the tree until I arrived. I'd follow the trail as best I could and vowed to get to the tree no matter how long it took, unless of course I died along the way, which at the time I felt was a definite possibility. I'd plod a couple hundred yards, throw up, and then spend 15 minutes or so munching snow and using the cold stuff to cool down before heading out again.

Fortunately, the cat traveled the mesa top much of the time, with only occasional jaunts off into a small side canyon or under a protruding rim to check for something edible. By noon, I could hear the sounds of treed hounds echoing out of a densely wooded canyon off in the distance. Amazingly, the closer I got to the hound racket, the better I felt. By the time I stood alongside Tony, admiring the huge cat 60 feet above, I felt fine.

To this day, I don't recall much about the beauty and exhilaration of most of the final segment of that 10-mile chase, but every time I look at the monstrous Boone and Crockett cougar glaring down from my trophy-room wall, I'm glad I didn't let a little thing like "barfitis" keep me from finishing the hunt.

Later that day, we found my hounds at a lady's cabin in another canyon five miles cross country from where they got "catfused." The Plotts had treed another lion and kept it treed up the canyon from the ranch house all night. The rancher's wife had watched the dogs and lion all day without going near them, and when they finally gave up late in the day, she fed them a good meal, making sure they stayed put.

Currently the cougar, mountain lion, catamount, panther, or puma (whatever you want to call this hard-muscled, stealthy, meticulous, deer-killing machine) population throughout North America is booming, and in many areas of the country, this dramatic and relatively undetected or ignored increase in big cats is having a drastic, detrimental effect on the deer populations, especially mule deer and blacktails.

Maurice Hornocker's studies on Idaho cougars showed the big cats would kill one deer a week, or approximately 50 deer per cat per year, and his words were taken as gospel by anyone spouting cougar kill rates on mule deer. Times are a-changing. California completed a study on cougars in that state, where all cougar hunting has been outlawed for a number of years. The California study showed the big cats killed a mule deer or blacktail deer every 1.9 days. In many areas, the increasing cougar population, coupled with the rise in coyotes and bear in many of the same areas, have virtually annihilated the mule deer and blacktail populations.

Dick and Mike Ray, a father and son team operating as Lobo Outfitters in Pagosa Springs, Colorado, are convinced that cougars are killing more game per year than ever before. According to Dick, when a lion makes a kill today, instead of getting to casually munch on it for a week or longer, the stealthy killer is fortunate to get more than a meal or two. It doesn't take long for some of the numerous aerial scavengers, such as ravens, crows, magpies, and eagles, which have also multiplied under the protection of federal and state laws, to locate the cat's fresh kill. Their raucous racket quickly attracts the attention of the local coyotes, which gang up on the cougar and drive him from the carcass. Within 48 hours or less, there's nothing left but scattered bones and pieces of hide. This forces the feline fury to kill more often than it would without the severe competition.

Dick and Mike often key off the birds to locate a fresh kill and pinpoint an area to start searching for a fresh track—if it is, in fact, a lion kill, and not that of coyotes. According to Dick, 50 percent of the deer and elk kills they find are made by coyotes. The old saw about coyotes only killing the sick and weak is pure hogwash! Most of the coyote kills that many of my lion-hunting compadres and I locate are healthy deer and elk in excellent condition, and many of them are mature animals.

The mountain lion is primarily a deer predator, but with the low population of mule deer due to the increase in overall predator populations, and human encroachment over much of its historical hunting grounds, the lion is switching to elk (the larger and seemingly more adaptable game) and living very well off the bigger ungulates. One winter, Dick and Mike took a large female that they had known about for some time. This particular cat had been producing two to three kittens per year for a number of years and had virtually eliminated the entire deer herd in her home area and switched to killing elk. Dick estimated her age at 10 to 11 years.

Several states are realizing the folly of protecting female cougars, with the rapid build-up in numbers, and are considering a quota system on females as well as toms, to better manage the population.

In many areas of Colorado, mule deer have found the best place to escape predators, such as the coyote and cougar, is the

Most cougars will climb a tree, hide in a cave, or go up on a ledge when pursued by hounds.

around human habitation, and some monstrous bucks have literally become urban deer because of the tremendous predator pressure in the wilderness areas they'd like to roam. This survival phenomenon brings the hunting cats right into mountain communities and subdivisions. Many animal lovers and protectionists are being forced to acknowledge the fact that a cougar roaming in and around back yards and playgrounds is an extremely dangerous situation.

According to the statistical summary of the Pope and Young records, Colorado is the all-time leader in producing record-book cougars, followed by Utah, Idaho, Montana, and British Columbia. If you're considering a cougar bowhunt, check out the Boone and Crockett and Pope and Young record books for the latest information on which states are producing the most and latest record-class cats.

It isn't just the overall numbers of cougars that are on the increase; the number of exceptionally large record-book cougars seems to be on the rise also. In the past 10 years, Arizona, New Mexico, Wyoming, and Colorado's state records on cougars have been exceeded, and in some states they've been blitzed several times within this period.

Dick and Mike Ray took a monstrous cougar in southwestern Colorado that scored a whopping 16 inches and wiped out the previous world record and the Colorado state record, held by Teddy Roosevelt for a cougar he killed near Meeker in 1901. At present, there are five cougars in both record books that score 16 inches. The Pope and Young world record 16 1/16-inch cougar was taken in Wyoming in 1993 and five of the top 10 cats in Pope and Young were killed in the '90s.

The cougar is not generally a "do-it-yourself" type big-game animal, and even though there are a few taken each year from blinds, by calling or even on rare occasions by still-hunting, tracking, and stalking, the cougar is a predator that lives and hunts by making use of its incredible eyesight and super stealth. Catching one of these big cats unaware is a task that most bowhunters would find next to impossible. Raising and training a pack of hounds capable of running and treeing a cougar is an expensive, labor-intensive, and time-consuming venture that few, if any, bowhunters are going to undertake. Hiring a guide or outfitter with a pack of trained cat hounds is by far the most practical way to get a record-class cat for your trophy room, as well as putting some fine eating in your freezer. (Cougar meat is delicious and should never be wasted.)

A cougar hunt can be the hunt of a lifetime and an education in how and where North America's most efficient predator travels and hunts, things few other bowhunters have a chance to observe. Few cougar-hunting clients experience the averages on a cougar chase. The hunts can range from easy, where you and the guide locate a smoking hot track in fresh snow and the dogs tree the cat before you can hike 100 yards from the truck.

On the other end of the stick, you and your guide may locate an old track that takes several *days* of cruising the canyons and back roads by 4x4, four-wheeler,

Cougars are territorial and have set routes on which they travel every week or so. They will traverse slopes where deer or elk feed on grasses and others browse.

horseback, snowmobile, or on foot, trying to cut down the distance between you and the traveling cat so the dogs can be turned out on a reasonably fresh track. Then you and your guide may spend several days on snowshoes or boot soles, slogging mile after mile through the rough, rugged, inhospitable terrain cougars love, before the tenacious hounds jump the cat and force him to tree or bay.

Mountain lions patiently bide their time until they locate an edible critter in the wrong place at the right time, and then with a short, furious burst of energy, they make a quick kill. Unlike bears that can run for miles and miles ahead of a pack of hounds, a cougar doesn't have the lung capacity or endurance for a long-distance fast-paced chase. Fortunately for hound hunters and people living in cougar country, these critters are not ferocious by nature. If a mountain lion had the demeanor of its cousin, the leopard, there would be fewer cougar chasers and a lot more wild cougar habitat.

Most cougars, when confronted by several hounds, will take refuge in a tree, cave, or on a rocky ledge rather than turn and fight. Occasionally, a big tom learns how easy it is to ambush and kill pursuing hounds and then becomes a hound man's worst nightmare. Generally, once a lion is jumped from its day bed or off a kill, the chase is of short duration.

Once the dogs are released on a cougar track, a responsible and conscientious guide or outfitter has lost control of the hunt. They are committed to follow the chase to its conclusion, regardless of weather conditions, terrain, or distance. If you as a hunter can't cut the mustard and get to the tree at the end of the chase, you've cheated yourself, the outfitter, and his hard-working hounds. All is not lost, however, as a good outfitter will pull the dogs off the cat and let him run for another client another day. This is one aspect of hunting with hounds that is often overlooked. If you tree a cat and it's a female or a smaller cat than you want, it's a simple matter to pull the dogs and leave the cougar to run another day, none the worse for wear but a bit smarter for the experience. Make sure you discuss exactly what size cougar you are hoping to kill with your outfitter, and the minimum-size cat you'll take, in the early stages of booking your hunt and confirm that *before* the hunt gets under way, so there are no misunderstandings. Be realistic and honest with yourself and your prospective outfitter. Establishing a good hunter-outfitter relationship early on in booking your cat hunt can go a long way toward assuring the success and enjoyment of this once-in-a-lifetime bowhunt.

Use the off-season time to carefully research areas producing big cougars, and then contact several outfitters specializing in cougar hunting those areas. Don't be bashful about asking questions, because the only stupid questions are those you don't ask. On this bowhunt, you're going to be totally dependent on the ability of your outfitter and his dogs, so spend some time on the phone to get acquainted and get a "gut" feeling for the type of hunt the outfitter runs. Don't hesitate to ask for references of both successful and unsuccessful hunters, and then contact them for further information on the outfitter's operation. Remember, individual clients may not have any idea of what an average cougar hunt is like, so the more hunters you contact and talk with, the better your knowledge of what to expect.

Make sure you understand fully what the outfitter expects of you on the hunt. Get yourself in the best physical and mental condition possible for your cougar bowhunt so that you don't miss out on a single aspect of what could be the most exciting and challenging bowhunt of your career, as well as the most physically demanding and exhausting one.

Cougars are heavily muscled but thin skinned and are not tough to kill with a well-placed arrow. A hound hunter's main concern is a wounded cougar hitting the ground in the midst of his hounds and killing or maiming some during its death throes. A lung-hit cougar will usually stay in the tree or ledge or wherever it's bayed until it expires, thus causing no danger to anyone.

Cougars can tree in some exceptionally oddball places that make for tough shooting, so take plenty of arrows on your cat hunt and, if you can figure out a way to practice shooting straight up or at a steep angle, do so.

COUGAR CALLING

Bowhunters having unexpected encounters with cougars when calling elk and deer are on the increase throughout the Western states, leaving little doubt that calling cougars is a viable way to get them within bow range. The prime prerequisite for successful cougar conning with a predator, elk, or deer call is *patience*. Both cougars and bobcats are slow, methodical hunters that rarely lose their cool and come racing to the sounds of a free lunch, regardless of how enticing.

I've called in lots of bobcats with a predator call, but the only cougar I called up came in and circled me 100 yards out and left without my even glimpsing him. I wouldn't have known I'd even had a big cat encounter if I hadn't seen his tracks in the snow when I hiked back to the truck. I followed his tracks for several hundred yards until I found where he'd laid on a small knoll where he could see his back trail. He evidently spotted me from more than a hundred yards out and took off at a hard lope. Following a fully alert, spooked cougar would have been an exercise in futility, so I headed back to the truck and easier, unsuspecting critters.

Setting up in good cat country is essential to success. If there isn't a cat within hearing, your chances are between zilch and zero. When you set up with the hope of calling in a big cat, choose a location where you have a bird's-eye view of as much surrounding country as possible. A mountain lion is the most sneaky and stealthy creature you'll ever call, and they have a penchant for getting within spitting distance unseen.

Tommy Freestone is an outfitter and predator hunter par excellence who specializes in calling fall bear in the rugged, cactus-filled canyons of southern Arizona. Freestone has had numerous encounters with cougars responding to his bear calling, and I was looking forward to the possibility when I hunted bear with him last fall. No such luck.

However, I'm not sure I would have wanted to be in his brother's boots several years earlier, when he and Freestone were trying to call a bear out of a steep oak brush and cactus-choked canyon. They'd hiked a mile from the truck (a favorite tactic of the lean and lanky outfitter) and set up in the predawn darkness, where the early morning sun would light up the canyon below.

When the morning gray brightened to good shooting light, Tommy filled the canyon with agonizing jackrabbit squalling and screaming, and kept up the distance-penetrating racket for over an hour. Other than a couple of curious magpies, Tommy and his brother seemed to be the only creatures enjoying the golden sunrise around that canyon. Freestone slipped out of his calling location and headed for the truck, while his brother continued to glass the area with the faint hope of spotting a bear.

He was glassing with his binoculars propped on cross sticks for stability when the warm rays of the rising sun soaking into his back lulled him into a bit of a semi-conscious stupor. He leaned across the top of his propped binocs and dozed off for a minute or two. When he opened his eyes and glanced in front of him, he went from stupor to shock in a heartbeat. Crouched less than 10 yards in front of him was a mature cougar, ears laid back and muscles quivering in full stalking mode.

The silently stalked hunter's first move, bringing his rifle into shooting position, brought the cat sliding forward, not the least intimidated, and ended all doubt about his intentions. Freestone's brother shot the cat right in the face from less than 10 yards.

When the gun went off, he sensed movement to his right and whirled to see a second cat, still 15 yards out, stalking boldly toward him. He'd had about all the sneaking cougars he could handle for one day, and when his adrenaline-charged shout didn't slow the second cat's approach, he shot it in the chest.

As he turned to look at the first cat, he caught another movement to his left, and a third cat stood up out of the buff-colored grass and looked at him. This time when he shouted, the cat turned and glided off.

Not sure I'd want to be in that situation with my bow and arrow set, but you can bet after hearing that story, I didn't do much dozing while glassing the canyons below.

For calling cougars, I recommend a coarse-voiced call that approximates the sound of an elk calf or deer fawn, such as the Critt'r Call magnum or Burnham Brothers Black Magic or the Circe Long Range model. My calling is very similar to Freestone's in that we both call continuously for one to two minutes, break for the same amount of time and then call again. When I start calling, I keep the volume relatively low for the first couple of series, gradually building it to maximum after five minutes or so.

Keeping this rhythm up for an hour can be exhausting. Where legal, an electronic call for cougar, bobcat, and bear will allow continuous calling with a lot less effort and give the bowhunter more time to keep a sharp eye on his surroundings. A remote electronic unit can also be set away from the bowhunter's location to attract the approaching cat's attention elsewhere and allow the bowhunter more freedom to move slowly without alerting the keen-eyed feline's motion detectors.

Adding a decoy to your cat calling set-ups can also enhance your chances of getting a cat within bow range without spotting you. I have had super results with a full-body mounted jackrabbit sold as a predator decoy and the Feather Flex foam fawn decoy. Both of these decoys are readily visible for several hundred yards and work great for attracting and diverting a cat's attention while you draw and shoot.

PREDATOR BOWHUNTING TACTICS

Predators are the ultimate wild hunters, and as such they face constant pressure from human hunters who are jealous of their skills and success at killing the critters the two-legged predators consider their own. The year-round hunting pressure results in an adversary that is not only good at hunting but equally adept at surviving through perfected escape and evasion tactics. If these attributes weren't enough, predators have keen, perceptive eyesight, phenomenal hearing, and a sense of smell more discerning than a whitetail. Add a predator's small size, tremendous agility, quickness, and endurance, and it's pretty easy to see why there are not more predator mounts and rugs in bowhunters' trophy rooms.

The best way to get these wily, fleet-footed, crafty critters is by using predator calls to bring them in up close and personal.

This past fall, I was bowhunting Iowa's late primitive weapons season along a river bottom on one of our leases. During the course of the morning I'd had half a dozen deer walk past and under my stand within 10 to 20 yards along with a flock of fifteen turkeys. Not a single one of these sharp-eyed beasties picked out my frozen-in-position, camouflaged form perched above them or showed the slightest interest in my tracks in the snow.

Mid-morning I caught a flash of red along the creek and a few seconds later a fluffy red fox came mincing along one of the two deer trails that ran along either side of my stand. I'd had to cross this trail to get to the stand, but my Scent Blocker-sprayed, rubber-bottomed boots had worked well enough to keep from spooking the deer that had come down the trail previously. When the skittish fox hit my cross trail 20 yards from the stand, he jerked to a halt, looked directly at me in the stand, and bolted like the hounds of Hades were after him.

The fox's nose was much closer to the ground than those of the passing deer, and he apparently had little trouble separating out the minuscule amount of scent my de-scented boots left on the trail from that of the turkeys and deer. He may not have positively identified the immoveable clump in the tree, but the whiff of scent and the fact that something was there was enough to kick in his survival instincts. Predators are tough.

I've taken a couple gray and red foxes, along with a coyote, by spot-and-stalk bowhunting or tracking them to their beds—and educated a whole lot more than I've killed. Still, each venture and encounter is a unique learning experience that has made me a more aware bowhunter. Wind and noise are the main deterrents to success in this type of hunting, so make sure you use a powder bottle religiously and move with less sound than a soft breeze.

PREDATOR CALLING

The best way to get predators within bow range is by imitating the sounds of their favorite prey in distress. I carry predator calls with me wherever I go bowhunting and have often added excitement and challenge to my hunts during lulls and at night. I've called in ringtails, coons, and gray fox at night on whitetail bowhunts in Texas and coyotes, and bobcats from deer stands during the mid-day lull. I've also called in foxes, coyotes and a wolf from stands over bear baits in Canada and Alaska.

One of the distinct advantages of bowhunting is the silence of the shot. Whenever possible and feasible on a big-game bowhunt, I generally end a morning's hunt by trying to call up some kind of critter, and I start an afternoon's bowhunt the same way. This gets the hunter instinct kicked into gear and keeps the anticipation from waning. Occasionally my calling efforts add a prime pelt to my collection and end the game-killing days of a predator.

CALLING TACTICS

When I set up to call, I make sure I have a clear field of view, good background with plenty of drawing room, and an open shooting area. Tree stands, pit blinds, and ground blinds all make excellent predator-calling stands.

I have several compadres who are successful callers and they call continuously. I feel that intermittent calling gives me a better chance to spot an incoming predator. My first series of calls is low in volume in case there's a critter close in. I call for a minute, gradually increasing the volume, and then remain quiet for one or two minutes.

I adjust my calling volume and frequency to the predator's actions. If it's coming in hard, I'll stop calling and get ready for the shot. I learned a long time ago to come to full draw while the predator is still quite a ways out, because these quick-to-react critters will spook at the slightest movement. Hitting a rapidly retreating coyote or fox at 30 yards is beyond my bow shooting capability most of the time, and I hate to see a game-eating predator get educated at my expense. When the incoming predator gets where I want it, I'll lip-squeak or whistle and be ready for an instant shot.

MOUTH CALLS VS. ELECTRONICS

I like a mouth-blown call because of its portability and handiness. I have these calls stashed in my pickup, daypacks, camera bags, and archery gear box. I may forget some piece of equipment on a bowhunt, but it won't be a predator call.

There are many superb mouth calls on the market today, and most of them will bring a predator close enough for a shot if you do your job and set up properly. I prefer calls with multiple voices: long-range (jackrabbit), medium-range (cottontail), and short-range (mouse squeaker) sounds incorporated into a single call. Haydel's, Sceery, Primos, Quaker Boy, and Lohman all make excellent multiple-voice mouth calls, with my favorites being the Lohman/Circe triple-voice call and Haydel's Government Hunter models.

Big game-type predators, such as wolves and wolverines, respond well to predator calls, and if you're planning a bowhunt where they live, make sure you include a predator call or two and give these primo predators a go.

Electronic tape callers have produced a number of good predator-calling sessions for me, but their size and weight limited their portability for many bowhunting ventures. With the new digital electronic callers, this is no longer the case. The digital electronic callers are small enough to fit in a jacket pocket, daypack, or fanny pack, with room left over for a cold soda or extra broadheads.

The most valuable feature of the new digitals is their capacity for multiple sounds. I have a small Foxpro digital caller that has 32 different sounds on it, ranging from deer bleats to antler rattling, snow geese honks and moose grunts to mouse squeaks. Any of these sounds are available almost instantly with the twist of a switch. The sound boards on many of these callers can be custom ordered with the sounds of your choice on them, so (where legal) you can use a single call unit for calling big game, turkey, waterfowl, and predators.

If you don't have a blind, use any available cover as camouflage when calling in predators to bow range.

NIGHT-TIME PREDATOR CALLING

Predator calling is a night-time adventure as well as a daytime challenge, and on many of my bowhunting trips, I've about burned myself out bowhunting big game all day and then calling predators most of the night. It's a tough job, but someone has to do it.

Night calling gives a bowhunter a lot more leeway with set-up, movement, and such. I use a red-lensed spotlight to pick up an incoming critter's eyes. Red light doesn't seem to spook predators or make them look away from the light as they approach. Almost all predators' eyes glow like red-hot coals in the bright light.

One way to maximize your big-game bowhunt is to do some predator calling during the mid-day hours.

Sometimes I mount a smaller red-lensed unit in my bow's stabilizer port. There are several light units that are adjustable and can actually be sighted-in for a given distance, and laser sights, where legal, are superb for nighttime predator bowhunting. Since I shoot (and miss) instinctively, night shooting is right up my alley. Raccoons, bobcats, ringtail cats, possums, and gray fox are mainly nocturnal hunters, making them prime targets for night calling. Coyotes and red fox will also respond readily to night calling, and in areas where they get lots of daytime pressure, they may be easier to fool at night than during the day.

Regardless of where or when you're bowhunting game animals or birds, there's always a no-season, no-bag-limit predatory-type critter around to test your hunting skills to the utmost and fill the lulls in your hunting day or night with plenty of challenges and excitement. ■

TURKEY

Thank God turkeys can't smell (I thought to myself) as the cantankerous gobbler "spit and drummed" to his heart's content a few yards from where I knelt comfortably, arrow strung and ready for a shot, and my aggravation grew. Half an hour later, I was still kneeling, but not nearly as comfortably nor as ready for a shot. I realized I'd been had by the longbeard, and there wasn't a thing I could do about it. The bird was so close, I didn't dare blink, and there wasn't room in the tight little blind to even think about turning around for a shot. That was the first time I had a gobbler near enough I could actually hear it breathing.

Two afternoons previous, I roosted the bird on the Ponderosa-studded slope. I'd found the ideal place for a set-up under a drooping spruce tree, just above an irrigation ditch where the gobbler scuffed the dry dirt to powder with his strutting and wing dragging. When I found the strutting ground, and even before I'd decided to ambush a turkey from under the adjacent spruce, I had already smoothed out the drag marks and tracks in the dirt so the area wouldn't show any fresh use. Old habits die hard.

The following morning, I was hidden in a cavernous pocket under the evergreen, 15 yards from the strutting ground, in perfect shooting position. As I listened to the vocal tom fill the valley below with his deep-throated gobbling, I just knew I was going to arrow that longbeard. Wrong! I'd tree-called softly in the paling gray of pre-dawn and gave a couple of quiet clucks just before fly-down time and was answered immediately by the "hot-wired" gobbler. I heard him fly down, hit the ground 200 yards up the hill, and the gobble a quarter of a mile in the opposite direction.

I made the beginner's mistake of chasing that ridge-running tom, and several other gobblers in the area, around the mountainside until late morning, without getting close enough for a shot. To add insult to injury, when I

Movement is a turkey hunter's biggest concern. A camo blind is an ideal tool to help conceal movement from keen-eyed turkeys.

got back to the blind to pick up a call I'd inadvertently left, there were fresh strut marks all over the knoll in front of my blind. Thirty yards farther down the ditch, I found an even more heavily used strutting area covered with fresh tracks, feathers, and droppings. I figured I had him cold now and proceeded to build a tight little blind in the oak brush, where I had a 10-yard shot to the strutting ground. I filled in the backside of the blind with thick oak and spruce branches, and even roofed it over so I would be kneeling in the blind's darkness, invisible to the sharp-eyed gobbler.

The second morning's scenario was much the same as the previous day, only I called a lot more aggressively, hoping to pull the tom away from his hens to the strutting area and make my bowhunt short and sweet. No such luck. This time, when the irascible gobbler strayed off with his harem, I stayed put, bound and determined to wait for him, or another one of the gobblers I could hear in the distance, to come investigate my calling.

I yelped excitedly on my box call every 20 minutes for the next three hours and got an occasional distant gobble to answer. My butt was numb and my patience had about petered out when my seductive yelping got a response from the ridge behind me. Within a few minutes, the sneaky tom was strutting, not on the strutting ground where he was supposed to, but right in back of my blind. That blooming bird kept me locked up and motionless while he strutted back and forth in the grass and weeds a few yards from the rear of the blind. His "spittin' and drummin'" and raucous gobbling in my ear aggravated me for over an hour as he moved back and forth and around the side of my blind, but never ventured out in front where he was supposed to go. Then he silently vacated the premises.

Not one to give up without a fight, I returned late that afternoon and set up in the shadowy confines of my first blind. On my second series of yelps, a gobbler answered from the hillside above and sounded off every minute . . . until he strutted onto the top of an irrigation dike at 10 yards and got skewered by a Thunderhead tipped xx75. I love it when a plan finally comes together in spite of the turkey's unpredictability and contrariness.

WILD TURKEYS IN THE UNITED STATES

Wild turkeys can now be found from the tip of Florida to the woods of Maine, from the rainforests of Washington to the brush country of south Texas, and the populations are thriving and spreading with each season.

There are four species of wild turkey found in the United States. The eastern turkey, as the name suggests, is predominately found east of the Missouri river. With the preponderance of cereal grains, mainly corn and beans, found in many of the Midwestern states, these turkey populations are increasing tremendously and, if anything, the overwhelming number of birds make them tougher to hunt than those in states where the population densities are much lower.

The Osceola subspecies is found only in Florida and is a similar-colored, smaller version of the eastern bird that has adapted to the swamps and sloughs of the Sunshine State.

Merriam's turkeys are the Western subspecies, found from the Dakotas west to California, Nevada, and New Mexico. Evidence discovered in the early Native Americans' southwest cliff dwellings (dating back several thousand years) shows that not only were Merriam's hunted by these early bowhunters, but the turkeys were also raised in captivity. The Merriam's turkey, with its contrasting white-tipped tail and body feathers, is without a doubt the most striking of the turkey species.

Rio Grande turkeys are mainly found in Texas, but have been transplanted (or transplanted themselves) to the surrounding states of Oklahoma, Colorado, New Mexico, and southern Arizona.

In addition to these four subspecies, Mexico boasts a couple more (if you are thinking of getting the world slam of turkeys with your bow and arrow). The Gould's, colored much like the Merriam's and probably pretty close relatives, live on the rugged slopes and timbered areas of Mexico. The Ocellated turkey is found farther to the south, in jungle-covered areas of the Yucatan, and has much different habits from the rest of the turkey clan, as well as brilliant, iridescent, greenish plumage with bright blue spots, similar to that of a peacock.

In order for us as hunters to rationalize getting skunked on our bowhunting ventures, we often anthropomorphize our adversary as being super intelligent and educated to the point of being unkillable, when in reality, most of their escapes are just plain luck or habit.

Several years ago, Bill Winke and I were hunting turkeys on a private ranch in Texas when we thought we'd run into a cagey, crafty, hunter-wise old tom. We gotten the gobbler going shortly after sun-up and he'd sounded off at every call we threw at him, obviously interested and coming to investigate. When the gobbler got 200 yards out in the dense brush he stopped coming but kept on gobbling with enthusiasm at our combined calling efforts. This went on for over an hour while Bill and I discussed his reticence to come the rest of the way in to our best calling efforts. We figured he might be henned up or maybe was just call shy. Either way, it was obvious he wasn't going to come to us so we might as well try going to him. He was making enough racket, so it was easy to keep him located as we circled out through the brush to approach him from another angle. When we got to the edge of the brush within 100 yards of the still gobbling gobbler and spotted him, we both broke out laughing. Our super cautious, henned up, hunter-wise adversary had run into a three-foot-high woven wire fence and was pacing back and forth along a 50-yard stretch completely baffled as to how to cross it. So much for turkey smarts. We quickly set up on the same side of the fence the bird was on. The first series of calls brought the gobbler running our way so fast that Bill almost missed him at 15 yards.

The main thing that separates the killability of the different turkey sub-species is simply hunter pressure. Generally, eastern turkeys are hunted much more than the other birds, but put a lot of pressure on a Rio Grande gobbler or Merriam's, and you will have a turkey that is equally difficult to call in and kill.

Almost all the turkey species follow the same year-round lifestyle pattern. In the winter, the mature gobblers are generally found in bachelor groups from two to 30 or more birds, while the hens and young of the year, along with the jakes, feed, loaf, and roost in much larger groups.

As the weather warms, the gobblers start separating and attaching them-selves to groups of hens or roaming around looking for unattached hens. As the breeding season gets into full swing, the gobbler hierarchy will have been established and a group of hens will usually be accompanied by a dominant breeding gobbler and one or more subdominant birds. During the early part of the spring breeding season, the hens and gobblers will roost together and spend the early morning hours together, at which time breeding occurs. This is usually the most difficult time to call in a mature longbeard, as they are all pretty well "henned up."

Prior to the onset of actual breeding, the hens will have located a well-hidden nest site. When they get into breeding mode, the hens stay around the gobblers in the morning until they are bred, then sneak off to lay an egg. They will lay one egg a day while still roosting with other hens in proximity to the gobblers. When there are several eggs in the nest, the hen will start spending most of the day on or around the nest and sit on the eggs at night. During the morning, they will move to the gobbler to breed and then go back to their nest and eggs.

Gobblers are the most vocal and responsive late in the season, when almost all the hens are on the nest and only spend a short time each morning with the toms. During this phase of the spring season, the "hot-wired" toms gobble more on the roost in the morning to let the nearby hens know where they are, and then, after flydown time, they vocally advertise their where-abouts so the hens can find them.

When the hens abandon the toms and head for their nests by mid-morn-ing, the toms really get vocal and respond readily to late-morning calling. During the late afternoon they gobble going to the roost and really fill the woods with their loud advertising once they are safe in their trees for the late afternoon. This should be the very best time for a bowhunter to seduce a gobbler into bow range. However, if I have learned one thing in my bow-hunting and outdoor career, it's Mother Nature's propensity for throwing a monkey wrench into sure things.

In Iowa and Nebraska, where I guide spring turkey hunters, the burgeon-ing turkey population, with lots of gobblers and even more hens, coupled with an equally elevated populace of turkey nest-destroying predators, has created a frustrating late-season problem. Over 50 percent of the turkey nests we find in the spring get hammered by varmints, such as coons, possums, fox, or coyotes. This puts the hens back to square one, starting the process all over again, which means that many late-season re-nesting hens are back roosting with gobblers and spending time with them until they get enough eggs laid to start full-time nesting. It puts a whole new spin on late-season hunting and can make the gullible gobblers of the normal late season as "henned up" as early-season birds.

Fortunately for bowhunters, turkey hunting has undergone some major changes that make it a whole new ball game now compared to 10, 20, or 30 years ago.

The turkeys are still the same sneaky, unpredictable, wary, contrary critters they've always been, but the expanding and booming turkey popula-tions, superb equipment, and unlimited turkey-hunting information available have brought about a new level of turkey bowhunting and greatly increased a bowhunter's chances of taking a hefty gobbler with a stick and string.

While there have been some major changes in turkey bowhunting techniques and equipment to help a modern day bowhunter be successful, the basics of turkey hunting are still pretty much the same as they were when the American Indians tangled with them. A turkey bowhunter has to know the rudiments of turkey habits, idiosyncrasies, scouting, calling, and hunting techniques, before venturing into the woods after one of the toughest and most challenging trophies a bowhunter can pursue. Hunting turkeys with a shotgun is tough enough, but when you decide to take on these feathered phenomena with your bow and arrow set, you've bit off a real mouthful. The turkey's eyesight and hearing are exceptional. Considering the fact that turkeys are right at the top of the menu on every predator's list, from great horned owl to bobcats, it's little wonder all turkeys are constantly on the alert, convinced that every unusual movement or shape in the woods is potential danger. Consequently, turkeys (especially gobblers) harbor little curiosity about unknown objects they can't readily identify as harmless parts of their environment.

Fortunately for all of us, a turkey's sense of smell is almost non-existent. If turkeys could smell, there certainly would be a whole lot fewer of them on dining-room tables at the end of the spring season, and bowhunting them would be a real exercise in futility.

CAMOUFLAGE

Good camouflage and its proper usage are more important to a turkey hunter than with any other type of bowhunting. You're going to have to blend perfectly with your surroundings or a gobbler will spot your outline in a heartbeat and be long gone by the time you get your bow drawn. It's never been easier to find a camouflage pattern to match the background cover you'll be bowhunting, from the palmetto swamps of Florida and rock canyons of Wyoming, to the rain forests of the northwest. Background is the most important aspect of your cover, and a full head net, or face paint and gloves, are mandatory for bowhunting turkeys without a blind. I make use of several different camouflage patterns during the course of a season, as the background color and vegetation changes in the locations where I'm guiding and hunting.

Movement is the turkey bowhunter's real nemesis. Imitating a lovesick hen with seductive calling pinpoints your location precisely for a sharp-eyed gobbler with the homing instincts of a laser guided missile. The slightest movement, drawing and releasing, while a gobbler is looking your way is an invitation to disaster and a running shot at a rapidly departing gobbler.

TURKEY CALLING TACTICS

Calling turkeys is not as tough as many turkey hunters would have you believe. Many books, videos, and articles deal with the specifics of how, when, and where to call spring gobblers. Take the time to study the available information and supplement what you learn with plenty of practice before the season; it'll go a long way toward the success or failure of your spring gobbler hunt. Don't get caught up in all the hype and wonder of turkey calling. Keep your patience lengthy and your calling brief, rather than vice-versa, and you'll be much more successful.

Learning to yelp and cluck on a box call, or a simple-to-use, push-pull type box call, is all that's needed to put you in the ball game bowhunting turkeys. Mastering a diaphragm call is a tougher proposition, but something that will make calling turkeys, especially for bowhunting, a bit more effective. With a diaphragm mouth call, you can make turkey sounds while you are in the process of drawing and holding on an incoming bird, without undue movement. On several occasions, I've been clucking and purring softly and had a gobbler walk within a few yards before I took the shot.

When I set up to call, I use a combination of three calls. During the initial calling phase, I use a box call. The box call is almost foolproof and can

A turkey's eyesight is sharp, so dressing in full camouflage from head to toe is essential to success.

produce loud, distance-covering sounds or quiet purrs and clucks for close-up use. A box call can make almost all the turkey sounds, such as yelps, clucks, purrs, cuts and even gobbles. My two favorite box calls are a Heartbreaker made by Will Primos and a handsome and realistic-sounding custom box made by Albert Paul of Greenville, Mississippi.

I also use several scratch-type slate calls made by Quaker Boy and Knight and Hale for soft purrs and clucks when a gobbler is getting close. I've pretty much settled on one diaphragm call the last couple of years: The Quaker Boy jagged-edge diaphragm's raspy sounds seem to get results better than any other diaphragm I've used, and I'm not one to change a winner. The diaphragm mouth call is a bowhunter's best friend, as you can keep calling with both hands free for drawing and shooting.

An experienced turkey hunter knows it's a good idea to carry a few turkey calls when afield. Some days the turkeys will respond more readily to one call versus another.

When I sneak in and set up to call a gobbling tom off the roost, I usually call very softly and let the gobbler carry the conversation. If he is with hens and the hens start sounding off, then I try to match the hens' calling, sound for sound, because if I don't get them curious or mad enough to come, the gobbler isn't going to come either. Let the gobbler's reactions or actions dictate your calling tempo and volume. Loud, forceful calling scares or turns off a lot more turkeys than soft, seductive calling combined with infinite patience. If you err, do so on the side of moderation rather than overzealousness.

One of the most successful methods of bowhunting spring turkeys is pairing up with a partner. One hunter does the calling while the second tries to ambush the turkey when its attention is on the caller. The key to making this plan work consistently is picking your calling location with turkey habits

A hen decoy will help add to the illusion when you are making seductive hen calls to bring in that boss gobbler.

and preferences in mind.

Turkeys will generally follow the path of least resistance in responding to a call or traveling from location to location. This characteristic makes easy travel routes, such as old logging roads, four-wheeler paths, cattle and game trails, narrow corridors in meadows, and open ridge tops, ideal places to try to draw a gobbler past a waiting bowhunter. When you set up to call a springtime tom, take your time and remember three of the most important aspects of ambushing a turkey: *location, location, and location.*

Set up where the advantages are yours and plan your ambush with care and thought before you ever make the first call. Turkeys have very little, if any, curiosity, and once they sense the slightest possibility of danger, they're history. You can swing a turkey off his chosen path of travel or direction, but it's darn difficult to get one to backtrack, so take the time to make it easy for a gobbler or his harem to come to your calling set up. Let patience work for you and against your feathered adversary.

DECOYS AND DECOYING

Some 30 years ago, I discovered the value of a turkey decoy for getting a gobbler's full attention and bringing him "up close and personal," at full strut, so I could photograph him. At that time there wasn't a turkey decoy on the market, and my pride and joy was a full-bodied mounted hen turkey, christened Henrietta. I wore the feathers off several skins carting this decoy over the mountainous terrain of Colorado and through the brush country of Texas on my quest for the ultimate turkey photo and to help fill my tags.

No longer do turkey hunters have to cart around a solid, bulky, full-bodied decoy that is forever snagging on brush and making more noise than hail on a tin roof. With today's lightweight, collapsible, realistic foam decoys or a photo-realistic, fold-up decoy, there is no reason a turkey bowhunter should take to the woods without several stuffed into his turkey vest or daypack, unless you're hunting a state where they're illegal, like Alabama.

My turkey vest contains Feather Flex's love triangle of two jakes and a hen, plus a Higdon Motion-Hen decoy with a flexible head and neck that can be manipulated with a pull string from 30 yards away. I also carry several photo-realistic Montana pop-up strutting gobbler decoys.

DECOY MOVEMENT

The lightweight Feather-Flex decoys swing seductively on their pointed anchor stakes in the slightest breeze, giving them life-like action to catch the eye of a distant gobbler. However, a stiff breeze can cause these ultra-light decoys to spin erratically and even blow off the stakes. Either of these occurrences will put an approaching gobbler into instant escape-and-evasion mode! To keep this from happening, simply screw a small wire connector nut down on the point of the stake, protruding through the decoy's back. This lets the decoy move seductively but holds it securely on the stake in the stiffest wind.

Just as movement can be a great attractant for a decoy set-up, too much of a good thing will spook the gobbler in a heartbeat. To prevent decoys from spinning or swinging back and forth too erratically, I *always* place two sticks or stiff weeds six to eight inches apart on either side of the tail. The stakes allow the decoy to swing back and forth enticingly, but eliminate a full spin or excessive movement. If there's no wind to provide movement, the Higdon hen decoy will provide enough action and realism to your decoy set to convince that reluctant tom to slip into bow range.

A motion decoy of some ilk will often con a gobbler away from hens or convince a reluctant tom to come that last few yards for a close look. Quite often the movement of the hen decoy will lure the gobbler's curious harem to your set-up, with the gobbler tagging along. A multiple-decoy set-up, with swinging or moveable decoys, is equally deadly when used on a travel-way between a roosting area and feeding area, or when set up right in the bird's loafing area. When located where there is long-distance visibility, I've pulled birds for half a mile without making a sound on my calls.

There are a number of motion-producing devices on the market, some practical enough and some questionable. Several of the small battery-operated units are very effective when used with lightweight foam or plastic decoys, and add just enough movement to calm a spooky tom's nerves and bring him to you. In a number of states, the use of any electronic devices for calling or attracting turkeys is illegal, so check your state laws before using such a device.

TURKEY DECOYING TACTICS

The best set-up I've used for consistently pulling in a lone, dominant gobbler, or both the dominant and sub-dominant birds, is setting out two jake decoys and a hen. The aggressive jake has a bright-red head, while the passive jake's head is muted gray. I try to position the aggressive jake decoy so it's between the hen and the approaching gobbler and 10 to15 yards slightly to the left of my shooting position (it's just the opposite for a left-hand shooter). This combination makes it seem like the aggressive jake is challenging the incoming gobbler by keeping between him and the hen, just inviting a confrontation.

I put the passive jake decoy off to the side, away from my position, to coerce the challenging tom closer to me and away from the second jake: the path of least resistance. The challenging gobbler will generally circle the hen and approach the jake from the front, presenting an ideal side or rear-end shot. Patience is tough at this point, but waiting for just the right moment is essential to making a killing shot. Make sure your decoy set-up is on level ground so, when the challenging and usually strutting tom turns tail end to you, he can't see over his fanned tail and catch the movement of your draw.

If I'm bowhunting a gobbler in an area where there has been little hunting pressure, I'll often use a single hen placed in an open area with maximum visibility from the most likely direction of the gobbler's approach. Good visibility is a vital part of successful decoying, so choose your decoy locations for maximum exposure. I try to set the decoy or decoys so the tom will pass my shooting position on his way to the decoys. With his attention on the decoys, he is less likely to pick up my camouflaged form or any slight movement I might make in getting into final shooting position.

When the dominant gobblers are "henned up," and later in the season when hunting pressure has educated many of the gobblers roaming my hunting area, I may add a couple more hens to my decoy set-ups. If I'm sure a gobbler is with hens, I'll often use a decoy set-up with three hen decoys and the two jakes, and use several different calls to convince the tom these hens are hot to trot and waiting for him to come and take care of their needs.

Some gobblers come in to your calls making all sorts of noise and sounds. Others come in on the sneak and don't make a sound at all. Blinds will help conceal a hunter's movement when a turkey surprises you and you have to get into shooting position.

The double-jake-and-hen decoy combination is extremely deadly in the late season, when the hens are nesting and the gobblers are roaming in late morning, mid-day, and late afternoon, looking for available hens. Even a wise old Alpha gobbler spotting this set-up will often throw caution to the wind and stomp in to kick butt and take hens!

TURKEY BLINDS

Today there are numerous superb, lightweight, portable pop-up blinds on the market for the turkey-hunting enthusiast to choose from. In the past, I've used the Double Bull, Invisiblind, Hide-Out, and Seneco blinds for turkey bowhunting and photography and had excellent results with all of them. Each of these blinds is sturdy, portable, lightweight, and quick to set up under hunting conditions.

Unlike deer and other big game, turkeys tend to accept a newly placed blind as part of the environment immediately. This means you can cart a pop-up blind along and set it up wherever and whenever needed to provide instant movement-hiding cover. Each spring on our Iowa turkey hunting leases, I set up a half-dozen blinds along the edges of food plots, watering areas, strutting grounds, and travel routes, for use by bowhunters and gun hunters alike. All it takes is a couple of decoys, some adequate calling, and lots of *patience* for these blinds to prove effective.

Blinds are effective for getting youngsters and beginners involved in bowhunting turkeys. They provide these inexperienced hunters with an almost foolproof hide, where they can get away with movement that would decimate their chances of getting a close-in shot at a turkey without them.

Utilizing a blind for bowhunting turkeys has taken many of the rocket-science aspects out of the equation. When modern-day pop-up blinds are combined with calling and decoy set-ups, the only variable left is the bowhunter's shooting ability and resistance to "turkey fever."

FALL TURKEY BOWHUNTING

Spring isn't the only time of year turkeys can be bowhunted, and I've taken a number of gobblers during the fall season in conjunction with deer and elk bowhunting, as well as specifically bowhunting turkeys.

Fall turkey bowhunting is a different proposition from spring hunting, as the birds (especially gobblers) are far less vocal than in the spring. This means you're going to be more dependent on your knowledge of turkey habits, daily movements, and habitat features: where they can be ambushed while traveling, feeding, or watering.

My favorite fall turkey-hunting method is to set up on a waterhole or food plot and ambush them as they come to feed or water. This type of bowhunting is ideal for making use of a blind. Turkeys have very set time-frames when it comes to feeding and watering, and a few days' scouting and glassing likely areas should allow you to pattern the birds well enough to choose a good site for your blind. Set the blind where there is little chance of being skylighted or outlined by the early-morning or late afternoon sun. Ambushing fall turkeys is a waiting game, and I've found the best way to make time pass is to read a book while you're waiting for turkeys to come.

Turkeys can be called in the fall, but the technique is quite different from springtime turkey calling. Generally, fall birds are in family groups of hens and poults, and bachelor groups of gobblers. The trick is to break up these groups by chasing after them, sicking your dog on them, or trying any other tactic that will spook the birds into flying in every direction.

Once the birds are scattered, set up near the point of dispersion and be patient. I generally sit quietly and wait at least an hour before starting to call. Call with a short series of plaintive yelps interspersed with the "kee kee run" call of a lost young bird. These calls will attract hens, poults, and gobblers alike. Be patient; it may take another hour before you pick up the movement of birds sneaking silently back to join the vocal birds. A couple of hen decoys in this situation will help draw the cautious birds into bow range. The returning birds are going to be spooky and looking for the slightest movement, and a blind will help greatly in keeping them from spotting your ambush.

An even more effective method of scattering fall turkeys is to locate the roost area of a group or two of turkeys. Just at dark sneak into the roost and scare the heck out of the birds, scattering them in every direction. The following morning, sneak into the area and set up. Start calling as soon as the woods come alive and call every 20 minutes for at least a couple hours. Stay alert, because incoming birds probably won't make a sound approaching your location.

I have, on occasion, had an old hen fill the woods with her coarse yelps in answer to my lost-turkey calls, as she tried to call me to her rather than come to me. Gobblers will occasionally pull this same stunt, but if you keep up your lost calls, they will eventually work their way to you. Fall turkey bowhunting isn't all that popular, and I can assure you that competition will not be a problem. The challenges and experiences are just as exciting as spring hunting, and fall turkey bowhunting adds another dimension to your fall deer and elk bowhunting.

KILL SHOTS

A turkey gobbler is certainly not in the same category as a bull elk for toughness, but they are *tough*. Nothing works better for bowhunting turkeys than a razor-sharp broadhead, properly placed. This is where a mechanical broadhead is advantageous. Several of my clients and I have used the Spitfire 100 Gobbler Getter, manufactured by New Archery Products, with good results from a 65-pound bow.

I've had several turkey-hunting acquaintances swear by head-shooting turkeys with blunts, and I have little doubt that a turkey shot this way is going to stay down for the count every time. However, I have trouble hitting bull elk at times and have missed the whole blooming turkey more than I like to admit, so hitting a turkey's weaving, bobbing head is totally out of my league. I try to put my arrow high in the center of the body mass, where it will get into the backbone, rib cage, and base of the wings to break bones and anchor the bird on the spot. A turkey shot through the breast will run or fly off, and it's tough to blood trail a flying turkey.

The only shot to take on a strutting turkey is to wait until it turns away, then use the base of the tail as an aiming point and try to put your arrow just above the white bull's-eye. I don't recommend a broadside shot at a strutting gobbler. Wait until he comes un-puffed and then drive your arrow slightly to the rear of the wing base to anchor them. Turkeys are tough. Take your time and make your shot count, because you aren't likely to get a second chance. A heavy-bearded, long-spurred trophy gobbler is a gorgeous addition to any trophy room and one a bowhunter can be proud of. ■

SMALL GAME
AND NON-GAME

It was everywhere, just as the lady in the village had told us, as Chuck and I slipped slowly through the undergrowth, trying to avoid the stickey bushes and impaling cactus. There were fresh tracks and trails in the sand and trails leading to the obvious den holes at the base of huge trees scattered through the dense jungle. An hour of sneaking quietly through the jungle-like forest hadn't netted us a single sighting of our elusive quarry.

We finally edged out onto a well-traveled trail between the little village and the nearby river, where we plunked down on a rock to contemplate our next move. A few minutes later, a leathery-skinned, old timer came down the trail with a water-filled olla precariously balanced on his shoulder, eyeing my bow and arrows with more than a bit of suspicious curiosity.

Fortunately, Chuck Cadieux, my partner in this questionable endeavor, spoke passable Spanish, and after a couple of minutes of listening to Chuck haltingly explain our unsuccessful bowhunting endeavors, the old man broke out in a toothless grin, set down the water jar, and motioned us to follow him.

Our chuckling guide led us back the way we'd come, to several large trees with gaping holes in their roots, worn smooth by four-legged critter traffic. Our guide started circling the trees bent almost backwards as he scanned the treetops.

"Alla alla," chortled the oldster, pointing upward. Sure enough, spread out on a limb, soaking up the hot sunshine, was our bowhunting quest: a huge, three-foot-long Iguana. Well . . . no wonder we couldn't find them. Nobody told us they spend most of their time living in the trees.

I'm not sure if one would classify Iguana lizards as small game, but a fresh lime-marinated and broiled lizard, dolloped with homemade salsa and washed down with an ice-cold brew, rivaled the best cottontail or squirrel I'd ever eaten.

Bowhunting small game can provide bowhunters with plenty of action, unbeatable shooting practice, and some delectable table fare. I've often wished that cottontail rabbits weighed 100 pounds or so or that deer tasted like cottontail.

I got a good start bowhunting bunnies in my hometown of Luverne, Minnesota, when I was nine years old. I had a small bow and a bunch of arrows made from dowel rods and tipped with homemade steel broadheads. I'd chased rabbits all over the neighborhood for several years before I finally hit my bunny "bonanza," a couple of blocks off Main Street.

The railroad ran through town, and there was a grain elevator alongside the tracks. There was always an abundance of spilled grain that attracted lots of pigeons (also fair targets) and cottontail rabbits from the nearby woods and old buildings. There were several piles of 20-foot by six-inch pipes laying alongside the tracks, providing an ideal hidey hole for the cottontails.

It didn't take me long to realize I could sneak up to a pipe and carefully check to see if it harbored a rabbit. If it did, I'd block the ends with rocks hauled up for just that purpose. Then I'd slip around and shoot into the open pipes until the rabbit expired . . . kind of like shooting fish in a barrel. As I proudly toted bow-killed trophies up the main drag, I got lots of comments on my prowess with a bow at nine years old, and the end result was a lot more important than the method. Don't think my folks ever did figure out how I provided so many bunnies for the table with my bow and arrow set.

Small game and non-game can provide beginning youngsters

Bowhunting small game is perfect for youngsters as it sharpens their shooting skills with plenty of action.

with bowhunting challenges commensurate with their size and abilities. When my son Blain was three, I got him a stout Bear Cub bow and made him some arrows. We lived on a ranch with several hundred acres of sage brush-dotted pastureland that was alive with Richardson's ground squirrels, or "picket pins" as they were more commonly known.

Blain would spend hours every day in the pasture around the house, stalking and shooting at the brazen little gophers. Most days he had to be seriously threatened to get him in the house for meals. It didn't take him long to mutilate and destroy his small supply of wooden arrows, so I took time one late afternoon to make him up a dozen classy little arrows, with full cresting and fluorescent orange fletching . . . figuring they'd be easy to find.

By noon the following day, he'd lost all but one arrow. With a seemingly endless supply of arrows in the little quiver, the tyke would shoot one arrow one way, another in a different direction, etc. Due to the bright colors, it only took the rest of the family three hours to gather all his arrows. From that point on, I gave him one arrow to hunt with. That way, he'd have to keep track of it every shot, and not let the overwhelming population of gophers exhaust his supply.

I never will forget the day he came running to the house with his first "big-game kill." I'd originally tipped his tiny arrows with cut-off 25-20 brass that made very effective and indestructible blunts. He swore he'd hit several gophers without killing them and wanted broadheads like his dad's arrows. I took several bent Bear Razorheads, ground them down to fit his arrows and put a razor-sharp edge on each.

We already had several safety discussions, and he was only allowed to take one arrow hunting. The second day, he came thundering up on the back porch holding his first gopher. Seems he'd missed a dozen or so and figured he had to get close, so he nestled into a thick clump of sage a few feet from a picketpin mound and waited. When the curious and probably overconfident gopher poked his head up, Blain slowly drew and put his arrow through the gullible gopher at less than *five feet* That kind of patience and perseverance makes good bowhunters.

There is nothing that will make a better shot out of a bowhunter than lots of shooting under hunting conditions, something that most bowhunters don't get. They practice and practice at paper targets or on a field range, shooting at full-bodied targets. There is no such thing as bad practice, but shooting at living targets, under actual hunting conditions, just can't be beat.

When I first started bowhunting in northern Colorado, I was lucky to live in an area that had a thriving population of cottontail rabbits, jackrabbits, picketpins, and prairie dogs. It was easy to grab my bow, a quiver of arrows, and head out in the pasture or drive a short distance to the nearest dog town. No limit, no season. At that time, rangefinders were a thing of the future, so the shooting was superb practice for judging range as well as learning what your bow and arrow were capable of at varying distances. It was this small-game and non-game bowhunting and shooting that made me a life-long instinctive shooter. The unlimited experience taught me the rudiments of range judgment and the effectiveness of long-range shooting.

Over the years, there have been a number of occasions when my big-game bowhunting suddenly took a back seat to small-game hunting with bow and arrow.

COTTONTAIL RABBITS

Cottontails are, without a doubt, the most popular small-game animal for gun and bowhunters, and at one time provided more meat volume for the hunter's table than whitetail deer. With the increase in whitetail numbers and the decrease in small-game hunting pressure, I doubt if that is still true, but cottontails are still number one on the small-game hit list.

There are numerous subspecies of cottontail rabbits, ranging from the largest swamp cottontail, weighing up to six pounds, to the pigmy cottontail, weighing a pound or less. Cottontails thrive from the east coast to the west, Mexico to Canada.

Snowshoe hares are cousins of the cottontails, but their propensity for changing from the dull brownish-gray summer pelage to white in winter puts them in the hare family rather than the rabbit clan.

I've bowhunted snowshoes in conjunction with bowhunting elk in the mountains of Colorado and whitetails in the birch, aspen, willow, and alder

Before heading out on your next deer hunt, bring along extra arrows because bowhunting cottontails is a fun activity during your mid-day break.

thickets of Alberta, Canada. One fall, I bowhunted whitetails in east-central Alberta during a full moon and unseasonable warm weather, which limited deer movement to the very early morning hours and late afternoon. The dense birch and alder thickets around camp were alive with snowshoe hares, providing hours of challenging and rewarding bowhunting during the long mid-day lulls.

Bowhunting bunnies and snowshoes is a great way to spend a sunny winter afternoon and a true test of your stalking and shooting skills, especially if you're bowhunting snow country. A missed shot at a rabbit or hare on snow-covered ground usually means down time searching for your arrow, or a lost arrow. So not only do you have to stalk carefully within bow range, you have to choose an angle that will give you the best chance of recovering your arrow should you miss. Of course, nobody plans on missing.

Cottontails and snowshoes are easily anchored with rubber bludgeon blunts, steel blunts, judos, or broadheads. Judos work the best in brushy country and are also very worthwhile when hunting in snow. When I'm bowhunting big game in good cottontail or snowshoe habitat, I generally carry two of my hunting arrows tipped with judos or rubber blunts for any unexpected encounter with these furry delicacies. To make sure I don't grab a blunt by mistake in the heat of action and try to kill a bull elk or buck with it, I carry the blunts with the feathers down and tips up where I can see them.

JACKRABBITS

If I had to choose my favorite small-game or non-game bowhunting target, it would be the jackrabbit. I've bowhunted jackrabbits from Mexico to Canada, and they never fail to give me all the bowhunting challenge a person could ask for. In addition to an exciting, action-packed bowhunting challenge, jackrabbits can

Jackrabbits are tough critters. I prefer hunting them with razor-sharp broadheads or judo points.

also provide some of the best hunting and shooting practice possible to hone your spotting, stalking, shooting, and ranging skills under actual hunting conditions.

There are four subspecies of jackrabbits in the United States. The common black-tailed jackrabbits found in the semi-arid west and southwestern United States stay the same dull-brown and white color year round, blending perfectly with the desert and brush country background they call home.

The white-tailed jackrabbit's range is farther north, from northern California eastward to Iowa, Kansas, and Minnesota. The white-tailed jackrabbit is actually a varying hare rather than a rabbit. It's lighter in color than its southern cousin and turns almost pure white in the winter, to blend it into the snowy background.

One of the most action-packed methods of hunting white-tailed jackrabbits in winter, when they are herded up in prairie shelterbelts or sagebrush and greasewood creek bottoms, is by pushing or driving. A couple of bowhunters sneak into the downwind end of the cover, and one or two more move through the patch, trying to stalk close enough for some shooting of their own. In the process, the drivers will move the jackrabbits to the standers, for plenty of fast action shooting. During the peak of jackrabbit populations in the Dakotas, I've seen several *hundred* jackrabbits come pouring out of a half-mile-long shelterbelt.

The antelope jackrabbit is found only in the desert regions of southwestern New Mexico and south-central Arizona. And the fourth subspecies, the white-sided jackrabbit, is limited to part of one county in New Mexico.

Jackrabbit populations are generally cyclic, with years of abundance when there seems to be a jack under every bush, and lean years, when finding a jackrabbit is as tough as locating a Pope and Young muley.

Jackrabbits are tough critters, and you don't need to feel over-bowed using your regular big-game bowhunting gear for them. In fact, bowhunting jackrabbits in conjunction with Texas whitetail, Wyoming antelope, Colorado mule deer, or even Arizona elk is an excellent way to fine-tune your shooting during the hunt.

I prefer either broadheads or judo points for jackrabbits. Black-tailed jackrabbits, with their thinner southern hides and fur, are easier to kill with blunts or judos. But the northern whitetails, that are bigger and heavier with dense winter fur, call for razor-sharp broadheads for consistent clean kills.

SQUIRRELS

Next to cottontail rabbits, squirrels are probably the most sought-after small-game critters with bow and gun. Find good whitetail country and you'll find good squirrel hunting. It is fast becoming a lost art, and seeing a squirrel hunter in the woods is getting to be a rare occurrence, except in the south and southeast, where gun hunting for squirrels is still a popular pastime.

The fox and gray squirrels are found from a bit west of the Missouri River to the east coast, with a wide variety of color phases occurring in each

When you're up in a deer stand, be sure to have a few arrows tipped with rubber blunts. They're ideal for some quiet squirrel hunting and you won't be leaving any arrows stuck high in surrounding trees.

species, from pure white albinos to a coal-black melanistic phase. Alabama has the most unique color-phase fox squirrels, with black and white faces, tails, and legs and every combination thereof. I got more engrossed bowhunting these gorgeous squirrels one fall than I did on my deer hunt. Never did get one of the critters for my den.

Patience is the key to getting one of these skittish, jumpy tree climbers into bow range. bowhunting squirrels from your deer tree stand is about as good as it gets. You can shoot at a dozen squirrels over the course of a morning or late afternoon bowhunt without spooking a single deer. You can make use of your regular big-game bowhunting equipment to fine-tune your tree stand drawing. A close miss on the squirrel-sized target should mean a good hit on a deer-sized target, if you pick the same-sized spot. If you're careful about your squirrel shooting, there's little chance of announcing your presence to deer in the area. Just be sure to carry enough ammunition in your quiver.

If you're specifically bowhunting squirrels, the best bet is locating a prime food source, such as a cornfield or oak tree the squirrels are hammering. Squirrels don't like to venture too far into the open. Find a corner or cul-de-sac where the squirrels can feed close to cover. Building a ground blind a couple days prior to bowhunting, or better yet, utilizing a pop-up ground blind for concealment, is ideal. These little fuzztails have super vision and will pick up the slightest, quick movement; they'll run first and look later.

If it's legal to use a feeder in your hunting area, you've got it made. Set up your blind 10 to 15 yards on the downwind side of the feeder, take lots of arrows, a fold-up chair, and a good book and enjoy a day of great squirrel hunting.

Stalking squirrels and picking them out of the trees with your bow and arrow is about as challenging as small-game bowhunting gets. This type of squirrel hunting is a great way to gain knowledge of your bowhunting area, improve your still-hunting and stalking skills, and keep your arrow supplier happy. It's also a great way to bowhunt with a partner. Use binoculars to spot feeding or moving squirrels. When a squirrel is located, one bowhunter tries to stalk close for

Rock chucks and other small non-game critters can provide a full day of quick shooting and fun.

a shot while the other keeps the squirrel in sight. If the squirrel spooks, the stalking bowhunter keeps the squirrel treed until the partner arrives.

The best way to get a shot at a treed squirrel is for one bowhunter to stand quietly on one side of the tree while the other circles out from the tree. The squirrel will usually try to stay on the backside of the tree, and when it moves around to stay out of sight of the moving bowhunter, the standing bowhunter should have a shot. Good camouflage is essential for spot-and-stalk squirrel bowhunting.

For this type of squirrel hunting, I prefer a rubber blunt and try to take shots where there's a tree trunk or limb behind the squirrel, in case I miss (which is generally the case). A broadhead or judo will stick in the tree, and you can kiss another arrow goodbye. Unfortunately, I don't always follow my own advice and have arrows sticking in trees in just about every prime whitetail and squirrel-hunting state in the country.

There are rock chucks, prairie dogs, groundhogs, gophers, and a host of other small non-game critters running around the country, just waiting to test your bowhunting mettle and provide you with all sorts of opportunity to sharpen your bowhunting techniques and skills. Don't leave home without extra arrows. ■

JAVELINA, HOGS, AND EXOTICS

 "You all ready, Billy?" I whispered as I stuck the Haydel javelina call between my lips. "Yeah," came the response, "Where they gonna come from?" I just shrugged and grinned over my shoulder at the ranch manager and my other hunting partner, Bill Bleakney. They were both standing by the edge of the sendero, backed into the heavy brush, waiting for the action to start.

I cupped the call in my hands to control volume and sound direction and started imitating the agonizing sounds of a javelina in distress. As I called, I kept swiveling my head back and forth to scan all possible approaches. Thirty seconds after my first hair-prickling squeals and squalls, I caught the first flash of movement, as several dark shapes scurried through the brush, headed in our direction.

Billy was scrutinizing a dense thicket in the other direction when I hissed to him and nodded toward the oncoming pigs. He immediately picked up the movement and jerked to full draw in anticipation of an easy shot. An instant later, two obviously agitated javelinas came bursting out of the dense brush with their hackles standing on end and their teeth popping and clacking like a pair of Spanish castanets. The large, old boar pig skidded to a dust-raising stop, squarely behind a prickly pear clump a scant 15 *feet* from Billy, almost totally obscured by the spine-covered pads. There was no way the hyped bowhunter could get off a decent shot.

The second equally irate little peccary javelina darted in and out of the brush and cactus, literally at our feet, while Billy was swinging his drawn bow this way and that, trying for a shot at first one and then the other of the darting, dodging, chuffing, snorting, salt-and-pepper colored pigs. Within seconds, the brush was filled with dust and the indistinct, blurred, bodies of the rest of the javelina herd, as they mass-attacked the sounds of another pig in dire straits.

I fluttered my hands over the call to vary the volume of my calling and increased the pitch and excitement of the squealing and screeching that filled the brush with noise. The increased terror imparted to my calling turned the already provoked pigs into gray blurs crashing noisily through the brush surrounding our legs and feet. I was about to gag on the call, trying to keep from laughing, as I watched my normally staid and steady bowhunting partner trying to decide whether to attempt a shot at the dashing, dodging berserk pigs or run for the nearest mesquite tree to avoid getting his pants legs shredded.

Just as suddenly as the action started . . . it was over! The javelina had gotten our wind, and while their eyesight is not the best, their noses are astute, and the drab-colored little porkers' ability to disappear into their brush-and-cactus habitat instantly is nothing short of phenomenal.

When we got back to the truck, we were still laughing at Billy's antics trying to get a shot at his first javelina at the same time he was trying to get both feet in the air. The only way Billy could get us to quiet down and get off his case was by shoving a couple of icy cold sodas into our hands. Not a bad trade.

JAVELINA

The javelina, or collared peccary (as they are properly known), is a herd animal that may be found in groups ranging from six to 30 pigs, with the average size around a dozen animals. The javelina's eyesight is designed to work best from his eyes to the ground in front of his nose, where he finds most of his food, and this limited visual capability makes these critters an ideal bowhunting quarry. However, their sense of smell is right up there with a wary old buck whitetail and right along with their keen hearing.

Javelinas' salt-and-pepper colored hair allows them to blend perfectly with their desert and brush-country surroundings, and a herd of javelina munching cactus on a

Javelina are short-statured and are difficult to spot. Glass for these small herd animals with the sun at your back to have the light work in your favor.

rocky Arizona hillside or feeding on a saladilla flat in south Texas will test your glassing and locating ability to the utmost. Adult javelinas weigh 30 to 65 pounds, and all javelina have a distinct musk gland, above the tail, that gives off a potent "skunky" odor when they get riled up.

Javelina have a reputation for being nasty, vicious customers that will charge a person at the slightest provocation. They are indeed fighters with a short fuse and a highly excitable nature when aroused. The peccaries' razor-like, self-sharpening tusks, or front canines, can do a lot of damage in a fight, and I've seen hounds slashed from one end to the other after a close encounter with javelina and many good bird dogs killed by a single javelina in a one-on-one fight. However, their reputation as a dangerous human adversary is exaggerated.

I've called numerous groups of steaming-mad javelina to within feet of my unprotected legs and had them popping their teeth and grunting in fury, seemingly looking for something to sink their two-inch tusks into. A truly hair-raising experience for the uninitiated, but I've never been chewed on or even felt I was close to it.

There have been numerous instances of people being badly bitten by javelina, but in almost all cases, the pigs have been closely associated with people, either by being raised in captivity or fed in someone's back yard. They lose their fear of people, and when they get pushed, surprised, or cornered, they can do a lot of damage in short order.

Javelina are found throughout central and south Texas, southern New Mexico, and Arizona. Texas has the most javelina by far, but the land is all private and strictly controlled by the ranchers, most of whom dislike javelina and will allow hunting on a day-hunting basis.

Arizona has lots of javelina roaming public land, however the state has a drawing or lottery on all of its public-land javelina hunting. Bowhunters are almost assured of drawing a javelina tag in most areas.

New Mexico also has a fair population in the southern part of the state, but most of the land is in private hands and hunting access is restricted. On public lands in New Mexico, javelina bowhunting is on a drawing basis.

JAVELINA HUNTING TACTICS

The most common method of bowhunting javelina is by spotting and stalking. This method requires a lot of time spent glassing the rocky hillsides and pear patches the pigs love. A good pair of binoculars and a spotting scope are essential for this type of bowhunting, and a keen eye is needed to spot the almost invisible pigs in their home territory.

In Arizona, the pigs can often be located by looking for freshly torn-up lechuguilla plants where javelina have been feeding. The light color and fresh appearance of the shredded plants is easy to spot at a distance, and closer inspection will verify the recent use by pigs. Arizona javelina like the rocky ridges where they can find shelter in the caves and niches in the rocks. They can also be found in the brushy streambeds and feeding along the edges of

A javelina's vision is poor, but its hearing and sense of smell are keen. Plan your stalk to keep the wind in your face.

croplands. Texas javelina can often be located by cruising the ranch roads and glassing water tanks, food plots, croplands, senderos, or saladilla flats.

Javelina are usually active morning and late afternoon during warm weather and tend to hole up in the shade during mid-day, which makes them almost impossible to spot. Glassing for javelina is a lot easier to accomplish if you have the sun at your back, lighting the areas you are glassing. A short-statured, grayish-colored javelina in the early morning or late afternoon shadows is a tough critter to pinpoint, even with the best of glasses and spotting scope. Make the light work for you and your positive results will increase dramatically.

Once you've located a herd of pigs or even a single javelina, plan your stalk carefully. Try to think of things from the javelinas' point of view. Their distant and close-range vision is not good, but make sure you keep your silhouette low so you won't be skylined, where even a myopic pig can pick out your human form. There's nothing wrong with their sense of smell or hearing, so keep the breeze in your face.

When you get close to your quarry, remember javelina are herd animals, and even if you think you're stalking a solitary javelina, take the time to closely glass the surroundings to make sure there aren't more pigs around. I've had a number of good stalks ruined by an unseen javelina bouncing out from underfoot or winding me at the last minute, and a spooked javelina may travel a mile or more before settling down again.

CALLING JAVELINA

The most exciting and action-filled method of bowhunting these little tuskers is to call them in with a predator call. Javelina will come to the same calling that will bring in coyotes and cats, and most predator callers in javelina country have found themselves in the midst of a pack of mad pigs on occasion while trying to call up other predators. Over the years, I've developed a method of calling that works exceptionally well for javelina, whether you are bowhunting in south Texas or the mountains of Arizona.

The reason most predator calls will work for calling javelina is that it's the cadence more than the sound that brings the agitated javelina on the run. My favorite calls are the Haydel Javelina model, which Eli Haydel developed after I told him what I needed, and the Lohman-Circe medium- or long-range calls.

The difference between predator calling and javelina calling is the repetitious and continuous *waaaa, waaaa, waaaa, waaaa,* imitation of a javelina in distress. Once I start calling, I don't stop as long as the pigs are coming, and when they get right on top of me, I muffle the sound of the calling but increase the tempo and intensity. I've watched pigs start coming at a full run from half-a-mile away, and when I stopped calling, the javelina stopped coming. Continuous calling will keep the pigs coming

A key factor when calling in javelinas it to keep the calling continuous until they are almost at your feet.

until they're right at your feet. A neophyte pig hunter who has never seen "hot-wired" javelina chomping around his legs is likely to forget all about shooting.

A few years back, we were bowhunting javelina in the mountains of southwestern Arizona when we glassed some freshly munched lechuguilla glistening in the early morning sunshine on a hill above the jeep trail we were following. Closer inspection showed it had been gnawed on a short while earlier so there had to be pigs close by. We eased to the top of a ridge above the feeding area and spotted a large herd of javelina feeding half a mile away across an open grassy bowl studded with yucca and prickly pear clumps. There were four of us bowhunting, so my calling compadre and I sent the other two bowhunters down the hillside to set up at the edge of the relatively open bowl. Dave Daughtry and I set up above them where I could photograph the action. When they were set, Dave and I both cut loose with our predator calls, and within seconds, the herd of twenty javelina was bounding our way full speed. Within a minute, our two companions were surrounded by leaping and running pigs as they tried in vain to get an arrow into one of the fast moving little targets. Dave and I were laughing so hard at their gyrations and gymnastics that neither one of us could call, although I did get some great photos of javelina within a few feet of the thoroughly bamboozled bowhunters.

On many occasions, I've surprised and panicked my hunting companions when I've set them up for a javelina calling session without letting them know what to expect. One minute they're calmly waiting for a bowshot at a harmless little javelina, and the next they're surrounded by a herd of agitated, jaw popping, bad smelling, grunting javelina. More than one of them has retreated in hilarious haste without getting off a single arrow.

HOGS AND JAVELINA—TEXAS STYLE

There's the scruffy longhaired Russian boar and then there's the feral hog, and Texas has plenty of both. Early ranchers imported the wild boar, mainly for a challenging self-sustaining game animal, but when the Depression hit, many of the ranchers turned cheap domestic pigs loose to crossbreed and provide low-cost meat for their ranch workers. Today, most of Texas is overrun with the hardy, destructive hogs, and most ranches allow unlimited hog hunting for a nominal fee.

The purebred Russian boars can still be bowhunted on private land with the use of bait and dogs in some eastern and southeastern states, but most of the purebred Russian strain has gotten diluted by crossing with domestic and feral hogs. But just because these hogs aren't purebred doesn't mean they are easy to bowhunt. Wild or feral hogs, wherever they are found, are some of the smartest four-legged critters you'll find.

My first experience with wild hogs took place on my first Texas bowhunting trip with Bob Lee, owner of Wing Archery. We flew to the Callahan ranch mainly for a deer hunt, but I got more engrossed in hogs and quail than deer.

The second late afternoon of our hunt, I was still-hunting along a sendero and spotted a humongous boar hog feeding along the edge of the road, where the rancher had been putting out grain for quail. I blithely tried to stalk the hog, and even though I had the wind in my favor and hogs aren't supposed to see well, that cagey old boar sensed something was wrong and took off before I got within 50 yards of him. Same thing the next late afternoon. According to the rancher, the immense 400- to 500-pound boar had been hard hunted for a number of years, was as cagey as they get, and rarely came out in daylight after gun season started. That was enough to get me "hog-wired." The third late afternoon, I got an early start and was waiting in a pile of brush on the downwind side of the hog's main trail, out of the impenetrable white brush thicket he called home. It was almost too dark to see when the behemoth appeared out of the brush 20 yards from me and caught a Bear Razorhead right behind the shoulders. The hog whirled and disappeared into the thicket of sticker bushes in less time than it takes to tell.

By the time I picked up the profuse blood trail, it was full dark, but I wanted that hog. I followed the blood into the unbelievably dense thicket

Texas allows baiting for javelina with feeders. This is the most effective way to bowhunt them. If you are on a do-it-yourself hunt, you can spread corn along a trail or road near a sight for a treestand or a pop-up blind.

that went from barely wadable to crawlable in only a few yards. I'd crawled 20 yards through a hog-hollowed tunnel following blood when I realized I was right in the middle of some of the best (or worst) rattlesnake country in Texas. If I got bit in the position I was in (front or back), it wasn't going to be pretty. It didn't take me long to cure my "hog fever" and decide to wait 'til morning.

After the morning deer hunt on another section of the ranch, we returned to trailing my hog and needn't have bothered. Every coyote in that county must have gorged on pork that evening, 'cause the only thing we could find was scattered hide and bones; we couldn't even locate the head in the thicket. Of course, I was the only one who crawled in and was looking, and the thought of those big rattlesnakes, even in daylight, didn't shorten my search radius too much.

Texas allows baiting for javelina and hogs, and this may be the most effective way of bowhunting them if you're on a do-it-yourself hog and javelina bowhunt. Most hogs and javelina are taken from stands over feeders and on the trails approaching the feeders, in much the same manner as whitetails. The little pigs and their larger cousins have fewer tendencies to sense danger from above or smell the presence of an elevated bowhunter. You can either use a commercial feeder that distributes feed on a timed basis, or simply drive the back roads and spread corn along the trail or road near a good site for a tree stand or ground blind. Pop-up ground blinds are ideal for this type of hog and javelina bowhunting.

Texas also allows the use of dogs for javelina and hog, and I can tell you a herd of javelina or hogs cornered in a brush or cactus thicket can make it tough on the best of dogs and test your mettle as a bowhunter to the limit.

I was bowhunting hogs and javelina with a Texas outfitter who had bought a couple of my Plott bear hounds for use on pigs when we ran into a boar that put us all to the test. A rancher friend of the outfitter's had called, complaining he had a crusty old boar that was running cattle off his feeders and tearing the heck out of his green fields, and he wondered if we might be interested in running him.

According to the rancher, the huge black and white boar stayed in the middle of a white brush thicket adjacent to the feeder and field, so that's where we turned the dogs loose. Within minutes they had the boar bayed in the thicket. That was the easy part. In order to get close enough for a bowshot, we had to push and bust our way through a couple hundred yards of stickery brush interspersed with equally vicious prickly pear.

The boar was king of the roost and not about to leave his sanctuary because of a bunch of yapping and yammering hounds. The interwoven, spine-sprouting brush kept the dogs from being able to leave enough teeth marks in the feisty hog to make him break cover, so we had no choice but to bust our way through and hope to be able to get a shot. When we got close to the melee in the brush, the dogs could hear our approach and went bonkers baying and harassing the humongous hog.

We'd been following hog tunnels the best we could through the chest-to head-high brush, and as we got within 30 yards of the fight, I queried my trusty leader as to what course of action I should take if the very irate porker decided to charge down the trail we were on.

"That's easy," he quipped. "Just jump up in the air as high as you can and don't come down."

Fortunately, I didn't have to test out that plan, because just about the time we got to where we could make out the form of the spinning, slashing hog and lunging, bawling hounds thrashing around in the brush, the hog decided enough was enough and tore through the brush like a runaway tank. It only took the dogs a few seconds to realize they'd been left behind, and then they lit out after their hoofed quarry with a vengeance.

When we finally flogged and flailed our way out of the sticker bushes, we could hear the dogs baying the hog again half-a-mile away. This time they'd driven the hog into a water tank and were churning the muddy bank to a quagmire, while the hog stood chin-deep in the water, slashing at any dog that swam close. When we burst out of the brush on the other side of the pond, panting and gasping from the half-mile run, the vengeance-driven hog centered his beady little eyes on us and came swimming across the pond like a hairy destroyer.

"You'd best be near a mesquite that'll hold you," gasped my guide, "'cause when he hits the shore, he's gonna come for one of us . . . hell-bent on serious damage."

Seeing the hog leave, the dogs plunged into the tank and were swimming in pursuit behind him. I couldn't believe a pig could swim that fast,

A razor-sharp, cut-on-contact broadhead is ideal for a quick clean kill on javelinas. Their long hair on the neck and shoulders make them appear taller than they are. So keep your shots lower rather than higher.

Hogs are a larger target than the javelina; but keep your shots away from the heavy-boned front shoulders. It is better to hit a little farther back than a little farther forward near the "shield" that extends over their shoulders.

but before the dogs were halfway across the pond, the mad pig hit shallow water and lunged to dry ground.

My compadre had moved 10 yards or so down the shoreline, and when the hog saw him moving, he turned his way. This gave me just enough time to drive a razor-sharp, two-bladed Zwickey through the two-inch hide, gristle, and fat shield behind his shoulders. The hog took a couple more steps in the direction of my guide and dropped dead. Neither of us could believe he went down that fast, but a later examination showed my broadhead had sliced through the aorta above the heart, causing an instant loss of blood pressure and immediate death. Of course, I claimed that's exactly what I intended to do in order to save my buddy's life. Ha!

Javelina dog chases are full of almost as much fun and excitement, and if you haven't tried either, get in touch with one of the numerous guides and outfitters who advertise hog and javelina hunting and book a hunt. You sure won't regret the experience.

A hog's eyes are also designed for close focus, and their distance vision is not too sharp, which make stalking hogs a viable method of bowhunting them. However, a feral hog or Russian boar's sense of smell and hearing is as good as the wiliest of whitetail bucks. They are far more intelligent and spooky than javelina, without a shred of curiosity when it comes to the unknown. The slightest sound or perceived threat will put them to flight without hesitation or a last look back. Complete blending camouflage, accurate wind monitoring, and slow, stealthy stalking tactics are essential for sneaking within bow range of hogs.

HOG AND JAVELINA BOWHUNTING GEAR

Hogs are tough, and the bigger boars have what's called a "shield" that extends over the shoulders and back of the front legs, covering most of the heart-lung area. This isn't to protect them from bowhunters but each other, as they are always hooking and tearing at one another with their razor-honed tusks, which can be four or five inches in length. The shield is made up of hide, gristle, and fat, and can be a bugger to penetrate with the wrong broadhead.

On his first hog hunt, my son Blain was 10 years old and shooting a 40-pound recurve with brand-new Savora broadheads. He shot a 300-pound Russian boar at 10 yards twice with this set-up, and the broadheads simply bounced off the boar's armor-like shield.

For my money, a razor-sharp, cut-on-contact broadhead is the best medicine for a quick, clean kill on large hogs. For smaller hogs and javelina, three-blade heads with a trocar point will do the job.

Javelina and hogs can be tough customers when poorly hit, and finding a wounded pig in the rough "stickerbushes" they call home can be next to impossible. Both hogs and javelina are not above going into caves or rock crevices or even a large hole in the ground when crippled, so make sure of your shots.

A javelina has a large head, and the long hair on the neck and shoulders make the little pigs appear much taller than they really are, so keep your shots low in the chest for best results.

Hogs are a little easier to pick a spot on, but keep your shots out of the shielded and heavy-boned front shoulders. A hit too far back will result in a lot higher percentage of recoveries than one too far forward.

Pigs may not have the allure of a bull elk or a whitetail buck, but they definitely are worth a bowhunter's time and effort. They can provide as much excitement and challenge as their larger big-game counterparts and some darn fine table fare to boot.

EXOTICS

My first experience with exotics on a Texas ranch, and several subsequent episodes, left such a bad taste in my mouth that I've never really gotten interested in bowhunting them. It has nothing to do with the animals themselves, as some of the exotics are as wild and elusive as any of the North American game. There isn't a more beautiful animal roaming anywhere than an axis deer or a more crafty and furtive critter than the aoudad or Barbary sheep. A graceful and speedy adult Indian blackbuck is every bit as unique and stunning as the American pronghorn, and a blue bull or Nilgai is as tough and resilient as any big-game animal roaming the wilds.

The problem with bowhunting exotics arises with the way they are hunted on many commercial operations abounding across the country. The high-fenced enclosures aren't extensive enough to be considered fair chase in my book.

On one of my first Texas bowhunts, I stopped at a ranch to look over their exotic bowhunting operation at the request of the outfitter running the hunts. We were glassing a herd of mouflon sheep on a hillside several hundred yards away. There were a number of good rams in the group and one that was outstanding in horn length, mass, and color.

The outfitter asked if I'd like to try taking the big ram with my bow, but I declined since it wasn't part of my planned hunting schedule and I didn't feel I could devote the time to making a good bowhunt of it. We were standing there discussing exotics when his hired hand drove up in a rattling, clanking, old pickup, got a couple feed buckets out of the back, and whistled shrilly.

Within minutes, the whole blooming herd of mouflon were nuzzling round the buckets and the big ram was feeding nonchalantly within 20 feet of where we stood. Some bowhunting experience that would have been. I had similar experiences on several other small ranches, and even had the same type of thing happen on several ranches when I was in Africa. That type of bowhunting isn't fair chase for the bowhunter or the animal, so if you're planning an exotic bowhunt, make sure you check out the hunting circumstances before you hunt. A trophy taken under such conditions certainly isn't going to be one you're proud to hang on the wall in your trophy room.

Fortunately not all exotic hunts are "canned," and the critters on large tracts of land can give a bowhunter all the challenges he wants and then some. I've had several good bowhunter friends return from bowhunting Nilgai on the huge King Ranch in Texas, shaking their heads and wishing they'd taken a .300 magnum with them.

One of the craftiest and most skittish animals I've ever bowhunted has been a free-roaming mature bull aoudad. I sat in a tree stand I'd hung near a remote feeder in the Texas hill country, where there was a herd of aoudad roaming the hills of several ranches. I had numerous good whitetail bucks within a few yards and lots of hogs and javelina, but the big bull aoudad I was after simply wouldn't come down while I was there, even though I had the wind in my favor and moved the stand on several occasions.

He'd stand on the hillside 200 yards away and watch as the rest of the band, including two other nice rams, moved skittishly into the feeder at the last tinge of daylight. Every aoudad in the group was as tight-wired and ready to bolt as a canary at a cat convention, and the slightest rustle of leaves, bird flying, or deer snorts sent them clattering back up the rocky slope. The last late afternoon of my bowhunt, with barely enough light for even my instinctive shooting, I took a shot at one of the smaller bulls and managed to hit the leg of the feeder dead center.

Exotics can definitely fill a void in your bowhunting year, as there usually is no season on them, so they can be bowhunted any time of year. Make sure you thoroughly check out the type of hunts offered and the hunting conditions on the operation before booking, so you don't short-change yourself or the exotic you're bowhunting. ■

GAME BIRDS AND WATERFOWL

Hunting game birds with a bow and arrow is about as challenging as the sport gets and quite often can add another component to your big-game bowhunt. Bowhunting most upland game birds often ties in beautifully with a big-game bowhunt, because an arrow is a silent killer, which means you can often hunt and shoot lesser small game and game birds at the same time you are pursuing big-game critters.

When I travel on a bowhunting trip anywhere, I make sure I have a supply of judo points (rubber bludgeon blunts), and if I'm headed into quail country, I'll toss in some snaro heads for these feathered bombs. I've often taken ruffed, blue, spruce grouse, as well as ptarmigan, quail, and sage grouse while bowhunting big game. The opportunity to add some challenging game-bird bowhunting to your big-game bowhunt shouldn't be overlooked on your travels. In many areas of the country, you can work it where you bowhunt your primary big-game species during the peak activity morning and late afternoon hours and spend the slack mid-day period bowhunting game birds.

PTARMIGAN

When I was bowhunting caribou on the North Slope of the Brooks Range, just south of Prudhoe Bay, I was amazed at the number of willow and rock ptarmigan we bumped while stalking caribou on the relatively open tundra. On the grueling and seemingly endless 700-mile drive from Anchorage to Prudhoe Bay, Curt Lynn and I broke the monotony by shoot-

ing several limits of spruce
grouse that we spotted as
they came into the open
to search for gravel along
the edge of the ribbon of
blacktop. Great way to start
a bowhunt and guarantee
some mighty fine eating at
the same time.

Judo points are the best
hunting head for shooting
ptarmigan in tundra country.
The springy wires on the
points snag and catch in the
dense vegetation and brush,
stopping the arrow from disappearing under the thick
blanket of moss and sedges.

Judo points are ideal for shooting ptarmigan.
The wires on the points snag on the brush so
the arrow doesn't get lost in the tundra or thick
undergrowth.

Numerous times when I was in the middle of sneaking cautiously
through the low-growing tundra willow and alders stalking caribou, I'd
find myself smack in the middle of a clucking, cackling flock of ptarmigan,
resplendent in their mottled white and reddish-brown fall plumage. (All the
species of ptarmigan turn white in the wintertime to camouflage them in
their snow-inundated habitat.) The noisy little grouse were so busy feeding
on ripe berries and buds that I could almost get close enough to touch them
. . . almost but not quite.

There were times I got so absorbed in watching and photographing the
antics of these intriguing tundra dwellers, I darn near forgot why I was there.
On several occasions, when I was still a safe distance away and well out of
sight of my antlered quarry, I couldn't resist the temptation and arrowed a
couple of ptarmigan. Bless the silence of arrows.

Another species of ptarmigan can be found around the alpine meadows
of the Rocky Mountains, extending from Alaska through Canada, and as far
south as the San Juan Mountains of southwestern Colorado. The white-tailed
ptarmigan is the smallest of the ptarmigan species and also a prime target for
bowhunters traipsing around the high country.

White-tailed ptarmigan are a lighter gray in color, with more vermicula-
tion in the feathers, and like their tundra-loving cousins, they change colors
with the seasons. The whitetails are a mottled-gray and white during the
summer and fall months, gradually changing to solid white when snow blan-
kets the mountains. During the winter there's very little protective cover in
their harsh mountain habitat, and their white plumage makes them virtually
invisible to the feathered and furred predators that hunt them.

During extremely frigid winter weather conditions in their harsh alpine
environment, the adaptable ptarmigan will aerial dive-bomb into soft snow

banks and stay buried for several days, using their dense feathers and the insulating snow to stay warm. Their fringed toes act like miniature snowshoes, allowing them the walk on the deep snow with ease and feed on the nutritious willow buds that are readily available at snow level. In many areas of the white-tailed ptarmigan's range, these unique and tough little grouse actually gain weight during winter.

Bowhunting the white-tailed ptarmigan calls for a bit more restraint than bowhunting tundra-dwelling ptarmigan if you want to make it back to camp or home with any undamaged arrow shafts. Whitetails prefer living and feeding in the rockiest areas they can find, where their plumage makes them virtually invisible amongst the rocks.

When I do locate a flock of ptarmigan in such an area, I try to push them slowly to a more open place where my arrows aren't going to be destroyed on the rocks with every shot . . . hit or miss. When I first started bowhunting ptarmigan, I was using a recurve and always carried a bunch of "disposable" wood arrows in my back quiver, especially for these rock dwellers. These wooden shafts were tipped with an empty .38 special case, which makes cheap and very effective blunts. I was happy when I got one ptarmigan for every three arrows ruined. There are times when a .22 pistol may be a ptarmigan bowhunter's best friend.

RUFFED GROUSE

Canada is noted for its big-game critters like moose, elk, bear, sheep, and caribou, but a bowhunter traveling north doesn't want to overlook its wide spread and plentiful populations of ruffed grouse, partridge, pat or ruffies, as they are locally known.

Ruffed grouse get their name from the feathered collar, or "ruff," which makes them look more intimidating to their challengers during the breeding season. Ruffed grouse have two distinct color phases. One is reddish brown and the other a soft gray. During the spring, the male ruffed grouse performs an elaborate, and noisy, mating ritual (called drumming) to attract females.

The first year Harvey McNally and I operated a bear camp deep in the northern part of Saskatchewan, we had ruffed grouse drumming all round our camp. One of our first bear hunters was from Louisiana, and early the morning after his first night in camp, he stumbled out of his tent surly as a pepper-sprayed bear. He was grumbling about some SOB running the roads around camp with his motor bike all night. Unbeknownst to us, there was a grouse drumming log about ten feet behind the hunter's tent.

When a male ruffed grouse drums or performs its mating dance, it jumps up on its "drumming log," rock, knoll, or other high point, and then primps, preens, and puffs up a bit. The grouse then stands bolt upright and starts slowly fluttering (drumming) its wings, gradually increasing the tempo until the wings are a roaring blur that sounds like a revved-up motor. Not exactly sounds to lull a hyped-up, uninitiated bear bowhunter to sleep.

Pressured ruffed grouse can be bearcats to bowhunt, as their variegated brown or gray plumage blends perfectly with the dull, leafy background, making a motionless ruffie almost invisible. You haven't lived until you've had a motionless, hidden ruffed grouse literally explode from under your feet in a flurry of leaves and reverberating wings. Wary ruffed grouse fly first and look around later, making them an extremely difficult bowhunting target. Anybody who can get an arrow into one of these jet-propelled feathered furies zigzagging through the trees should be in Ripley's Believe It or Not.

Back country grouse that haven't had many run-ins with hunters or hikers can be a bowhunter's delight. They're relatively imperturbable and accommodating, as long as a bowhunter doesn't make quick moves or startle them. Most of the time, when they do spook and fly, they'll fly into a nearby tree and can be approached again, with caution and patience, for another shot. I've killed many treed grouse by using rubber bludgeon blunts and

When shooting a treed ruffie, use rubber bludgeon blunts so, in case of a miss, your arrow doesn't get lodged high in a tree.

moving around until I have the tree trunk directly behind the grouse. If I miss (heaven forbid), there's a good chance my arrow will hit the tree and I can recover it for another shot.

'Course, there have been times when I've missed the grouse and the whole dang tree. Broadheads will often skip under the leaves and forest duff on a miss or pass through and be a bugger to locate. Judos work great for ground shooting grouse but will penetrate a tree trunk and hang up. Unless you're a good tree climber, stick to blunts on treed ruffies.

BLUE AND SPRUCE GROUSE

Blue grouse and their cousins, the spruce grouse, are commonly known as "fool hens" because they don't seem too bright when it comes to avoiding close encounters with humans. Blue grouse are common in the Rocky Mountains, western states, and Canadian provinces, while the spruce grouse is found a bit farther north, in Canada and Alaska. The two may look alike, but the spruce grouse is not nearly as good eating as the blue grouse.

When I was outfitting for elk hunters, I had to caution my clients that when they stumbled onto a flock of blue grouse, they made sure they saved enough arrows for an elk encounter. Might seem like a no-brainer, but I had one bowhunter who, after partaking of some of my wife's creamed blue grouse the afternoon before, got so engrossed in trying to fill his daily limit of three grouse that, when he finally brought the third grouse down and the feathers cleared, he only had one broadhead-tipped arrow left for his late afternoon hunt. I couldn't believe it when I met him at mid-day and saw the one arrow in his quiver, but he was so proud of his morning's harvest, there was nothing I could say. Fortunately, we didn't get into a situation during the late afternoon bowhunt where he needed more than one arrow; unfortunately, he didn't even need the one he'd saved.

During the early big-game bow seasons in much of the western United States and Canada, blue grouse are still in family groups, with a hen and full-grown poults hanging together. When I run into such a family group, I try to arrow the poults first, as they are the best eating and their chances of surviving the year are much lower than that of the mature hens.

In late August and September, blue grouse can generally be found around creeks, beaver dams, and other water sources, especially at the lower elevations, where water sources are limited. A high-country bowhunter glassing and stalking the ridges near timberline is more likely to run into single males or small bachelor groups. Blue grouse have an inverse migration during the fall and early winter. They move to the higher elevations during the winter, where the buds and leaves of the low bushes they feed on are readily available above the snow. If you're planning a big game bowhunting trip into blue grouse country, make sure you have a small game license so you don't miss out on some great grouse hunting and even better gourmet grouse cuisine.

SAGE GROUSE

One of the easiest bowhunting game-bird targets is the largest member of the grouse family, the sage grouse. These hefty grouse (weighing up to six pounds) are found on the prairies, plains, and foothills, from southern British Columbia, Alberta, and Saskatchewan southward to western Colorado, Utah, and Nevada. In all of these areas, sage grouse and antelope can be found using the same sagebrush and greasewood-choked bottoms and watering from the same waterholes.

When the fall sage grouse and archery antelope seasons coincide, a bowhunter can combine his pronghorn hunt with some great grouse shooting. Water is the key to locating sage grouse in the semi-desert country they love. The super-sized grouse generally move to water shortly after daylight and again just before dark, so a pronghorn bowhunter has only to set up on a well-used water source and wait them out.

If you really want a challenge and some great wing shooting, work the dense thickets of sagebrush and greasewood during mid-day, when the grouse will be holed up in the shady brush, loafing through the heat of the day.

Sage grouse are big and tough, so stick to razor-sharp broadheads for shooting them. I've used flu-flus fletched for 30-yard shots with broadheads but prefer standard-fletched hunting arrows, as the open country makes finding the arrows from missed encounters a fairly easy proposition. If you get into a flock of sage grouse, try to shoot the smaller, younger birds, as they are much better eating than the older hens and cocks. A

Sage grouse, the largest member of the grouse family, move to water just after daylight and again before dark. If you're set up for pronghorn in a pit blind, you'll find yourself in perfect position for these birds.

six-pound male sage grouse makes a great trophy for your den, but it's a little like eating a boiled 7x16 mud and snow tire.

QUAIL

If only quail weighed as much as sage grouse, I'd be a happy bowhunting camper. Not only would they provide a lot more fabulous eating, but I'd be able to hit them a lot better. The quail's superb taste works against them as serious bowhunting targets, because not many hunters are willing to let them fly off after near misses with an arrow, and bird targets don't get much tougher than these skittish, flighty little feathered bombs. Numerous times, when I've been bowhunting whitetails in Texas from a stand overlooking a feeder, I've had to climb down and retrieve my arrows after sticking them into the ground around feeding quail.

Scaled or blues, bobwhites, Gambel's, and mountain quail are all pretty much the same when it comes to hunting them with a bow and arrow. Tough targets. The snaro head, with three or four wire loops sticking out, is the only way to go for serious quail hunting, as a hit anywhere on a quail with one of these unique heads will usually put them down, and they give you a much better chance when shooting into a group of birds (not unsportsmanlike with these delicious desert denizens).

The most effective way to bowhunt quail is sitting within bow range of a feeding station or a waterhole and taking them as they come in. I've had quail keep coming back to a waterhole until I had all my arrows sticking in the bank around them. After a few such encounters, bowhunting quail takes on a very personal "do-or-die-trying" quality.

Quail can also be glassed and meticulously stalked in the open brush and cactus country. One way to have your cake and eat it, too, is let your hunting companions follow behind with a shotgun. After you get a chance with your bow and arrow set, they can follow up and get some of the birds you didn't kill. Ha! You might have to eat a bit of crow during the quail feed, but a little crow mixed with golden-brown fried quail is a lot better than the peanut butter and jelly sandwiches most quail bowhunters eat.

PHEASANTS

Pheasants are probably hunted more with bow and arrow than all the other game birds combined and can provide challenging shooting regardless of where you live. Many private shooting preserves offer excellent pheasant hunting behind trained dogs. This will challenge your shooting skills to the maximum with fast action and excitement, not to mention the excellent table fare provided by these Chinese imports, should you be proficient (lucky) enough to skewer a bird or two.

Hunting behind a well-trained dog that will hold the birds until you move into position for a quick shot is an experience all bowhunters should enjoy. However, hunting behind an ill-trained dog can be a frustrating disaster.

Years back, Nebraska used to hold an annual (invite-only) pheasant and duck hunt that featured a wide variety of four-member teams. There were governor's teams, race car driver teams, movie-personality teams, etc. One year I was chosen to join bowhunters Jim Dougherty, Darryl Imhoff, and Jeannie Lloyd on the bowhunting team.

On the first day of our hunt, we drew a local guide who had just spent $1500 for a new pointer and, boy, was he proud of that dog. By mid-morning, that damnable dog had flushed over 100 pheasants, and the only pointing he did was with one paw as he ran past them at 30 mph. The hyper dog flushed most of the birds so far in front of us that we couldn't have reached them with a three-and-a-half inch twelve-gauge magnum, let alone an arrow. Darryl and Jeannie finally sneaked in on a small weed patch and jumped several roosters, one of which Darryl arrowed cleanly in the air.

By noon, the totally frustrated and hoarse (from yelling) guide, knowing I raised hounds, made the mistake of asking how I'd handle a dog like that. "I'd have shot it at 10:30," I replied.

I built my own flu-flu arrows and fletched them for 20- to 30-yard shots. Flu-flus can be fletched to maintain top speed for different distances by using either three or four feathers and varying the width of the full feathers used. Arrows fletched with four wide feathers slow down faster than those fletched with three narrow feathers, which maintain arrow speed for farther distances before air resistance slows them down. Test different fletching combinations to get the distance that works best for your type of bird hunting and use bright-colored feathers to aid in locating your arrows. Unfortunately, flu-flu arrows do not work worth a darn from compound bows because the cables tend to strip the feathers.

Pheasants are tough birds and I heartily recommend razor-sharp broadheads for flight or jump shooting. For stalking and shooting birds on the ground, you can get by with judos or rubber bludgeons in the early season when their plumage is fairly thin. During late season, when the birds are winter ready and wilder than a March hare, I recommend broadheads only.

The colorful pheasant is a tough bird and should be hunted with razor-sharp broadheads.

Pheasants are a great game bird for bowhunters, and if you want to have some fun and excitement and get a youngster turned on to the sport of bowhunting, take them to a shooting preserve for a day of bowhunting pheasants. If you can work out a deal with the operator, whereby you only pay for birds killed, so much the better. Should be a cheap bowhunt.

WATERFOWL BOWHUNTING TACTICS

Kill a decoying goose with a sharp stick! This I've got to see!" chortled my host in the pre-dawn darkness as we unloaded our gear at the edge of the narrow pit blind in the middle of a goose-trodden, winter wheat field. Several hundred greater Canada geese had been using this field totally undisturbed for the past week. The evening before, we'd watched the flock leave the field at dark and head for their Missouri River roost area. They would be returning at first light to feed in the same place the following morning. The plan was to place just a few decoys in front of the old previously dug pit blind to pull the first geese arriving within bow range. My host at Big Bend Ranch, just south of South Dakota's capitol city of Pierre, had agreed to let me bowhunt geese on this section of the ranch with the understanding that I could try my luck on the smaller groups of early arrivals. Once the large flocks started arriving from the nearby Missouri River, I had to switch to a camera and stay in the pit until the birds returned to the river for their midday rest in order to avoid spooking the geese away from their primary feeding area on the ranch. Don't think the rancher was much worried about my reducing the population with my bow and arrow.

The following morning it was still black as the inside of a coal mine when the rancher and I set out a dozen full-bodied decoys around the edge of the pit and climbed down to get settled. It didn't take long to realize that shooting a bow from the narrow confines of the trench blind, specifically designed for shotgun hunting, was going to be a problem. The only way I could manage to draw my bow and shoot was to crouch just below ground level where the pit sloped down at one end. I'd have wait until the geese were set to land and then rise up, jerk to full draw, and shoot.

It was barely light enough to see and only a couple minutes past legal shooting time when four gigantic Canadas materialized out of pre-dawn grayness and filled the quiet South Dakota morning with their honks of greeting to the feeding honeys surrounding the trench. They set their wings and dropped over the opening in the decoy spread 15 yards from where I crouched in eager anticipation. When the huge birds stuck out their webbed feet and started back flapping to slow their downward momentum I lunged up, jerked my 85-pond Hoyt compound to full draw, concentrated on where I wanted the arrow to go, and released. The Thunderhead-tipped XX75 zipped right over a thoroughly startled goose that actually crashed into the ground before frantically launching itself back into the air. "Man, you damn near got him!" hissed my host from his end of the pit blind. "Get ready! Here comes three more!"

The silent flight of my hunting arrow hadn't alerted the incoming geese in the slightest. The three huge incoming Canadas set their wings 100 yards out and lost elevation rapidly as they headed for the same landing zone as the previous group. When the geese were still ten feet in the air, necks extended and feet reaching for the ground, I jerked to full draw and raised up for the shot. This time I gave the plummeting goose in the center a bit more downward lead and released. The arrow slashed through the center of the goose with a solid sounding thwaack and the 13-pound bird slammed into the ground, bounced once, and never twitched again.

Waterfowl bowhunting is an extremely challenging and exciting day afield with long seasons and liberal bag limits.

Ducks and geese can be bowhunted by three methods: jump shooting, pass shooting, and decoying. Decoying and pass shooting are the most productive for bowhunting geese, while decoying and jump shooting work best for the for the smaller, faster flying, harder-to-hit, duck species.

Jump shooting ducks is hard to beat for an exciting and challenging bowhunting experience that can be employed throughout the country. When your big game bowhunt coincides with the waterfowl season, midday jump shooting ducks can add a whole new dimension to your big game bowhunt.

I can remember one late season whitetail bowhunt in the south, where the waterfowl season was still open during my deer hunt. The second day, I was still-hunting along the creeks, hoping to find a cottonmouth or two, when I discovered the steep-banked creeks flowing through the hardwood bottoms were filled with wood ducks. It didn't take me long to add a bird-hunting license to my deer license, and since I already had the necessary waterfowl stamp, I was in business.

I couldn't wait for the morning deer hunt to end so I could sneak along the creeks bowhunting the gorgeous woodies. I'd ease along a creek, glassing ahead for a telltale ripple of disturbed water or sight of a duck. Once I pin-pointed the location of my feathered quarry, I'd circle out 30 yards or so from the creek bank, being careful to stay out of sight of the unsuspecting ducks. When I got opposite where I figured the ducks were located, I'd ease quietly toward the edge of the bank and come to full draw before I got within sight of the creek or ducks.

If there was a tree or other cover along the edge of the bank, I'd try to make use of it to cover my approach and help break up my outline. On several occasions, I caught the woodies by surprise and got an arrow off before they burst into the air. Most of the time, my shot was at a panicked, rapidly rising duck. I managed to limit-out on ducks several days in a row while everybody else was back in camp taking a mid-day nap. I used regular hunting arrows with broadheads for this hunting, because I had a good backstop for my arrows and the speed was a definite advantage.

I've spent many a pleasant fall day in Colorado jump-shooting ducks off high-mountain beaver dams. During the late duck season in the Colorado mountains, the many warm-water springs and irrigation ditches also provide some fantastic jump shooting with a bow and arrow for mallards drawn to the lush sedges and tepid water.

JUMP SHOOTING TECHNIQUES

The real key to successful jump shooting is locating your quarry before it sees you. Binoculars and a spotting scope can aid dramatically in this endeavor. Look for the ducks themselves or for rippling water that indicates feeding or loafing ducks. Ducks have excellent eyesight, so plan your stalk carefully to keep yourself completely out of sight until the last possible moment. Complete camo, including gloves and a head net or face paint that blends with the background, can often make the difference in the success or failure of your stalk.

DECOYING TECHNIQUES

Decoying works well for bowhunting both ducks and geese. However, the same blind or pit set-up that works for shotgunning won't necessarily work for bowhunting. A bowhunter needs a blind with room enough to draw, swing, and shoot without interference. I prefer a blind open on the front with a good dense background that allows my camouflage form to blend with the background cover. Concentration is a real key to arrowing incoming ducks or geese dropping into a decoy spread. It's tough to concentrate on a single bird, and then to further concentrate on picking a spot to place your arrow on a rapidly descending bird in the middle of a flock.

The decoy spread should be placed a bit closer to the blind, with the primary landing area for ducks and geese situated 10 to 20 yards directly in front of the bow shooter's position. In many areas, a bowhunter can make use of a boat, hip boots, or waders and a few strategically placed decoys for some fantastic duck or goose bowhunting.

Small creeks, sloughs, or swamps are ideal places to set out several lightweight decoys and make use of the available cover for concealment, much as you would for ambushing a whitetail buck. Having a smidgen of skill with a duck call can add a lot of drawing power to your decoy set-up. However, the old saying, "Remain silent and let people (or waterfowl) wonder about your intelligence or open your mouth and remove all doubt," might hold true for duck and goose calling. Silence in conjunction with waterfowl decoying is more likely to pique waterfowl's curiosity and bring them within bow range than atrocious calling.

PASS SHOOTING

I've taken several snow geese and a couple of Canada geese by pass shooting. This type of waterfowl bowhunting gives you plenty of shooting and bowhunting action. There's a lot of anticipation as your arrow streaks skyward toward a passing goose and even more frustration as the goose seemingly sideslips your homing shaft with ease.

One day, pass shooting at geese coming off the Missouri River south of Pierre, South Dakota, another bowhunter and I had 50 or more arrows grouped in a 30-yard circle 100 yards or so below the pit blind, looking like a bunch of bright-colored flowers sticking out of the prairie. We were shooting at passing geese out of a pit blind dug on the ridge top and managed to empty our quivers several times during the day's shoot. After 100 practice shots, give or take a few, we finally zeroed in on two hapless snow geese.

WATERFOWL BOWHUNTING EQUIPMENT

Forget flu-flu arrows for waterfowl bowhunting. Ducks and geese are fast flyers and you need all the arrow speed you can muster to get your arrow in the same place as the target while it's still there. I've taken ducks and geese with both recurve and compound bows shooting instinctively. I'd recommend using the type of bow you can shoot best instinctively or with the least amount of sighting equipment.

Waterfowl are tough birds, with dense feathers and muscled bodies that can take a lot of abuse. Regular hunting arrows with razor-sharp broadheads are the best medicine for waterfowl, and I'd go so far as to recommend trying one of the mechanicals broadheads. Blunts, bludgeons, and snaros might work for jump shooting smaller duck species, such as teal or wood ducks, but I still prefer the deadly efficiency of a razor-sharp broadhead. If you're going to be waterfowl bowhunting over open water, check to see if your hunting arrows float. If they don't, you're going to run out of ammunition in short order.

If you haven't given waterfowl bowhunting a try, you're missing an extremely challenging and exciting bowhunting avenue with no competition, long seasons, and liberal bag limits. Who could ask for more? ■

BOWFISHING

It's hard to holler without making a sound, but that's just what I was doing as I carefully plucked out the needle-pointed sand burrs buried in the palm of my hand and both knees. I should have worn leather gloves and protective kneepads in this god-forsaken desert country, where everything either bites, stings, or sticks you. I really hadn't planned on having to creep and crawl up the backside of a tank dam to get close to my quarry on this trip.

Only had a few yards to go and managed to brush most of the hellish little stickers out of the way, until I crouched below the top of the dam. Using a clump of greasewood to break my outline, I peered cautiously over the top. Ha! My unsuspecting quarry was still dozing in the hot, New Mexico sun (back to me) in perfect position for a shot. I slowly raised up, drew my bow, double-checked to make sure everything was in shooting order, picked a spot in the middle of my target and sent the barbed arrow on its way.

Dead center hit! With as little fuss and noise as possible, I reeled in my prize and proudly admired my first bow-killed bullfrog.

New Mexico bullfrogs . . . who would've thunk it? I'd gotten an invite from Jack Niles, a well-known Albuquerque bowhunter, to join him and his son for a desert bullfrog bowfishing trip. At first I wasn't sure he wasn't putting me on. Who ever heard of bowfishing for bullfrogs in Gila monster, scorpion, and rattlesnake country? After Jack explained the little-known circumstances of the bowfishing venture, I jumped (no pun intended) at the chance to try this new and challenging bowfishing endeavor.

We bowhunted (fished) the small tank dams, built to hold water from the numerous artesian wells in the area. Each small pond held a dozen or more jumbo bullfrogs. The bowfishing was so good, we were actually trophy hunting bullfrogs, taking only the biggest and fattest from each pond we sneaked in on. In several areas, there were a dozen or more ponds in a half-mile radius, so we each had our own bullfrog bowfishing bonanza.

We'd drive within a short distance of a waterhole and then sneak carefully to the top of the dike, trying to keep our camouflaged silhouettes broken by the brush on top of the dike. The giant frogs were evidently prime targets for the local hawks and were easily spooked by any quick movement against the skyline. A lesson we'd learned on the first pond we hunted.

Once we glassed and located several large bullfrogs, we'd separate and each sneak on a different frog. A number of times during the day, we'd all have a frog on our arrow at the same time. If there were lots of big frogs in the pond, we'd keep shooting until they all disappeared in the moss and sparse reeds, and then retreat for a cold drink or break in the shade of the truck. After giving the spooky frogs 15 minutes or to settle down, we'd sneak back, arrow a couple more, and then move to the next pond.

At the end of a long day of almost constant sneaking and shooting, we had a 100-quart cooler full of some choice-eating frog legs. If only the quail season had been open, we'd have been able to add some of the hundreds of quail we jumped that day and had the makings for my favorite "south of the border" meal . . . fried quail and frog legs.

There have been numerous trips when having a bowfishing rig and fish arrows tucked into my bow case has added an exciting and challenging episode to my general travels, hunting, and photography trips. You never know just where you'll run into some great bowfishing. I certainly never expected such a bowfishing bonanza in the arid cactus and greasewood desert of New Mexico, nor did I expect a totally different bowfishing bonanza when I headed in the opposite direction, a couple of years later.

Saskatchewan is a province well known for its superb fishing for walleye, northern pike, and lake trout, as well as its outstanding trophy whitetail deer and spring black bear hunting. However, I'll bet you've never heard about its best-kept secret . . . unbelievable bowfishing for carp.

I'd booked a spring bear hunt in northeastern Saskatchewan during the early part of June and driven to Regina, the capital city of the province. I'd gotten in a couple of days early to visit friends, do some shopping, and see the sights.

At the dinner table one evening, my host asked if I had any bowfishing equipment with me.

"You bet, I never travel anywhere without a bowfishing reel and dozen fish arrows. I left my wife in Pierre, South Dakota, with her folks and there's some spectacular bowfishing waiting there when I get back off this trip," I replied, wondering what he was getting at and hoping we weren't going to be bear hunting in such thick cover that I needed a fish arrow and reel to find my bear.

"I just chatted with a buddy, and he's been having some pretty good carp shooting on a lake 40 miles north of here. If you're up for it, we'll head up tomorrow morning and give it a go . . . eh?"

According to my host, the lake we were driving to was excellent for walleye and northern pike but also had a good population of carp. I figured a cold-water lake this far north would probably produce small to medium-sized carp at best, but bowfishing is bowfishing. Boy was I wrong!

The lake was a typical glacial-moraine type, filling the bottom of a flat valley, with rocky shoreline, sandy beaches, and a few scattered trees in sight. Not exactly my idea of good carp water. The ever-present prairie wind was raising whitecaps on the long narrow body of water, and I wondered how we were going to see cruising carp in the waves. My questions were soon answered.

As I walked along the sandy, rocky shoreline, I spotted the tail of a carp waving just under the surface, as carp feed on the bottom. The tail was a good six inches wide, indicating its owner was one very large fish. Before I could get an arrow into the water, the fish submerged but was immediately replaced by an immense shadow just below the surface of the roily water. When my arrow sliced through the water and into the lunker carp, line started sizzling off my bow reel and the fight was on.

I kept setting the drag tighter and tighter on the wild running fish and finally, after a 10-minute tug-of-war, I dragged the 30-pound lunker onto the sand. What a way to start a bear bowhunt. That sunny, windy afternoon, three of us arrowed 20 or so carp. The smallest was 15 pounds and the largest was a whopping 34 pounds. Bowfishing doesn't get much better than that, especially when your primary objective is a Pope and Young black bear.

Bowfishing is a great way to get youngsters started in archery and bowhunting. Mud, water, fish, and a bow and arrow set, combined with lots of shooting action and excitement, make an almost irresistible combination for youngsters with a smidgen of interest in the outdoors. There are few areas of the country that don't have streams, lakes, sloughs, or ditches with an abundance, or overabundance, of rough fish just waiting for kids to test their shooting skills.

My grandsons, Zane and Cole, spent many days and countless hours stalking carp along ponds and ditches when they lived on a farm in Iowa. Even now, when we drive past a carp-filled irrigation ditch near our whitetail hunting-camp house in Iowa, they're craning their necks to spot carp in the shallow water and mumbling about not having their bowfishing rigs along.

Having a bowfishing rig readily available while traveling has provided me with some unique and exciting fishing opportunities where I least expected them. One such memorable trip occurred when my wife and I traveled to Pierre, South Dakota, to combine a visit to her parents with whitetail and pheasant hunting in early October. Oahe Dam on the Missouri River, adjacent to Pierre, is well known for its fabulous walleye, northern pike, and king salmon fishery. I've spent many pleasurable hours summer and fall bowfishing above the dam and in the tail waters below the dam for cruising buffalo and carp in the 10- to 15-pound range.

On several occasions, during the fall bowfishing and hunting trips, I'd observed lunker king salmon cruising along the shoreline of the bays of the huge reservoir as they got into the spawning mode. That particular trip, I'd been invited to participate in the Governor's Pheasant Hunt and managed to find myself attending a meeting of the state's fisheries biologists. I'd attended college with most of them, and during the bull session after the meeting, I learned that bowfishing for king salmon had recently been legalized on Oahe reservoir after September 1.

The following afternoon, at the end of the public boat dock on the west side of the reservoir, I sent a dozen arrows into the clear water and hauled in my five-fish limit of silvery king salmon, weighing from 10 to 14 pounds. The locals around the shore who had been trying to catch the elusive and non-feeding salmon on lures gaped in amazement. One totally enamored old timer quipped emphatically, "Been here three hours and ain't had a strike from one of them persnickety salmon . . . by gosh, I'm getting me a bow and arrow to fish with."

That was the beginning of adding bowfishing for the challenging and delicious king salmon to my annual combination fall hunting trip for deer, pheasant, and waterfowl in this prairie-outdoorsmen's paradise.

At the other end of the country, I ran into another unexpected bowfishing Mecca while I was photographing Rio Grande turkeys in Texas one spring. I was stalking a gobbling turkey along the banks of Wolf Creek, a small limestone creek running through the ranch where I was working, when I spotted a fish tail undulating above the deep moss of a small pool below me. I set my camera down and stood against the trunk of a live oak, overlooking the quiet stretch of river below. I couldn't believe my eyes when I spotted several humongous carp voraciously bottom-feeding in and out of the moss covering the bottom of the clear, flowing stream.

After the warm, rich, morning photography light turned hard and flat, I uncased my trusty bow, attached the fish reel, grabbed a couple of fish arrows, and headed up the creek. The serpentine creek had numerous undercut ledges, moss beds, and still pools that all harbored a monstrous carp or two. The clear water and elusiveness of the wary carp made stalking them close enough for a sure shot a real challenge. The solid rock bottom also made missing a real arrow-shattering experience.

I ended the first day with a half-dozen 10- to 25-pound carp for the smoker and an equal number of bent, splintered, mushroomed, and generally unusable fish arrows. Talk about frustrating; there I was with some of the best bowfishing right at my feet, and I'd ruined every fish arrow I had on the first day. This was Texas deer and turkey country, and there wasn't another fish arrow to be found within 200 miles. I probably spent as many hours daydreaming about the carp bowfishing on that ranch and that beautiful stream, as I did the turkey photography, deer, and hog hunting.

Over the next several years, I bowfished that unique and productive little stream every time I was in the area and consistently took carp over 15 pounds. You can bet I was a lot more careful with my shooting and carried an extra supply of fish arrows on subsequent trips. Couldn't ask for a more exciting or challenging way to fill the mid-day lull when turkey hunting or photographing.

Some of the most exciting bowfishing I've encountered was on salt-water fishing trips, where I just happened to have my bowfishing rig along. One time, off the coast of Destin, Florida, I got so engrossed in shooting sharks, rays, and various other salt-water species, I didn't get much trolling or jigging done. The highlight of the trip was when the skipper motored up on a basking 14-foot hammerhead shark and I got an arrow into it. Sharkskin is unbelievably tough, and even though I was using an 85-pound compound bow at the time, the prototype stainless-steel fish point I was testing only penetrated a few inches. After an exciting five-minute tug-of-war on the big-game rod, the monstrous shark pulled loose and disappeared.

Later we arrowed and boated several smaller sharks, in the three- to five-foot range, as well as rays and surfacing triggerfish. On the same trip I made contact with a local game warden and we spent an exciting day bowfishing for gar in the backwater sloughs off the coast. An exciting addendum to a run-of-the-mill fishing jaunt.

Bowfishing isn't strictly a daytime activity, and on several bass-fishing trips, I've worn myself to a frazzle working a bass lure from morning until evening. Then, after a good supper and a bit of rest, I've jumped back in the boat with my bowfishing rig and a spotlight and spent the night bowfishing for carp, gar, buffalo, and, best of all, bullfrogs. Nothing like a mess of fresh frog legs to make you appreciate your bowfishing rig.

Some of my acquaintances have found a way to pay for their bowfishing expenses, as well as a few hunting trips. They started out just enjoying the challenge of bowfishing the lakes in their home cities for huge carp, buffalo, and gar during the night hours, when they had entire lakes to themselves. The huge bottom dwellers moved into the undisturbed shallows and provided plenty of action-filled shooting.

One morning they had bowfished until almost daylight, and after loading their boat on the trailer, along with several garbage cans full of carp and buffalo, they stopped at a 7-Eleven for some coffee and donuts. A gentleman came up to them and inquired what they were going to do with their load of fish. When they told him they were headed for the dump, he proceeded to let them know they were missing out on a good way to make some cash money.

It didn't take them long to glom onto a good thing, and after a night of bowfishing, they'd take their fresh-killed fish to a nearby housing development and sell them. Once word got out, they'd sell several hundred rough fish in less than an hour and make enough to cover all their expenses plus some surplus to put away for their fall big-game bowhunting trips. Business got so good they rarely missed a weekend night of bowfishing, and they had a list of phone numbers to call so that the people would be waiting for them when they arrived with the fresh fish. Nothing better than having a ton of fun and making money at the same time.

BOWFISHING EQUIPMENT

Bowfishing isn't rocket science and doesn't require a lot of expensive equipment for participation. When I first started bowfishing (either the year they invented electricity or lightning; I'm not sure which), I used an old, straight yew-wood bow with a tin can taped to the front to hold the line and solid-fiberglass fish arrows that weighed a ton. Even with this inefficient and archaic outfit, I got plenty of carp in the sloughs and backwaters along the Rock River near my hometown.

Today, I use my hunting compounds, equipped with a Zebco 808 reel, filled with 80-pound Dacron line. The reel is mounted on an adapter that screws into the stabilizer bolt hole on the front of my bow. Another good bowfishing reel is the AMS Zero Drag Retriever reel, which attaches to the side of the bow via the sight-mounting holes.

There are a number of excellent bow reels available for all types and styles of bows, and you shouldn't have any trouble finding a unit that works perfectly with your hunting bow. I used solid-glass fish arrows for years because that was the only thing available. Now I get much better results using the heavyweight Easton aluminum fish arrow shafts, which can be straightened if they get bent. The string attaching through the nock gives much better arrow flight and water penetration.

However, a word of caution: When using a bowfishing outfit with the line attached to the nock, you have to be extremely careful to make sure your line is clear and your reel released and functioning properly. If the line snags or is stopped suddenly by failure of the reel to release, the arrow can rebound. When bowfishing, I always wear Polaroid glasses to cut the glare off the surface of the water and allow me to see the fish better. These glasses also provide eye protection.

Years ago, we had a different set-up when bowfishing for heavy-weights, such as shark and gar: a slider attached to the 200 to 300 pound stainless or heavy monofilament leader. The leader was looped through the hole in the fish point and then a leader sleeve was clinched on it to hold the loop. The can tab was slipped over the shaft and a second, smaller loop was formed through the tab, so that it reached just below the nock. The leader was then fastened to the running line attached to the bow reel, or, in the case of sharks and larger fish, the line that came from the fighting rod and reel.

When you draw this rig back, the tab slides down the shaft, allowing the leader to hang free under the bow. When the arrow is released, the tab and leader slide back up the shaft, keeping the leader and fish line straight to permit good arrow flight. At present, there are several commercial varieties of these sliders on the market, and I highly recommend their use in your bowfishing ventures.

Any good, retractable-barb fish point will suffice for bowfishing carp, buffalo, small gar, etc. However, the bigger the fish, the more durable your

Bowfishing provides plenty of off-season shooting practice. The fish point you use will vary depending upon the size of the fish and its hide—whether it's the thick hide of a shark, a thin-scaled fish, or the tough hide of an alligator.

fish point needs to be. The barbs should be retractable for good arrow flight and water penetration without planing and yet stay locked in position during a tough fight on big fish. After all this, they need to release easily when it comes time to remove the fish. The Muzzy Stingaree is one of the best all-round bowfishing points on the market. Muzzy has a complete line of bowfishing equipment available, as do many other outlets. For a look at what's available for bowfishing today, go online and type in "bowfishing equipment."

If you're going after big fish, such as sharks, gar, or even alligators, make sure to use the stoutest and sharpest fish point available. These denizens of the deep have tough hides or scales that only a solidly built fish point will penetrate.

On my second shark-fishing trip to Destin, Florida, I was accompanied by Bob Lee of Wing Archery. Bob and I had discussed the trials and tribulations of trying to arrow and hold a big shark, and he had spent considerable time and effort researching a super, big-game fish point that was designed along the same lines as the old-time whaler's harpoon.

The stainless-steel head had a point that rotated back into the body in flight and opened into a locked position when reverse pressure was applied. The only way this head was going to come loose was to be cut out or pushed completely through the unlucky fish in which it was stuck. Bob only had one prototype on the trip for photography, but in the excitement of sticking his first shark and getting it close enough for another shot, he inadvertently grabbed the prototype and shot it into the 300-pound shark. That would have been okay, but the enraged shark managed to roll up in the 120-pound test fishing line and break loose, taking the $1,500.00 prototype to the depths with it.

Bowfishing not only provides lots of off-season shooting practice for yourself and the whole family, but can add a whole new dimension to your trips and traveling, whether on a family outing to Florida or a big-game bowhunt in Texas or South Dakota. Think bowfishing and you might just find yourself packing your bowfishing rig *first* on your next vacation, hunting, or fishing trip. ■

AFTER THE HIT

I was kibitzing with the crowd waiting for the banquet bell to ring in the lobby of a Eugene, Oregon, hotel when a guy I'd never seen before came up and blurted out, "Man, I owe you an apology. I thought you were plumb full of BS advising bowhunters to get after an arrow-punched critter as soon after the hit as possible in one of your recent magazine articles on blood trailing." Can't say that's the first time someone's felt I was full of it, and unfortunately it's probably not the last time.

Seems the gentleman had been bowhunting blacktails the previous morning and got a hit on a Pope and Young buck at the head of a grassy valley bisected by several brushy draws. He thought he'd made a good chest hit but like many bowhunters under the adrenaline rush of fast action, he wasn't absolutely sure. Normally he'd have followed the time worn and, in my estimation, the wrong premise to give the buck 30 minutes to lay down and either stiffen up or die. He'd just read where I advised bowhunters to get on a hit animal as soon as possible after the shot. Since I was the guest speaker at the annual blacktail bowhunt and banquet the following evening, he figured he'd give my advice a try, and if it didn't work out, he'd let me know in short order the following evening.

The hyped bowhunter took off after the buck, and when he topped the ridge overlooking the valley, he spotted the wounded buck moving down the valley several hundred yards below his vantage point. Instead of bedding down to stiffen up or die, as the bowhunter expected, the buck slipped into cover along the edge of a draw on the hunter's side of the valley and disappeared. The hunter figured he'd find the buck in the brush dead and couldn't believe his eyes when the buck reappeared at the upper edge of the draw on the ridgetop and disappeared over the top. The bowhunter ran along the top of the ridge and got to the spot where the buck disappeared just in time to see him stagger and collapse in the middle of a small scrub thicket. The thoroughly amazed archer sneaked up on the thicket and found his high-lung-and-shoulder-hit buck down for the count.

The elated bowhunter bought me a cold beer and stated for all to hear that if he hadn't followed the buck immediately, he would never have found him. He'd tried to back trail the buck from where it succumbed and couldn't find any blood trail or tracks to follow. He acknowledged that he would never have searched over the ridge in the direction the buck took, as it was headed back in the general direction where it had been shot.

There's considerable controversy on whether to *wait* or *go* with arrow-hit animals, and I have tried unsuccessfully for years to find out where the waiting rationale first originated. In a discussion with Fred Bear years ago, I stated that I figured one of the first vocal bowhunters (not Fred of course) had to be a smoker. When this bowhunter finally hit a deer, he was so nervous that he took half-an-hour to smoke a couple of cigarettes and settle down. When the bowhunter found his deer, he decided this was the thing to do and promoted the idea until it became gospel to the gullible bowhunters of the day. Unfortunately, this myth has been perpetuated over the years and is still around.

To understand the evolution of broadheads and their killing ability, we can look at the surgeon's tool, the scalpel. Years ago, when I first started bowhunting, there were many bowhunters (including some pretty well-known names) who promoted a rough-edged broadhead that would tear and rip its way through an animal. Wrong.

At the same time, surgeons were using scalpels that were sharpened in the hospitals and reused. By today's standards, those scalpels were like rip saws. During surgery, infection was more of a concern than bleeding, because the rough scalpel blades carried microscopic particles of infectious material into the wound, and if the surgeons weren't exceptionally careful, the incisions became infected. Excessive bleeding wasn't as critical a problem at the time.

However, when hospitals and surgeons modernized with microscopically honed replaceable and disposable scalpel blades that were used for one cut and then discarded, problems with infection lessened considerably due to the precision and cleanliness of the incisions. But bleeding became more of a problem because the exceptionally smooth, clean cuts didn't seal up as readily as the ripped and torn incisions of old. (Now laser scalpels have virtually eliminated both problems.)

A razor-sharp broadhead has the cutting edge honed into the steel of the broadhead, while a file-sharpened or rough-sharpened broadhead has a feather edge that may feel sharp to the touch, but is actually sitting *on* the metal edge of the head rather than honed *into* the steel. This feather edge can peel off on initial contact with hair, hide, muscle, and bone, leaving a dull, inefficient broadhead pushing through the vitals. The rough edges and metal feathering get clogged with the hair and hide particles (along with fat and muscle tissue) as it penetrates, drastically reducing its cutting and slicing efficiency and eliminating its secondary cutting effectiveness.

To see for yourself the drastic difference between a rough-cut wound and one cut with a razor-sharp broadhead, take a piece of pliable plastic garden hose or clear plastic tubing (simulating large arteries and blood vessels in a game animal). Saw through the hose or tube with a hacksaw or regular crosscut saw (like a rough-sharpened broadhead) and then make the same type of slice with a razor blade (simulating a razor-sharp broadhead).

Check the edges of the cuts to see the difference. Dab the ends of the severed hoses or tubes with glue (agglutinated blood), stick them back together and let set. You'll find the rough-cut section of hose will glue together much easier than the smooth-cut section, and provide a much stronger bond because there are more rips, gouges, and stringers to increase the bonding surface for the glue and provide a faster-sealing, stronger glue joint. The clean, smooth razor-cut edges don't provide the nooks and crannies for the glue; consequently, the joint isn't as strong and will generally come unglued under flexing or pressure.

A rough-sharpened broadhead, or one that needs tremendous pressure to "punch" through the outer hair, hide, and muscle to get to the vitals, also produces more shock to the animal than a razor-sharp "cut-on-contact" type broadhead. The more shock from an initial arrow hit, the quicker the animal's brain registers damage and starts the survival process, where anesthetizing endorphins are released and blood chemistry starts to change near the wound sites.

When a critter's survival system starts reacting to an arrow injury, the blood near the wound sites thickens or agglutinates and acts as glue, sealing the cuts and rips. The rougher the edges of the broadhead cuts, tears, and rips, the quicker and more effectively the thick sticky blood is sealing the site and stemming the loss of blood.

Next to the invention of the compound bow, nothing compares to the introduction of precision-sharpened, replaceable-blade broadheads that come from the package razor-sharp as the most valuable innovation to aid bowhunters in their endeavors. I feel fortunate in being able to get a razor-sharp edge on almost any broadhead with minimal effort. However, I've found that most bowhunters don't have the touch and or the willingness to expend the time and effort to learn proper sharpening techniques. Hence they can't sharpen their broadheads worth a darn.

At the peak of my guiding and outfitting days, I checked every client's broadheads. If they weren't razor-sharp (and most weren't even close), I made the clients sharpen them or, in most cases, I did it for them. I am convinced this stringent policy kept our wounding loss much lower than most other outfitters I knew. Today, there is absolutely no reason for a bowhunter to be hunting with anything but razor-sharp broadheads. Even though your broadheads are sharp when you put them on the shafts prior to hunting, check them in the field occasionally, as the super-sharp fine edges on the blades can lose their edge over time bouncing around in a bow quiver. If they don't feel perfect, replace them with new blades.

"Should I get another arrow into the animal if I get a chance? What should I do after I get a hit on an animal?" These are the two most common questions asked by bowhunting friends and clients as they head out for their hunt.

My answer to the first question is pretty much the same regardless of the species of big-game animal being bowhunted. As long as your intended quarry is within bow range and still able to move, don't hesitate to get as many arrows into it as you possibly can. Once the initial hit is made, the more arrows you can get into an animal, the quicker the hunt will come to a successful conclusion.

In reality, however, only on rare occasions will a big-game animal give you enough time for a second shot after the initial strike. Most of the time, your intended target is going to be long gone before you've recovered from your first shot, let alone gotten a second arrow on the string. *Don't* think about a follow-up shot before you make certain you follow through on your first! There have been many easy shots missed because of this split in concentration at the "moment of truth."

The question of an immediate course of action after hitting an animal varies a bit with the situation and the animal being hunted. When I have a bowhunter in a tree stand, bowhunting whitetails, bear, or elk, I advise him to concentrate on observing, as closely as possible, where the arrow hit the target and the animal's immediate reaction, and then *remember* these details. More importantly, I want him to make sure he observes precisely where he last saw the arrowed critter disappear from sight into the brush or timber.

In most situations, my clients have radios and are instructed to stay put and call us for immediate assistance, so we can get on the animal's trail together as soon as possible after the hit. As an avid bowhunter, guide, and outfitter, I abhor losing any wounded animal. Considering the toughness and unpredictability of all wounded game animals, I don't take any unnecessary chances on losing one that has been hit by myself, a hunting partner, or a client.

When I was guiding and bowhunting bears, if I didn't find the bear dead within a couple hundred yards, I'd get two of my best blood-trailing Plott hounds and let them do the job I raised and trained them for. If you haven't been in on a midnight chase after a wounded bear in the mountains, then you haven't really been bear hunting. Sometimes it's almost as much fun as being in a car wreck, and other times it can get plumb miserable. Seems, after bear bowhunting, clients have been on such a hair-raising, heart-thudding night-time venture, they tend to concentrate on better shot placement on their next bear hunt.

After 30-plus years of guiding clients and bowhunting bears myself, I can count on several fingers the number of arrow-punched bears we failed to recover, and I'm proud of that fact. Unfortunately, those days in many of the "protect-the-poor-bear" states of the west are long gone with the outlawing of dog hunting. This recovery factor was totally ignored by the antis in their smear campaigns against bear hunting with hounds.

WAIT OR GO?

For bowhunters without the advantage of a guide or blood-trailing dogs, my advice is the same for all big-game animals. *Don't wait!* In my experience, the *only* time a bowhunter should wait any appreciable length of time before getting on the trail of a hit animal is if he knows *for sure* the animal is hit too far back, in the liver, paunch, or intestines. In more graphic terms, a gut shot!

The other circumstance of not following an animal right away occurs when a bowhunter takes a late afternoon shot and is not certain where the animal was hit. I'll spend a little time quietly looking for the arrow in the immediate vicinity of the hit. If I find the shaft with blood on it indicative of a fatal hit, and there is a copious blood trail, then I'll cautiously follow it for several hundred yards. The minute the blood trail peters out or I feel the hit may have been marginal, we'll get the heck out of there and wait until morning.

One of the hard, cold, after-the-hit facts I've learned from my outfitting and guiding experiences with bear, elk, antelope, whitetail, and mule deer bowhunters is to take everything a client tells me about the location of the hit on a big-game animal with a grain of salt and start the recovery job with a completely open mind. I've had dozens and dozens of instances where the arrow hit wasn't anywhere near where the hunter thought after we recovered the animal. The distance between our eyes and brain isn't far, but some-

More times than not, don't wait to trail your game. Assess the sign from where you last saw the animal and begin tracking.

times, by the time this combined information exits our mouth, it's been unintentionally but seriously compromised.

One spring I had a bowhunter shoot a bear from a tree stand over a bait. When I quizzed the ecstatic bowhunter about where he hit the bear, he was emphatic that his arrow was buried to the bright red fletching, halfway up the bear's body and slightly behind the shoulder. A perfect hit. He painted a vivid picture of the bear running off, then stopping 50 yards out and slumping down with the bright fletch still easily visible.

I tried to work out the skimpy, almost non-existent blood trail by lantern light, and after an hour without finding much blood or a dead bear, I got Skunk and Toughie out of their boxes and turned the job over to my four-legged experts. Several hours later, my client put a second and final arrow into the treed bear and ended the hunt. His first perfect, behind-the-shoulder hit had actually hit the bear in the front paw and sliced the top of his foot open. That bear would have been back on the bait later that night, but once a hunter draws blood, it's an outfitter's responsibility to use every legal means possible to recover the animal. Even if it isn't the law, it's still the right thing to do.

After a number of these situations with all species of big game, I learned to go by what I personally saw at the site of the arrow hit and let my instincts and experience guide me. Most bowhunters certainly don't mean to lie or mislead themselves or their companions, but in the adrenaline-pumped, mind-racing few seconds at the peak of a bowhunting quest, the eye sometimes sees and records what the minds wishes was true.

I've probably learned more about animal reaction to arrow hits and how to recover hit animals by bowhunting and guiding for antelope hunters than by any other means. In the wide-open spaces that pronghorns call home, you can generally keep the antelope in sight from the time it's hit until you load it in the pickup. In antelope country, by using a good pair of binoculars and a spotting scope, coupled with patience and a desire to learn, I was able to study each and every type of arrow hit and learn much about how to handle the same hits on other big-game animals.

In our antelope camp, we seldom lost an antelope that had been hit with an arrow. Throughout my 30 years of bowhunting pronghorns, we've recovered many animals with relatively minor hits simply because we could, and did, stay with them in the open country.

On one such occasion, I had a female bowhunter on her first pronghorn hunt slice a Pope and Young buck's lower front leg with a razor-sharp, two-bladed broadhead from her 42-pound bow. Around the supper table the previous evening, we'd discussed my philosophy about getting after an arrow-hit antelope and staying with it as long as possible. She took this to heart when she hit the buck, knowing full well that the hit was superficial. Six hours and four miles later, she was able to slowly walk within 30 yards of the dehydrated and shocky buck and put an arrow through the lungs. Her perseverance coupled with open country, where she could keep the antelope in sight and often shortcut the distance between them, and the warm weather were all were factors in recovering that buck.

On another occasion, my good friend M. R. James sliced a Pope and Young buck's cheek open with his broadhead when the flighty buck whirled and jerked its head around just as M. R. released, a common occurrence with the phenomenally quick-reacting pronghorns. He was thoroughly bummed when I came to pick him up at midday, but three hot, weary hours and several miles later, M. R. was able to get close enough to the thoroughly whupped antelope to add a beautiful, hard-earned trophy to his collection.

Occasionally, we'd back off and leave an arrow-hit antelope simply because the hit was so superficial that there was little bleeding, virtually no chance of recovering the animal, and zero chance the wound would incapacitate the pronghorn in any way. In several such cases, another bowhunter took the same animal later in the hunt. In almost all instances, the original arrow wound was almost completely healed, with no sign of infection.

Waiting for the hit animal to "stiffen up" is another hunting myth that costs bowhunters untold lost animals each hunting season. If the arrow hits the vitals, the animal will be down for the count quickly and immediate follow-up will not change that fact one bit. If you get a bad hit, the minute the animal gets over the initial shock and has a chance to lay down, he is *not* stiffening up. On the contrary, he's calming down, his survival instincts are engaging, and his recovery and healing system is kicking into high gear.

By giving the animal 30 minutes to an hour before going after him, you've let him recover from the initial surprise of the hit, given his system time to start the chemical and physical process of coping with the wound, and let him begin recovering. You've also given him time to re-engage the gray matter between his ears and tune his eyes, ears, and nose to alert him of any approaching danger.

Worst of all, his endorphins (neurotransmitters in the brain that produce pain-relieving properties similar to a dose of morphine) have gotten a chance to work, and his blood chemistry has changed and started the coagulation process that can seal the wound and diminish or eliminate a blood trail if he can sneak slowly and carefully away from his bed. When the wounded critter sees, hears, or smells you approaching, it will more than likely sneak away from its point of observation or bed, often in an unexpected direction, leaving little, if any, blood trail to follow.

STUDY THAT SHAFT

Quite often the arrow shaft can be an important indicator in determining just where an animal has been hit and how you should proceed in recovering it. Bad hits are a fact of life that none of us like, but sooner or later, it's going to happen. Once you open those fingers or trip that release, the situation is beyond your control and anything goes. Hopefully, you'll never get much experience at this aspect of bowhunting, but the more knowledgeable you are about it, the better your chances of turning an unfortunate situation into success.

The *first* thing a bowhunter needs to do after making a hit is to find and study his arrow. Combining the information provided by the arrow with what he observed during and after the shot should provide enough information to formulate a plan of after-the-hit action. When I arrive at the site where an arrow hit a critter, I strive to get all the information about the shot and hit I can from the bowhunter and then spend time studying the shaft to verify that information.

Gut-shot animals are a bowhunter's nightmare and I would venture that more bow-shot animals are lost to "gut" hits than any other type of arrow wound. The shaft is a valuable asset when it comes to confirming a gut hit and its severity. The shaft from a gut-hit animal will usually feel a bit greasy, may be streaked with faint blood smears, and can have a sharp, sour smell. Ungulates, such as deer, elk, caribou, etc., have four separate stomachs, and quite often it's possible to tell just where the hit is located by the condition of the stomach material on the shaft. If the hit is through the paunch or forward stomach, the material will be grainy and might even have small pieces of undigested vegetation or grain clinging to it.

One of our Iowa clients had a whitetail buck jump the string and wasn't sure where his arrow hit. A study of the shaft showed coarse material and even some small bits of well-chewed corn. This was proof the deer was hit in the paunch and the only course of action was to back off and leave him alone for

After the hit, find and study your arrow to further verify where you hit your quarry.

24 hours. The following morning, we recovered the dead deer in a dense cedar thicket 300 yards from where it was hit. Evidence and sign indicated the deer had expired a few hours before we found it. Had we given that deer the accepted few hours to "stiffen up," we would probably have jumped him in the thick brush, spooked him out of the area, and lost him.

The shaft from a hit farther back, in the large and small intestines, will usually have a slick feeling, smears of fine, almost-liquid, green gut contents with a sour smell and a very sharp taste, due to the strong acids involved. Yes, I quite often taste the stuff covering the shaft, as it can help determine what's on it. (Not pleasant, but a heck of a lot better than finding a dead animal a week later that should have been recovered.) I've found that an animal hit farther back will expire much sooner than one hit forward in the paunch, unless the liver is involved in the hit. This is due to the strength of the acids and the more-liquid nature of the large and small intestine contents, which spread more rapidly through the body cavity causing high fever, dehydration, and peritonitis to set in at an accelerated rate.

There is nothing good about a gut hit, as the wounded animal is doomed. However, knowing how to handle a gut-hit animal will result in almost 100 percent recovery.

The arrow shaft from a liver-hit animal will usually be heavily covered with a smooth coating of very dark, almost black-colored blood. Again, the situation calls for patience and time to ensure recovery. A liver-hit animal may bleed profusely for a short time, but if the animal has a chance to bed down for any length of time, the hide, muscles, or fat layer may seal the outer wound and stop any further blood trail. If the liver-hit animal is left alone, it won't be far from where it was initially hit.

Broken shafts often give a good idea of where your arrow is in the animal and the possibilities of secondary cutting damage. Over the years, I've recovered a number of elk, deer, bear, and antelope where the initial hit would not have been fatal, but by keeping the animal moving and the arrow working within its body, the secondary cutting of the razor-sharp broadhead created additional hemorrhaging that led to recovery.

Every shaft that's hit an animal has a tale to tell, so don't overlook this aspect of your after-the-hit actions.

LATE HITS AND PAUNCH SHOTS

If I even suspect a gut shot or it's an unknown late afternoon hit, I will not attempt to search for the animal for a minimum of 18–24 hours. The standard is to wait four to six hours but that is simply not long enough. Leave a gut shot animal totally unpressured after the arrow hit, and it will bed down and stay within a few yards of its first bed until it gets too far gone to move fast or far. No bowhunter worth his salt wants to see any animal in pain for an extended period, but pushing a gut shot animal will cause it to keep moving without leaving much in the way of a blood trail. This lack of a good trail slows down trailing, giving the stricken animal a chance to sneak off undetected and reducing your chances of recovery to near zero. A hard-pressured, gut-shot animal will generally head for the thickest, most impenetrable cover it can find, which makes it even more difficult to find. Generally when a gut-shot critter begins to fever-up and dehydrate, it will seek out water, so if there's a stream, tank dam, or lake in the vicinity of the initial hit, and you don't find the animal close to where it was shot, concentrate your efforts around the water source.

PUTTING IT TOGETHER

The main attributes for recovering arrow hit animals are patience, perseverance, and as much luck as you can muster. The axioms for successfully following a blood trail to its conclusion are simple. No. 1: Find the *first* drop of blood. No. 2: Find the *second* drop of blood. No. 3: Find the *third* drop of blood. Simply follow this procedure until the animal is within sight of the last blood droplet. What could be simpler? Yeah, right.

Almost every bowkill results in a blood trail of some kind. Depending on the bowhunter's skill, his quarry's cooperation, and *luck*, blood trails can be good, bad, or impossible.

Blood trailing is serious business with me, as it's where my expertise as an outfitter is put to the test and can make the difference between the success or failure of a client's bowhunt. When I am searching for or on a blood trail, I don't want anyone talking or making undue noise. I don't want to alert a nearby animal and I want to center my undisturbed concentration on the job at hand.

Two people on a blood trail is good and three is workable, more than that is asking for trouble. My guides and I generally do the trailing while the client brings up the rear. They often times don't like this, but unless they are proficient and experienced they're more trouble than help. We communicate quietly with whistles or whispers, and while one or two of us search for blood sign, the next person stays with the last blood until a new spot is found. We generally use toilet paper to mark the trail in dry weather and plastic biodegradable tape in wet weather. If the blood trail is lost, circle out in front using the marked trail to get a line on direction of travel. Keep a sharp eye on the top and back side of logs, fences, or other obstacles where a critter might jostle another drop of blood loose in crossing.

Making a clean hit in the vital area of a big-game animal and a clean, quick, kill is the ultimate goal of every bowhunter; unfortunately the uncanny reflexes and speed of most game animals can turn a good shot into a bad hit in the blink of an eye or the trip of a release. The bowhunter who does his homework and uses his head and a good measure of perseverance *after* the shot is the bowhunter who will consistently bring home game. ■

FIELD CRITTER CARE
AND TROPHY
PREPARATION

You've just found your arrowed critter, and whether it's the trophy of a lifetime or meat for the freezer, the first piece of equipment you want to reach for is not a knife, saw, rubber gloves, or axe, it's your *camera!* If I've learned one thing in over 40 years of bowhunting, guiding, outfitting, writing, and photographing, it's the importance and lasting value of photos.

Hundreds of times over the past years I've had hunters, their wives, and their parents call or write and want photos of their hunt and kill for a hundred different reasons. When you get to your downed animal, take the time, right then and there, to get *lots* of photos . . . you won't be sorry.

Photographing yourself with your bow kill, as soon as is practical after you locate it, will provide a visual record that will show the animal as presentable and imposing as possible. These on-site photos will catch the hunter's excitement, pride, and exhilaration at their peak, with a background that will trigger detailed memories of the hunt for many years to come.

Take the time to clean up your bow kill and give the animal the same respectable look it had in life. Wash or wipe away *all* the blood and move the animal away from the bloody ground and leaves. Dab water or saliva on the eye to give it that life-like glint, and shoot photos from several different angles to show its trophy qualities and, hopefully, catch your best side.

This process is easy if there are at least two hunters present, but it can

 190

still be accomplished by one hunter alone if he carries a small tripod or camera clamp to hold the camera and uses the self-timer. Getting *good* photos takes time and a bit of work, but I'll guarantee you the effort will provide you with some of the most valuable and longest-lasting memories of your hunts.

Peak-of-the-moment photos are much better than those of a bowhunter sitting on the tailgate of a pickup in the driveway, with a stiff, milky-eyed, tongue-protruding, blood-dripping buck. Ever been shown any of these by a fellow bowhunter? Nothing turns non-hunters off more than seeing repugnant photos of dead animals, so start your field critter care with good photos.

Taking detailed photos of your trophy animal while it's still fresh will also give your taxidermist a much better chance to get the final details of the mount as life-like as possible.

FIELD DRESSING FACTS AND FICTION

When you walk up on a downed animal, there are many reactions and emotions that take place, ranging from sadness at seeing a majestic creature dead, to panic at the thought you've just killed a 700-pound animal, five miles from your vehicle in 80-degree temperatures and you're all alone in the mountains.

Before you grab your knife and start hacking, give some thought to the situation and how best to handle the job ahead. There are a number of myths when it comes to handling game animals . . . myths that can cause later problems, and some that can add a whole new taste sensation to your game meat.

One of the most prevalent myths, when it comes to deer, is that you must immediately cut off the oily, odiferous tarsal glands and the animal's testicles to keep the meat from having a gamey taste. Wrong! The glands on the insides of the back

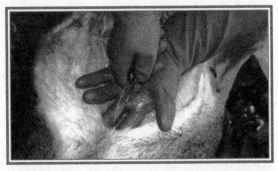

A razor-sharp knife will help make the field dressing job that much less of a chore. Use one hand to help lift the hide away from the paunch so you can cut the hide more easily.

legs and the testicles are non-circulatory glands. There is no way they can carry their strong smell to the meat—unless you get the secretions on your knife, hands, or clothes and transfer it. In many of the western states, a bowhunter must leave a testicle on each hindquarter as evidence of sex, so make sure you're familiar with the laws before you start slicing and dicing.

Cutting the throat on a freshly arrowed animal to let it bleed out is ludicrous. An arrow kills by hemorrhaging or bleeding out, and if the animal hadn't already bled out you wouldn't be in a position to gut it. This is a good way to ruin a good cape for trophy mounting. Don't do it.

Each animal is different when it comes to field dressing, and what is best for a whitetail deer in Iowa may not be best for an antelope on the plains of Wyoming or a moose in the arctic outback.

The basic tools for field dressing a big-game animal are: a sharp knife, bone saw or axe, several lengths of rope, rubber gloves (thanks to Chronic Wasting Disease-CWD), and wire ties or strong cord.

Over the years I've used about every size and shape knife made for field dressing. One fall, I killed a bull elk on a spur-of-the-moment hunt, where I heard a bull bugle from my truck, took after it, and, an hour later, killed him a mile from the road. I'd left my daypack in the truck and the only thing I had to field dress the elk was a Bear Razorhead broadhead. I not only gutted the elk with the broadhead, but completely quartered him with no problem at all. While I was in Alaska, I skinned and cut up a harbor seal (they were classified as varmints then) with a broken bottle I'd found on the beach. Any quality, sharp knife will work for field dressing deer, bear, and antelope-sized game.

A folding meat saw, such as the super-sharp Gerber interchangeable blade saw, doubles as superb limb trimmer with the coarse blade and an efficient bone saw with the fine-toothed blade. A quality, packable saw is essential for field dressing larger animals or when you need to quarter a game animal to pack it out.

For larger animals, such as elk and moose, I prefer an axe like the narrow bladed, all steel Estwing models. These can be bought at most good hardware stores in medium and regular sizes and are worth their weight in gold when it comes to serious field dressing and quartering. The narrow blade holds a razor-sharp edge and will cut through hide, meat, and bone like they were butter. I can strip the loins out of an elk and skin a quarter faster with this axe than with a knife.

Several hanks of rope are essential for field dressing larger animals when it's a one-man job, and it's always better to carry too much than not enough. Tying the back legs to keep them spread or keep the animal from rolling downhill is just one use for rope. In my pack, I carry a 20-foot length of 5/16-inch braided-nylon mountain-climbing rope, with three aluminum snap links. Using the rope and snap links as pulleys, I can (by myself) hoist a 250-pound deer completely off the ground or pull elk quarters up into a tree where they can be tied off and left hanging.

Camouflage pants usually come with ribbon ties to pull the pants legs tight around your boots, which I never do. As I pointed out to Realtree designer Bill Jordan in our Iowa hunting camp, the only practical use I could ascertain for these pant-leg ribbons was to tie the anus shut on a deer when you're field dressing it. Carrying some small diameter cord or wire ties will work just as well for tying off the bladder or anus when needed, and will probably make your camo clothes designer much happier.

With the proliferation and scare of CWD in many areas, the use of rubber gloves for field dressing has become more advisable. This past year, I got a supply of quality, latex camouflage gloves from Charlie's Own. These disposable gloves are ideal for field dressing, handling scents, setting up and removing decoys, and keeping your hands dry in wet weather, and they should be an integral part of your hunting gear.

Another essential for my field-dressing kit is Liquid Game Bag. This oily pepper formulation has saved many game animals from getting fly-blown and ruined, for both me and my clients. You simply rub it on the exposed meat to keep flying critters away. Liquid Game Bag has no lasting effect on the meat and is the best and most efficient meat protection I've found.

I like to dress or gut an animal as soon as possible after recovery, but that doesn't necessarily mean that the minute I find a client's or my own whitetail buck in Iowa, I'm going to jerk out my knife and start slicing. There are many times when you may want to load and move the animal before gutting. Game animals are not necessarily afraid of blood or the scent of blood, as this is an integral part of their environment, so a gut pile in your bowhunting area isn't going to drive the deer out of the country.

However, on our Iowa leases we have many food plots to attract deer, and I don't want several gut piles in the vicinity of the stands for one reason: coyotes. We have enough problems with these four-legged deer killers spooking and running deer without attracting or giving them additional reason to hang around the food plots by leaving gut piles for them. In such situations, we'll move the deer out of the area or even haul a deer back to camp and gut it there, then haul the guts to a thicket where I can trap or snare coyotes and help to manage the predator problem.

Antelope are another animal we often haul to camp before gutting. In the open prairie, we can generally drive to the kill site, carefully load the antelope and then haul it to camp. Antelope have very oily and fragile hair and have to be handled with extreme care to avoid damaging the cape and transferring any of the gamey hair oil to the meat. We place the un-gutted carcass of a trophy buck on a clean tarp and very carefully cape it out. Then we finish skinning the rest of the carcass, gut the antelope, wash it thoroughly, wipe it down with Liquid Game Bag, cover with game bags, and hang it in the shade.

Another myth is that you should never wash a carcass or get it wet after it's gutted and skinned. Hogwash (pardon the pun). Meat-processing plants spray-wash carcasses many times throughout the process of killing, skinning, gutting, and cutting livestock carcasses. There have been several times when I've immersed elk and mule deer quarters in cold mountain streams to help get the initial body heat out of the meat when the early archery season temperatures were in the 80s.

Field dressing a big-game animal can be quick and easy or a major undertaking, depending on the animal involved and the situation.

The first step is to get the critter in position, lying on its back, with the rear legs spread. Your ropes will come in handy for this if you're working alone, especially if you're dealing with a large deer or elk-size creature. At this point, you have to determine how you are going to field dress the animal.

If you have to drag a deer-sized critter any distance to transportation, you want to make as small an opening as possible (to get the guts out) to keep dirt and debris out of the body cavity. If you don't have to pack the animal, you can be a bit more liberal with your cutting and sawing. If it's an elk or moose and you're going to have to quarter the critter to get it out of the woods, you have a lot more leeway in field dressing.

You also have to decide, now, if your bow kill is going to the taxidermist and for what type of mount. More mounts are ruined at this stage than at any other time. If there's any doubt whether you want to save the skin for a mount or not . . . save it!

Take plenty of photos and get the measurements as recommended by your taxidermist, so he can make the mount as realistic and close to live dimensions as possible. If you're on a once-in-a-lifetime bowhunt for

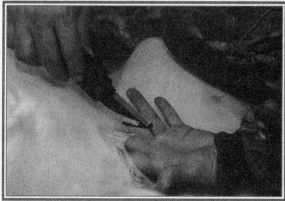

such things as sheep, big bears, goats, etc., check with a taxidermist *before* you leave to find out what type of photos and measurements he needs to do the mount properly. Don't just bring him a salted hide, as most hunters do, and expect the best he can produce.

Some hunters prefer to use a knife with a gut hook to cut the hide. Just make sure that its blade is razor-sharp and that you use your other fingers to help lift up the hide so you don't puncture the organs or intestines in the body cavity.

For maximum meat protection, once you have the animal stabilized in position, make an incision completely around the anus, pulling it out while you carefully cut it free from the pelvic walls. Pull it out far enough to securely tie it shut with string, wire ties, or your pants-leg ribbons. This will keep feces from getting into the body cavity and giving the meat an indescribable flavor and color.

Next, carefully cut through the skin at the lower end of the sternum and, even more carefully, open this incision several inches. At this juncture you can do one of two procedures.

For deer, antelope, sheep, etc., that have short, clean belly hair, stick two fingers in the hole you've made and spread them in a V, with the tip of the knife blade between your fingers. Lift the hide and underlying belly muscles up and away from the paunch and intestines as you cut from sternum to pelvis, keeping upward pressure on the knife blade to prevent puncturing the paunch or intestines. A number of hunters like a gut hook-type blade for this chore, but I can do it faster, and surer, the old-fashioned way, so that's what I do.

When you're dealing with bull elk or moose that have spent considerable time urinating over their chest, belly, and legs, or wallowing in urine-saturated mud to intimidate their competition and impress the cows, you'd best be a bit more careful. Wearing rubber or leather gloves, carefully make an incision through the hide at the base of the sternum, only this time do not cut through into the body cavity.

Don't forget to throw in a pair of long gutting gloves. You'll appreciate keeping your arms and clothes clean and dry (as much as is possible).

Split the skin only from sternum to pelvis, and carefully skin the rank hair and hide back away from the belly muscles for six inches or so to each side of the centerline. Once this is done, discard and replace your rubber gloves or wash your hands, then use the same two-fingered procedure to open the belly muscles and tissue to the pelvis.

When you have the body cavity open, lay your knife blade alongside a finger and run it around the diaphragm on both sides to free the heart and lungs. Reach far up into the neck, where you find the corrugated-feeling windpipe and esophagus, and cut these off in the throat to free them. This can be a real chore for a short-armed person on an elk-size critter. You may have to use your axe or saw to open the chest and rib cage a bit farther up to reach high enough to cut these organs loose.

Grasp the windpipe and pull the heart and lungs downward as you use your knife to cut any adhering tissue loose from the top of the rib cage. If everything is cut loose, the heart, lungs, paunch, and intestines should all roll out of the carcass easily. At this point, find the bladder and tie it off with another piece of string, then ream around the lower end of the small intestine, where it passes through the pelvis, to free up the anus so you can pull it back through the opening.

If transportation out of the woods is readily available or you are going to have to quarter the critter to get it on a four-wheeler or horse, you can open the pelvis and rib cage with your saw or axe to make the gutting job easier, since you are going to end up doing this anyway when you quarter the animal.

If you intend to leave the animal in the woods for a period of time until you can get back to it and pack it out, getting the body heat out of the meat and allowing it to cool is essential to prevent spoilage.

I personally do not like to take the hide off an animal until I get it packed out, as the hide offers protection to the meat, keeps it clean, and prevents it from drying out. However, with an animal the size and bulk of a moose or elk in warm weather, sometimes there is no choice. *Do not* place still-warm game meat quarters in plastic bags, as they will spoil in short order. Wait until all the body heat is out of the meat and it's thoroughly cooled before placing quarters in plastic bags for protection from dirt, debris, or the elements.

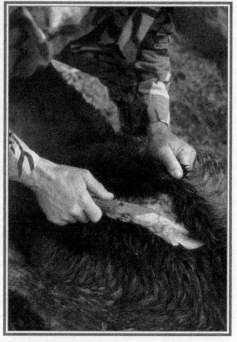

With big game like elk, it is important to open up their body cavity as soon as possible to get it cooled down and minimize/prevent any spoilage of the meat.

When an animal dies, the bacteria in the alimentary canal immediately start to migrate into the neck and throat. Ninety percent of game spoilage starts there and progresses. I've seen field-dressed elk lay on six inches of snow and spoil in the neck and front quarters. So it's extremely important to get air circulating through the chest and neck of larger game animals. If you aren't going to quarter your elk or moose immediately, open up the throat from chin to brisket and cut out the windpipe. Even if you plan on having your trophy moose or elk mounted, the long hair of the neck makes the slit easily repairable by a taxidermist. The open throat allows air to circulate through the chest cavity and throat, to cool out the meat and prevent spoilage.

If possible, also get the critter off the ground, propped on logs or rocks or hung in a tree, where air can circulate completely around the carcass to cool it out. This is where a rope and three snap links can save the day. A lone hunter can hoist an animal the size of an elk far enough off the ground to allow good air circulation and easily haul the quarters into a tree.

Quartering an animal is just what it says: cutting the critter into four pieces for hauling out. However, with an animal the size of a moose or elk, many bowhunters aren't going to be able to carry or backpack a whole quarter, and you may end up cutting the beasties into sixths or eighths.

To quarter a big-game animal, with or without hide, open the animal from pelvis to front of chest to gain full access. If the animal has been caped, the head is off; if not, cut the head from the carcass to facilitate quartering.

With a knife, slice between the second and third ribs, from the rear to the backbone, and then chop or saw through the vertebra to separate the front half from the rear. Easy. Roll and hold or tie the hindquarters upright and saw or chop downward through the center of the pelvis, keeping as close to the center of the back as you can. I generally carry a small plastic tarp to lie under the carcass to keep the meat as clean and free of debris as possible.

For splitting the front quarters apart, start at the rear of the front quarters and slice along the vertebral processes to free one side of the loin. The loins can be left attached to the front quarters, but I prefer to strip them both out and handle these choice chunks of meat separately. Either way, chop or saw through the top of ribs, where they join the vertebrae, and work your way forward to the base of the neck.

With an axe or regular meat saw, it's easy to continue and split the neck from top to bottom. However, if you're using a folding saw, you may want to cut the neck free at the juncture of neck and chest and just split the front quarter this far . . . that's it. Now all you have to do is get the sections back to camp or home.

TROPHY PREPARATION

Field trophy preparation is often a necessary part of getting your bowhunting trophy of a lifetime home and to a taxidermist for mounting. Trophy preparation is also a time-consuming and meticulous endeavor best left to experts, so if at all possible, take care to keep your kill clean and fresh and get it to a taxidermist whole. Then let him take care of it.

Every bowhunter should know the basics of caping-out a trophy big-game animal. It's not rocket science and can be accomplished with nothing more than time and a sharp knife. Caping is best done when the critter is fresh, as soon as you have taken a sufficient number of photos and measurements, as recommended by your taxidermist.

The first cut in caping an animal for a head and shoulders or head mount should be made along the centerline of the neck, from the top of the skull slightly below the antlers or horns (if the critter has them) to slightly behind the shoulders. I prefer to work from the head downward (with the lay of the hair) to prevent damage to fragile hair.

Next, cut around the chest behind the shoulders, making sure you have plenty of cape for the taxidermist to work with. Always cut upward when skinning or caping to avoid cutting off hair. Split the skin down the back of the front legs and run these cuts back to intersect with the cut around the bottom of the chest. From this point to the base of the skull, it's simply a matter of carefully skinning the hide away from the carcass to the back of the head. Skin the cape as clean and free of fat and clinging tissue as possible, to save having to strip this material off later.

Skinning around antlers and horns is painstaking work. Make your

If your field dressing is done right, you can pull the innards out in one large pile.

If you can't wrap your meat while at camp, be sure to have some Liquid Game Bag to rub on the carcass to keep off flies.

neck cut to the base at the backside of the horn or antler and carefully peel and pry the hide away from the base. I use a flat-bladed screwdriver for this chore in hunting camp and do a lot more prying than cutting. Keep the hair on the hide and not the base of the antlers. When you reach the base of the ears, cut them off as close to the skull as possible and continue carefully down to the eyes. Take extra care here, as this is the most critical part of caping.

Feel around through the skin so you get a sense of the shape and form of the eye *before* making the first cut. Start at the backside of the eye and cut perpendicular to the skull, keeping your cuts small and precise. When I get the eyehole started, I stick my finger in to pull it away from the skull. This also makes me more careful with my cuts so I don't slice my finger in the process. If you have any fur or hair showing around the eyehole, you've gotten careless. Once past the eyes, keep skinning down to the nose and lips, again being careful not to cut through the thin skin. The only way to get proficient at caping is through practice. If you're a serious bowhunter, practice your caping on non-trophy animals and even non-game animals.

Skinning the heads out on all critters is much the same, whether it's a bull elk, coyote, or prairie dog. The smaller the

When at camp, remove as much of the hide as possible to keep the carcass cool and minimize bacterial growth.

animal, the more precise the skinning job must be. For fine caping work, I use a scalpel with replaceable surgical blades. It makes for easier skinning and cutting in touchy areas, such as eyes, nose, and lips. Remember, if you see fur or hair protruding through your cuts around these areas, you need more *practice*.

Skinning out and turning the lips and ears is generally a job for the taxidermist or your outfitter, but it doesn't hurt for you to spend some time watching them perform this task so you learn how and can practice on your own, in case you ever want to do it yourself.

Once you have the cape off, roll it with the hair-side out, place it in a plastic bag and freeze until you can get it to a taxidermist. Do not salt before placing it in the freezer.

RUG MOUNT SKINNING

Bears are obviously the top candidate for a rug or flat mount, but there are many smaller critters that also make super rug or flat mounts for the bowhunter's trophy room. Coyotes, fox, badgers, bobcats, cougar, coons, and many others should be skinned flat for this type of mount.

If you are contemplating a full-body mount of any bow-killed animal, consult a taxidermist as to how he wants it skinned. Some taxidermists prefer an animal skinned with a dorsal cut and others with the normal belly and inside leg cuts. Don't leave on your trip without a full understanding, including precise notes on how to take care of your trophy for the best results.

For smaller fur-bearing animals, such as fox, coyotes, cats, etc., you might want to simply case the hide out for tanning and hanging in your trophy room. Case skinning is similar to pulling off a sock, in that you make your initial cut between the hind legs and from the front pads past the critter's elbows. You then carefully cut and pull the hide off the carcass, inverting the hide as you go. Skin the head out to the tip of the nose, leaving the ears, eyes, and nose on the hide just as you would a head mount. Freeze and get to a taxidermist. What could be easier?

Odd as it sounds, there's another critter that is often the target of bow-hunters that can make a conversation piece in a trophy room, and that's a tanned snakeskin. You case them the same as a fur-bearer, by peeling them like a sock. You can easily home-tan a snakeskin with one of the commercial preparations offered in magazines, or you can have your taxidermist do it for you.

TURKEY CAPING

Among the most asked-about mounts in our Iowa hunting camp are the turkey capes we have hanging on the walls to show the differences in the coloration of Merriam's, Eastern, and Rio Grande turkeys. These turkey capes are simple yet attractive do-it-yourself mounts.

This is a good place for a sharp cutting instrument, such as a scalpel or Exacto knife, because of a turkey's (or any bird's) thin skin. Hang the turkey by its head, back side out, and locate the featherless tracts running down both sides, much like the part in a person's hair. Start your cuts at the upper end of the feathers, below the bare neck, and cut down the center of these tracts along the side of the bird. Skin away, from body to base of tail, and cut off tail at base, leaving it attached to the feathered back skin. Handle carefully and keep feathers as clean as possible during the skinning, as a turkey has lots of oily fat between skin and body that will mat the feathers.

Lay the skinned cape feather-side down and clean all meat and fat from the skin and base of the tail. Do not cut bases off any feathers in the process. Once the skin is as fat- and tissue-free as possible, rub Borax (available at any grocery store) thoroughly into every crack and crevice of the skin, especially around the base of the tail. Don't worry about getting the white powder on feathers, as it will shake out easily later.

While the cape is still damp and flexible, spread it skin-side down on a large piece of cardboard covered with more Borax and, using pushpins, fasten it in position. Spread the tail and arrange all feathers where you want them, and tack down the spread tail with more pins between the tail feathers to hold it in place. Leave it in position until dry and shake out excess Borax. A lightly dampened cloth will clean any powder residue off feathers.

The cape can either be hung as is or backed with colored felt for an even more striking display. Hot glue works well to fasten a turkey cape to felt, or it can be carefully sewn on.

A tremendous number of wildlife trophies taken by bowhunters are wasted and lost because the hunter didn't know how to take care of them in the field. Don't let this happen to you. Spend some time with a taxidermist, ask questions, and *practice* what you learn. The next trophy you get might be the best ever, and you certainly don't want to lose it to ignorance. ■

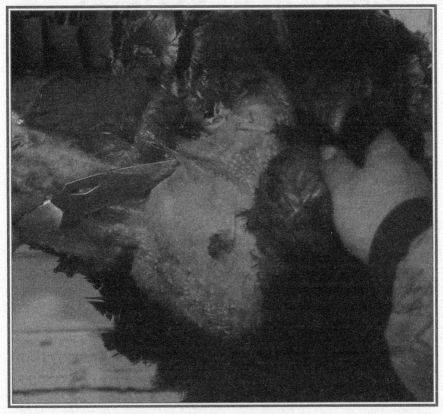

Caping a bird to display the tail feathers is an easy task you can do right at camp. Be sure to have a razor-sharp knife or razor-type knife to get clean cuts on this thin-skinned bird.

AUTHOR'S ARSENAL
AND ACCESSORIES

I f I'd written this book when I first started thinking about it, there would have been nothing in it about compound bows, replaceable-blade broadheads, mechanical broadheads, fiber-optic sights, laser rangefinders, digital trail cameras, or much of the bowhunting equipment we consider essential parts of our hunting gear today. However, being a world-class procrastinator, I put off doing the book until I felt I had a bit more experience bowhunting and all the gizmos and gadgets had been invented. Ha . . . I should live so long.

I am a firm believer in the KISS (Keep It Simple, Stupid) principle of bowhunting, regardless of whether my quarry is whitetails in Illinois, moose in Alaska, pheasants in South Dakota, or sharks in the Sea of Cortez. This belief has been reinforced dozens of times by clients and friends who have put their trust and faith in the latest and greatest bow sight, rest, mechanical broadhead, scent eliminator, or other new bowhunting tool, only to face malfunctions or the product's failure to live up to its hype.

MY BOW AND ARROW SET

I started out using a hand-made longbow my mom shot in college, and then I graduated to a recurve in the early '60s and took lots of big- and small-game animals with it while I learned the basics of instinctive shooting. When I switched to a compound bow, I remained an instinctive shooter.

As a writer and photographer, I deal with testing various types of equipment, including bows. It's much easier for me to pick up a new bow and start shooting without having to mount sights, string peeps, release loops, drop-away rests, etc. I simply install a nock and arrow rest and shoot. I can switch from one bow to another without a lot of fuss or bother and evaluate a bow's potential a lot quicker and easier.

However, the main reason I've stuck with instinctive shooting for all of my bowhunting is *simplicity* and *dependability*. I can bowhunt and shoot much earlier and later than a bowhunter using a peep and sights (even the fiber-optic or lighted-sight pin types), and range judging is not nearly as critical. Anyone can learn to shoot instinctive, and those who say they can't are kidding themselves. You don't use a sight or rangefinder for throwing a football or hitting a golf or tennis ball. The average person can throw a baseball five yards or 50 yards with reasonable accuracy, so why shouldn't you shoot an arrow with the same ease?

True, instinctive shooting is simply concentrating on where you want the arrow to hit, pointing with the bow, drawing the arrow, and releasing. Start practicing at five yards until you can group your arrows in a two-inch circle, then move to 10 yards and repeat. Keep doing this, varying the distance back and forth, until you get your brain programmed for the various distances, and you're on your way to becoming an instinctive shooter. A working knowledge and proficiency for instinctive shooting should be a necessity for any serious bowhunter, even sight shooters, in case of equipment malfunction.

I have shot many brands and models of bows over the years. Almost all the bows on the market today will perform and shoot better than I (or most bowhunters) can under hunting conditions. Go to a well-stocked archery shop and check out several bows in your price range. (To find a dealer near you, visit archerysearch.com on the web). Choose the bow that feels the best in your hands, and then get it in the proper draw length and weight. Spend whatever time it takes to become proficient with it. What could be simpler?

Since I shoot instinctively, I need a longer bow to avoid acute string angle and the resulting finger pinch. I've been shooting a Mathews Conquest for the past few years with excellent results and have it backed up with Golden Eagle, Renegade, and Champion bows that have all taken several big-game animals.

There are a lot of great, high-tech arrow rests on the market, but I continue to use the simple flipper rest. It does everything I need it to, and I have one taped unobtrusively to the riser on my bow as a spare. In the unlikely event the one on my bow breaks, it would take only a few seconds to replace, and once again I'm ready for action. I've had a number of clients over the years that have had arrow rest failure ruin their bowhunts.

My first set of hunting arrows were over-spined, Micro Flight fiberglass arrows that accounted for numerous missed deer the first couple of years I bowhunted. I graduated to aluminum and took dozens of big-game animals with these superb arrow shafts over a long stretch of time. I had misgivings about carbon and graphite shafts when they first hit the market, but after exhaustive testing and hunting use, I'm sold on them and wouldn't use any other kind. Carbon shafts provide superior strength, durability, and, most importantly, unbeatable penetration on game animals.

The only other essential attachment to my bow is a quiver. Here again I've chosen simple and foolproof models. I have several of these quivers full of arrows, with different-colored fletching and broadheads for hunting and photography. With the simple addition of a Kwikee bracket screwed to the side of my bow, I can change quivers at will.

A great feature of some quiver systems is the screw-in bracket caddy that holds the quiver solidly when it's off the bow. I *always* screw the bracket to a tree or log and lock my quiver in, where I can reach it easily with little movement. I've taken several Pope and Young animals with a quick second shot because of this handy, quiver-holding accessory.

Broadheads are undisputedly the most important bowhunting tool in my arsenal, and I always opt for the best. I started out with Bear Razorheads because I could get them razor-sharp with little effort. This head is still one of the best on the market. Many other broadheads are also effective, provided you can keep them sharp.

Hunting with dull broadheads (the worst sin a bowhunter can be guilty of) has been virtually eliminated by replaceable-blade broadheads. I want a broadhead that cuts on contact, and Andy Simo's Thunderhead 125 was one of the first and best with a trocar point that could be sharpened, along with quality construction and heavy replaceable blades that could be touched-up or resharpened. Bob Barrie's Rocky Mountain Razor was another quality broadhead that fulfilled my requirements.

Spotting the Phantom broadhead was love at first sight. The basic two-bladed head, with hefty bleeder blade insert, was and still is my idea of the *perfect* broadhead. The blades and inserts came razor-sharp, and the head was almost indestructible. Coupled with small-diameter carbon shafts from my 65- to 85-pound bows, I shot completely through every big-game animal I hit. I used the same shaft and single (re-sharpened) Phantom broadhead on six different big-game animals, from moose to antelope, over a two-year period before losing the arrow on a hunt. Steel Force broadheads are in the same category as the Phantom and are as easy to tune and shoot the same point of impact.

BROADHEAD SHARPENING

Nothing works better than a sharp tool and nothing is worse than a dull tool, whether it's on the end of your arrow shaft or in the sheath on your hip. Every bowhunter should know how to sharpen a broadhead, knife, or axe to a razor-sharp edge . . . few do.

The proper sharpening tools are few but necessary. A good six-inch mill bastard file; a double-grit, medium, and fine Carborundum or diamond sharpening stone or hone; and a leather strop or razor hone. If you plan on resharpening replaceable-broadhead blades, an Exacto tool handle will hold the blades and reduce the chances of cutting your fingers.

Use the mill file to make four or five level swipes *into* each side of the blade to be sharpened, to remove nicks or tool marks and flatten the edge evenly. Next, take the blade and run it down the medium side of your diamond hone or Carborundum stone. I spray the surface with WD-40 or use a light cutting oil to float the metal particles out of the stone. Simulate trying to cut thin slices from the hone and keep the blade at the same flat level on both sides for six to eight strokes. Make sure you cut *into* the edge of the blade and not away from it.

Next, take the blade and stroke it back and forth on a leather belt, strop, or piece of slick leather attached to a block of wood. This operation is to work the fine feather or wire edge off the blade so you polish the edge *in* the steel and not on it. As previously stated, a rough featheredge might feel sharp but will

Having a backpack or daypack with plenty of pockets–inside and out–is a must for me.

lose much of its efficiency when it fills with hair, tissue, and muscle fiber. If you can't shave the hair off your arm easily, work on the blade some more. Once you get the feel and touch, you should never go bowhunting again with a dull knife or broadhead. Sharp equipment is the sign of a good hunter in my estimation.

BACKPACK AND FANNY-PACK ESSENTIALS

I carry too much stuff for a fanny pack, so I got the best daypack I could find: a waterproof, camouflaged, Non-Typical pack from Crooked Horn Outfitters, with enough room to carry everything I need in a tree stand or day hunt in the mountains of Colorado. Certain essentials stay in my daypack, whether I'm bowhunting whitetails in Iowa or moose in Alberta.

Without a doubt, the most used tool in my pack is a folding saw and ratchet-type clipper combination. I use the clippers for trimming trails into stands and cutting small limbs around tree stands and ground blinds. These sturdy ratchet-style clippers will cut thumb-sized branches and limbs with ease. The saw gets regular use cutting limbs in shooting lanes, opening the chest cavity and pelvis (with included meat blade) in game animals, and a host of other chores. I often use the rope I carry in the pack to fasten the saw to a limb or branch, for longer reach in trimming shooting lanes.

My 20-foot hank of 3/8-inch braided-nylon climbing rope, and companion hank of 1/8-inch braided-nylon rope, are accompanied by three climbing snap links and several small snap links, hooked to the outside of my pack. These get used for everything from hanging a deer or elk carcass to tying packs on a four-wheeler or pulling gear into a tree stand when someone forgets to add a pull-up line.

I always carry a good safety belt (by Game Tracker) in the pack and make use of it every time I get both feet off the ground. This is the best and easiest-to-use safety belt I've found for all purposes and wouldn't be without it. When my guides and I are setting up and constantly moving 30 to 40 tree stands each fall, we need a safety belt that is dependable, quick, and easy to use, and this one fits the bill exactly. It doesn't take up much room in my pack and is an integral part of my daypack, regardless of where I am bowhunting.

There are a couple of little pockets on the front of the pack that are just the right size for two Diamond Machine Technology folding sharpening hones. One has a medium (blue) grit and fine (red) grit, while the other is fine and extra fine (green). They are indispensable for tuning up broadheads while you're in the stand or keeping your knife sharp while field dressing a critter.

My daypack contains an indispensable roll of toilet paper in a Ziploc bag to fulfill several important functions, one of which is as a biodegradable marker for marking blood trails. If you can't figure out the other use, you probably ought to stay close to home. In addition to the trail-marking TP, I carry a roll of plastic trail-marking tape in bright green or orange for marking blood trails in inclement weather.

I also tote a kit with highly reflective tacks for marking trails into tree stands, and tape for marking the trees or ladders so my clients and I have no trouble locating stands in the pitch black of early morning. These brilliantly reflective little markers can be picked up with a flashlight beam at 1000 yards and are equally effective in fog and rain. I wouldn't be without a supply of them in my daypack.

My field-dressing kit contains several pairs of rubber gloves, a packet of Handi-Wipes, a hank of stout cord, and a packet of industrial-strength dry wipes for cleaning up blood, etc., before and after dressing an animal. It also contains a small scalpel and extra blades for splitting the lips, turning the ears, and skinning around the eyes on animals to be mounted.

The other small pouch holds two small, but powerful, penlights, one white and the other green. The green is brighter and better for use traveling through the woods or finding things in a stand and can't be readily seen by big game. The white light is best for finding blood and general use. I carry a couple of sets of extra AAA batteries in the zipper pouch of the pack, but these little lights seem to burn forever on a single set of batteries. I also carry two bright headlights in the pack, along with extra batteries, for blood trailing at night and general hands-free use when a more powerful light is needed for gutting or skinning a beastie in the dark.

The inside zipper pouch carries a half-dozen hand warmers, a flint and steel with a sealed package of waxy fire starter, a super-hot butane lighter for torching scent sticks, and a compass.

The two outside pouches carry a water bottle on one side and a bottle of

Liquid Game Bag on the other, along with a sheathed knife.

On extended trips, I carry a couple of screw-in tree steps and a half-dozen small screw-in hangers that always come in handy—and usually end up getting left behind. I also carry several extra quiver holders.

I never go anywhere without at least three predator calls on a lanyard. I usually carry a variable tone call, along with a jackrabbit call and a cottontail call with mouse squeaker voice. These ever-present predator calls have accounted for a variety of predators over the years and added a lot of excitement to many bowhunts.

I have a small archery kit bag that contains extra bow wax, an extra string or cable set-up, rests, a spare arm guard, and a shooting glove. I carry a small custom leather case that holds half-a-dozen extra broadheads and a couple of rubber blunts.

One little item that I've taken on all my flying hunting trips is a Bowmaster portable split-limb bow press. This easy-to-use, lightweight press, which fits in the palm of your hand, saved the hunt for one bowhunter with a broken string in northern Alberta and for another in Alaska, where there wasn't an archery shop within 1000 miles.

My pack also contains several spare squeeze bottles of talcum powder. As discussed in many of the preceding chapters, I'd be lost if I didn't have a powder bottle to determine the idiosyncrasies of the wind when I'm bowhunting, and a couple of spares in my daypack makes sure this doesn't happen to me or a client.

The item I've added most recently to my pack is a small package of Tear Aid, a unique patching material that will repair anything from neoprene waders to pop-up blinds, rain gear, leaky gas tanks, and brush-torn camo pants. This waterproof, gasoline-proof, ultraviolet-resistant clear polymer tape stretches but will return to size, and it has an unbelievably strong bond with a variety of materials. There have been a dozen instances in the past where this patching material would have saved the day for me and my clients. Tear Aid is a product that deserves a place in any bowhunter's daypack and traveling archery kit.

In addition to these essential "travel-everywhere" items, my daypack still has enough room to pack a full set of rain gear, in case it's needed, my rattling antlers, which stay in the pack from beginning to end of the deer season, as well as a hefty lunch and drink when warranted. I might forget my bow and arrow, but it's doubtful I'll go afield without my fully stocked daypack.

Over the years, I've observed bowhunting clients, friends, and other bowhunters show up in hunting camps with nothing but a bow and arrow set and a camouflage outfit (consisting of three different brands of camo). They get by, borrowing everything else they need from others in camp. Some have lugged out a daypack loaded with enough stuff to set up a full-fledged camp, everything but the kitchen sink . . . for a week. Finding the mid-point, where you tote enough equipment on your bowhunts to provide for your needs, without overdoing it, comes with experience and education. Even then, it's difficult to leave that extra pair of binoculars, knife, or chunk of rope at home. Guess that's why they keep making larger and larger duffel bags, daypacks, and fanny packs. ■

DESKTOP SCOUTING
AND PLANNING

H ow's the elk and mule deer bowhunting in your area? And where do you
suggest I bowhunt to kill a Pope and Young bull and muley buck?" the
caller asked in all sincerity. Geez . . . some request! If only it were that
easy, I'd have a heck of a lot more trophy bucks and bulls hanging in my own
trophy room. Yet, when I was conservation officer for the Colorado Division of
Wildlife, that was fairly typical of the calls I received about a week before the
season opened. My first inclination was to tell the inquirer that the bowhunting
in my whole district was top quality. This would have been the truth, since the
quality of the bowhunting never varied; it was only the hunter success that
varied.

The bowhunter on the phone had never been to Colorado, nor had he
even looked at a map of the general area about which he was inquiring. I was
supposed to verbally guide him to a record-book bull elk and mule deer buck
over the phone! Yeah, right.

Each fall, I gladly provided many bowhunters with explicit advice on
where they should bowhunt in my conservation district. The information was
based on helicopter and fixed-wing plane game counts and surveys, horseback
and backpack trips, along with my own bowhunting experiences in the area. I
may have told them all they knew about the area, but naturally I didn't tell them
all I knew of the area.

Over the years, I helped many bowhunters locate spots where they were
able to harvest a buck, bull, or bear. Unlike the first caller, these bowhunters had
done their homework and had a rudimentary knowledge of bowhunting conditions in Colorado. It wasn't magic to guide them to a specific area where they
had a good chance of finding an animal, when I could refer to specific locations

on United States Forest Service or United States Geological Survey maps. They could locate the desired spot and study the maps to familiarize themselves with the lay of the land and access before they left home.

If you're at all like me, you probably have a sincere aversion to research, office work, correspondence, and anything else that is liable to keep you house-bound when you could be outdoors in the fresh air and sunshine. However, quite possibly the most important aspect of your pre-season preparation, planning, and scouting is going to be carried on under the roof of your own home.

A major part of intelligent planning and preparation is gathering pertinent information on your particular hunting area, and in the case of some species, such as whitetail deer, studying the surrounding areas well. You may be able to scout out your local bowhunting area during various times of the year, but how about the surrounding property that belongs to someone else and is off limits to your on-the-ground scrutiny? Often, knowing the key land features of neighboring properties, and how they can affect deer movements into your hunting area during various seasons and under varying circumstances, can be vital to your close-to-home bowhunting success.

If you're planning an out-of-state bowhunting trip, the most important elements in the success of your trip are the time spent at home, mentally preparing for your hunt, and physical preparation, such as hiking, climbing, shooting, etc.

One valuable source of information to get you started on your quest is the harvest data for the various states or provinces you're interested in bowhunting. Many states and provinces provide this comprehensive information on a yearly basis for free or a very minimal fee. Harvest or kill figures will show you the top harvest areas, by game management unit, hunter pressure by area, and hunter-success ratio. Not all states provide the same info, but this type of data can narrow your search for prime bowhunting locations.

What you are looking for is an area with high success ratio and low hunting pressure. Good luck. Many such choice locales may be limited-license areas with a lottery drawing or other limitation involved, requiring further patience and perseverance to even obtain a license. States such as Illinois and Iowa for whitetails, Arizona, New Mexico, and Montana for elk, Wyoming and parts of Colorado for antelope, all have drawings for their best trophy-producing areas. However, that doesn't mean you can't find an exceptional bowhunting area where licenses are readily available . . . with a little in-depth research and digging.

Unfortunately, most states do not make any attempt to separate out Pope and Young animals in their harvest figures, so you can't narrow your search down for record-producing areas within a state. The best place to further define your search for record-class animals are the Boone and Crockett and Pope and Young record books.

Boone and Crockett is for rifle-harvested game, but the information is of definite value for locating areas that historically have produced record-book animals. A copy of the Pope and Young club's biennial big-game awards and statistical summary is available from the Pope and Young office and can provide current harvest data on Pope and Young record-class animals of each species.

Even these valuable sources of information won't narrow your trophy search to a specific game-management unit or drainage within state or provincial borders. The Pope and Young summary will give you a synopsis of which states have produced the largest and greatest number of record-class animals over the past two-year biennial competition, as will the Boone and Crockett summary. Even more valuable, Pope and Young will give you the names of the bowhunters who took them, which the persistent bowhunter can put to use.

Once you've chosen the best state for your bowhunt and then defined your hunting area to one or more places within the borders of that state, you can get serious about honing your home-base bowhunting skills by studying available maps, familiarizing yourself with the country you'll be bowhunting.

For public lands in the western United States, the Forest Service and Bureau of Land Management offer general-use maps that show a broad picture of each National Forest BLM unit scattered across the western states. These maps are invaluable for orienting yourself to the basic features of the locale and giving you a broad picture of the country you'll be hunting. Forest and private land boundaries, wilderness areas, roads and trails, timbered and open areas, drainages, mountain ranges and peaks, campgrounds, and numerous other general features, encompassing a huge chunk of country, can be found on these maps.

You can correlate the information you've gleaned from your harvest-data research with a public land map to narrow your search for a quality hunting area. Once you're familiar with one or more locations and the pertinent data that matches them, it's time to get on the phone for some first-hand information on your proposed hunting area.

The best source of information is the local conservation officer, but realize that if you approach this person the wrong way, you'll get zip. Conservation officers get hundreds of calls from hunters each fall, and most are like the one in the opening paragraph of this chapter. You have to convince the CO that you are a serious bowhunter who has done your homework, that you are looking for basic information and not expecting him to put you within bow range of a record-book critter over the phone.

Ask for input on the different areas you've researched and get the names of local sporting goods stores, Chamber of Commerce members, ranchers, or bowhunters in the area who might provide additional info. Use your public relation skills to the best of your ability, because good information at this point can really improve your chances for a successful bowhunt.

United States Geological Survey maps or topographical maps are unparalleled for providing an accurate visual look at the terrain features in your proposed bowhunting area from the comfort of your own home. It's amazing how much you can learn from such maps when you really apply yourself.

For several years, Dr. Kowalski, a close family friend and avid elk hunter, spent several weeks with us in Colorado trying to outsmart the local elk bulls.

I'd advised him where I thought he should hunt and outlined the general area on a USGS map. Doc would judiciously study the maps for three or four hours while he poured down prodigious amounts of coffee. When he got through with his intense examination of the maps, he could tell me more about the area in detail, without ever having set foot in that part of the mountains, than I knew from having flown, hiked, and horse backed the country. If I hunted with him and agreed to meet him at a specific rock pile, meadow, or saddle between two drainages, he always showed precisely on time and I damned well had better be there when I was supposed to or I got a lecture. Unfortunately, USGS maps don't show the exact location of living breathing critters.

To outfit yourself with a set of maps for your hunting areas, order a state map catalog, which also lists map dealers, and an index map of the state or states of interest. Once you get the index, it's easy to pinpoint the exact location you need and order specific maps. The most useful maps will be of the standard quadrangle type, in a scale of 1:24,000: one inch on the map equals 24,000 feet on the ground. These maps are 22 by 27 inches and give a detailed view of the lay of the land from above.

DeLorme mapping company produces an atlas and gazetteer for each of the 50 states, containing a complete series of individual topographic maps covering the entire state along with additional valuable information for the traveling bowhunter. The individual maps are produced in either a 1:160,000 scale or 1:320,000 scale. A selection of these atlases and gazetteers should reside in every serious bowhunter's library.

There's a psychological aspect of desktop scouting and planning that should be understood and taken into consideration when choosing a hunt location and finalizing your plans. Planning and deciding to bowhunt a high mountain valley in Colorado, Idaho, or even the Brooks Range of Alaska, while studying the country on a large-scale, flat map in the comfort of your Pennsylvania or Florida home, is a far cry from encountering the reality of actually roaming and bowhunting the rugged, physically exhausting, and difficult terrain you've chosen.

I've had numerous clients voraciously study maps of our elk, mule deer, bear, and whitetail deer bowhunting country during the off-season and assure me they were physically ready for the country. When they arrived in camp, they were totally awe struck by the ruggedness and inaccessibility of many of our hunting areas and weren't quite as well prepared for the challenge as they thought, physically or mentally.

Keep this factor in mind when studying maps and contemplating hunt locations: Try to mentally envision what the terrain will be like on the ground as you study your maps and photos, so when you get to your bowhunting area, the shock won't be quite as great.

I have a real *love/hate* relationship with computers, and there's rarely a day goes by that I don't threaten to shoot holes in the one I'm using or think about getting a new one with more speed, bells, and whistles and the latest technology.

One of the best things to come with modern computer technology is a couple of new companies that deal with mapping and aerial photos.

Up-to-date aerial photos give you a broad overview of your hunting area, unobtainable by any other method, and can be used to pinpoint the location of key land features, such as waterholes, saddles between valleys, travel corridors, feeding and bedding areas, potential stand locations, and more. When used in conjunction with topo maps, aerial photos can give you even more precise information on your hunting locale.

If you have a Global Positioning System unit and a modicum of skill in its use, you can use the topo map coordinates to enter waypoints of various locations of interest on your aerial photos. It will facilitate your finding them with ease and assurance on the ground, regardless of weather or other adverse factors that seem to plague bowhunts.

Mytopo.com is a company that specializes in producing high-quality, up-to-date, custom United States Geological Survey maps and aerial photos that are the greatest thing for bowhunters since replaceable-blade broadheads. You can go into www.mytopo. com on a computer and–by selecting one of the lower 48 states and using lat/lon coordinates, UTM coordinates, the name of a town, a mountain peak, or other prominent feature in your chosen area–you can pull up a map or aerial photo of it.

There are web sites and software programs available to help you pre-plan for your hunt. Try to visualize the type of terrain you will be hunting and prepare for it.

After you've pinpointed your area of interest, you can view and adjust the map or aerial photo from a very large-scale map down to a small scale, like 1:5000, which will show a car in someone's driveway. Once you delineate your target area on the map or photo, you can customize your map order with the name of the area, ranch, or your name on the map or aerial photo, simply by punching a couple keys on your computer.

The maps and aerial photos are reasonably priced and come in various sizes and materials. Glossy, exceptionally high-quality 36 by 44-inch maps and photos, designed for wall mounting in dens, hunting camps, offices, etc., are the largest size produced. My favorite maps and aerial photos are 18 by 24 inches, printed on ultra-violet and fade-resistant, waterproof paper, ideal for carrying in the field. These maps and photos can also be printed on heavy, glossy paper suitable for wall mounting or carrying in a file.

MapCard is a companion company with an even more valuable service for bowhunters. You purchase a year or longer membership direct from the company or one of their representatives, such as Cabela's. This membership allows you to go into their website and pull up maps or aerial photos similar to MyTopo, only with MapCard you can download and print as many maps or aerial photos as you want.

The unique feature of this program is that, once you have a section selected, you can put different colored icons in place to delineate tree stands, game trails, food plots, ground blinds, feeders, kill sites, etc. You can add the icons and their captions to each individual aerial photo or topo map and print them out on your computer. The chosen map and icons can be stored and revisited whenever you want to change or update the information.

There is also a program that allows you to outline an area, such as a ranch or lease boundaries or food plots, with the cursor and MapCard will figure the acreage . . . neat. These maps work great for our hunting camp in Iowa, and I've printed aerial photos of all the leases, complete with stands, blinds, food plots, etc. for each of my guides. I print my maps and aerial photos on heavyweight, matte paper for durability and ease of use and keep them filed by lease and hunting area in an accordion-style portable file.

As valuable as these programs are for the traveling bowhunter, they are even more valuable when adapted to bowhunting your own back yard. You can peruse maps and aerial photos on the computer endlessly–actually scouting and exploring adjacent properties better, with the sharp, clear photos, than you could on foot–and you don't even have to worry about getting caught.

You can get a large-scale look at the overall lay of the land in conjunction with your particular bowhunting area or properties. You can locate travel-ways, feeding areas, corridors, bottlenecks, and other features on adjacent properties that will let you anticipate the game movements to and from your ground. Then, with more accuracy, you can improve your chances of setting up a stand or locating a food plot in precisely the right place. The amount of information you can glean from these superb programs is endless, and the fact that you can get a hard copy of whatever you deem necessary is invaluable.

These programs are worth far more than the nominal price of the membership or maps to the serious bowhunter who wants to be armed with the latest and best knowledge obtainable. The maps and photos are great for bowhunting clubs and hunting leases; they can't help but make any bowhunting operation more efficient, and planning any hunt far more enjoyable and effective.

Another item that can be of value, whether bowhunting in your backyard, traveling to adjacent states, or flying farther afield, is a county plat directory that gives you the ownership status of every private farm and home in the county. Most counties have these available at the county court house. Having one in your possession when you head for new bowhunting country, especially in the eastern and Midwestern states, where most of the land is privately owned, is invaluable. Many times I've passed up bowhunting a choice piece of ground because I didn't know who to contact and later found out it would have been easy to get permission from the landowners.

We're constantly using the plat book in our Iowa whitetail hunting operation to put us in contact with the landowners of properties we'd like to hunt. There have been several times in past seasons when we spotted a good buck on unfamiliar ground, located the owner with the help of the plat book, and got permission to hunt the property. Check with the county farm agent or local conservation officer to find where you can obtain a current plat book for the county that you're interested in bowhunting.

Off-season desktop scouting may not be habit forming, but it definitely can become hazardous to the health of your quarry, whether it's a bull elk roaming a hidden valley deep in the Colorado wilderness or a crafty old whitetail buck, secluded in an isolated slough in the middle of an Iowa cornfield. The effort expended and the time spent scouting and planning your bowhunt from the comfort of your own home might just prove to be the most valuable contribution to the success of your bowhunting venture. ■

Alabama Department
of Conservation and
Natural Resources
64 N. Union Street
Montgomery, AL 36130
334-242-3486

Alaska Department
of Fish and Game
PO Box 115526
Juneau, AK 99811
907-465-4100

Arizona Game and Fish
Department
5000 W. Carefree
Highway
Phoenix, AZ 85086
602-942-3000

Arkansas Game
and Fish Commission
#2 Natural Resources
Drive
Little Rock, AR 72205
501-223-6300

California Department
of Fish and Game
1416 Ninth Street
Sacramento, CA 95814
916-653-7664

Colorado Division of
Wildlife
6060 Broadway
Denver, CO 80216
303-445-0411

Connecticut Department
of Environmental
Protection
Wildlife Division
79 Elm Street
Hartford, CT 06106
860-424-3000

Delaware Division
of Fish and Wildlife
89 Kings Highway
Dover, DE 19901
302-739-9910

Florida Game and Fresh
Water Fish Commission
620 S. Meridian Street
Tallahassee, FL 32399
850-488-4676

Georgia Wildlife
Resources Division
2070 US Highway 278 SE
Social Circle, GA 30025
770-918-6400

Hawaii Division
of Forestry and Wildlife
1151 Punchbowl Street
Honolulu, HI 96813
808-587-0166

Idaho Fish and Game
PO Box 25
Boise, ID 83707
208-334-3700

Illinois Division
of Wildlife Resources
One National Resources
Way
Springfield, IL 62702
217-782-6384

Indiana Division
of Fish and Wildlife
402 W. Washington
Street
Room W273
Indianapolis, IN 46204
317-232-4200

Iowa Fish and Wildlife
Division
900 E. Grand Avenue,
#502
Wallace Building
Des Moines, IA 50319
515-281-5145

Kansas Department of
Wildlife, Parks, and
Tourism
512 SE 25th Avenue
Pratt, KS 66612
602-672-5911

Kentucky Department
of Fish and Wildlife
Resources
#1 Sportsman's Lane
Frankfort, KY 40601
800-858-1549

Louisiana Department of
Wildlife and Fisheries
PO Box 98000
Baton Rouge, LA 70898
225-765-2800

Maine Department of
Inland Fisheries and
Wildlife
284 State Street
Augusta, ME 04333
207-287-8000

Maryland Department of
Natural Resources
Tawes State Office
Building
580 Taylor Avenue
Annapolis, MD 21401
410-260-8367

Massachusetts Division
of Fisheries and Wildlife
100 Hartwell Street
Suite 230
West Boylston, MA 05183
508-389-6300

Michigan Department of
Natural Resources and
Wildlife
PO Box 30444
Lansing, MI 48909
517-373-1263

Minnesota Division
of Fish and Wildlife
500 Lafayette Road
St. Paul, MN 55155
651-296-6157

Mississippi Department
of Wildlife, Fisheries,
and Parks
1505 Eastover Drive
Jackson, MS 39211
601-432-2400

Missouri Department
of Natural Resources
PO Box 176
Jefferson City, MO 65102
573-751-3443

Montana Department of
Fish, Wildlife, and Parks
1420 E. 6th Avenue
PO Box 20071
Helena, MT 59620
406-444-2535

Nebraska Game and
Parks Commission
2200 North 33rd Street
Lincoln, NE 68503
402-471-0641

Nevada Department of
Wildlife
11 Valley Road
Reno, NV 89512
775-688-1500

New Hampshire Fish
and Game Department
11 Hazen Drive
Concord, NH 03301
603-271-3422

New Jersey Division of
Fish, Game and Wildlife
Mail Code 501-03
PO Box 420
Trenton, NJ 08625
609-292-2965

New Mexico Department
of Game and Fish
PO Box 25112
Santa Fe, NM 87504
505-476-8000

New York Division
of Fish and Wildlife
50 Wolf Road
Albany, NY 12233
518-457-3730

North Carolina Wildlife

Resources Commission
1701 Mail Service Center
Raleigh, NC 27699
919-707-0010

North Dakota State
Game and Fish
Department
100 N. Bismarck
Expressway
Bismarck, ND 58501
701-328-6300

Ohio Division of Wildlife
2045 Morse Road,
Building G
Columbus, OH 43229
614-265-6300

Oklahoma Department
of Wildlife
1801 N. Lincoln
Boulevard
Oklahoma City, OK 73105
405-521-3851

Oregon Department
of Fish and Wildlife
3406 Cherry Avenue
Salem, OR 97207
503-947-6000

Pennsylvania Bureau
of Wildlife Management
2001 Elmerton Avenue
Harrisburg, PA 17110
717-787-5529

Rhode Island Natural
Resources Management
22 Hayes Street
Providence, RI 02908
401-277-6605

South Carolina
Department
of Natural Resources
Robert C. Dennis Building
1000 Assembly Street
Columbia, SC 29201
803-734-3886

South Dakota Game,
Fish and Parks
Department
523 East Capitol Avenue
Pierre, SD 57501
605-773-3387

Tennessee Wildlife
Resources Agency
Ellington Agricultural
Center
440 Hogan Road
Nashville, TN 37220
615-781-6500

Texas Parks and
Wildlife Department
4200 Smith School Road
Austin, TX 78744

512-389-4800

**Utah Division
of Wildlife Resources**
1594 W. North Temple
Suite 2110
PO Box 146301
Salt Lake City, UT 84114
801-538-4700

**Vermont Department
of Fish and Wildlife**
103 S. Main Street
10 South
Waterbury, VT 05671
802-241-3700

**Virginia Department
of Game and Inland
Fisheries**
4010 W. Broad Street
PO Box 11104
Richmond, VA 23230
804-367-1000

**Washington Department
of Fish and Wildlife**
600 Capitol Way N.
Olympia, WA 98501
360-902-2200

**West Virginia Division of
Natural Resources
and Wildlife Resources**
324 Fourth Avenue
South Charleston, WV
25303
304-558-2754

**Wisconsin Department
of Natural Resources**
PO Box 7921
Madison, WI 53707
608-266-2621

**Wyoming Game
and Fish Department**
5400 Bishop Boulevard
Cheyenne, WY 82006
307-777-4600

CANADIAN PROVINCES

**Canadian Wildlife
Service**
Inquiry Center
10 Wellington, 23rd Floor
Gatineau, QC
Canada K1A 0H3
819-997-1301

**Alberta Fish
and Wildlife Services**
Main Floor, Great West
Life Building
9920 180th Street
Edmonton, Alberta
Canada T5K 2M4
780-944-0313

British Columbia Wildlife

Branch
PO Box 9391
Victoria, British Columbia
Canada V8W 9M8
250-387-9771

**Manitoba Department of
Natural Resources and
Wildlife**
Box 24
200 Saulteaux Crescent
Winnipeg, Manitoba
Canada R3J 3W3
204-945-7775

**New Brunswick
Fish and Wildlife Branch**
PO Box 6000
Fredericton, New
Brunswick, Canada E3B
5H1
506-453-3826

**Northwest Territories
Wildlife Management**
PO Box 1320
Yellowknife, Northwest
Territories
Canada X1A 2L9
867-873-7401

Nova Scotia Wildlife
PO Box 698
Halifax, Nova Scotia
Canada B3J 2T9
902-679-6091

**Ontario Ministry
of Natural Resources**
300 Water Street
PO Box 7000
Peterborough, Ontario
Canada K9J 8M5
705-755-2000

**Prince Edward Island
Fish and Wildlife
Division**
183 Upton Road
Charlottetown, Prince
Edward Island, Canada
C1A 7N8
902-368-4684

**Quebec Department of
Recreation, Fish and
Game**
880, chemin Sainte-Foy
RC 120-C Québec
Canada G1S 4X4
418-627-8600

**Saskatchewan
Environment
and Resource
Management**
3211 Albert Street
Regina, Saskatchewan,
Canada S4S 5W6
306-787-2309

**Yukon Territory
Department
of Renewable Resources**
Box 2703
Whitehorse, Yukon
Territory, Canada Y1A
2C6
867-667-5652

WEBSITES & MAPS

To locate websites by
state: www.state.co.us/
Insert the two letter
abbreviation per state.
The above example is for
Colorado. Then follow the
links to the hunting page.

To locate websites by
Canadian province:
www.gov.ab.ca/
Insert the two letter
abbreviation per province.
The above example is
for Alberta. Then run a
search on the home page
for hunting.
www.mytopo.com
877-587-9004

www.mapcard.com
info@mapcard.com
406-294-9994
One South Broadway
Billings, MT 59101

**US Geological Survey
Info Services**
PO Box 25286
Denver, CO 80225
888-ASK-USGS or 303-
202-4700
ask.usgs.gov

DeLorme Mapping Com.
Two DeLorme Dr.
Yarmouth, ME 04096
800-511-2459
www.delorme.com